THE LAST CHANCE RANCH

A Story About Football, Gang Members, and
Learning to Play by the Rules

THE LAST CHANCE RANCH

A Story About Football, Gang Members, and
Learning to Play by the Rules

MARK EMMONS

LONGSTREET PRESS
Atlanta, Georgia

Published by
Longstreet Press, Inc.
A subsidiary of Cox Newspapers,
A subsidiary of Cox Enterprises, Inc.
2140 Newmarket Parkway
Suite 118
Marietta, GA 30067

1st printing 1996

Printed in the United States of America

Library of Congress Card Catalog Number: 96-76496

ISBN: 1-56352-334-5

Book design by Jill Dible

Jacket photo by Dave Cruz

Digital film prep and imaging by Advertising Technologies, Inc., Atlanta, GA

For Sandy, who had the Faith
For Jill and Caitlin, who gave the inspiration

PREFACE

I was paid to be a wise guy. That was not exactly the description of my old day job, but those generally are the unwritten marching orders for any newspaper sports columnist. When you come right down to it, sports is the one part of the newspaper, other than maybe the comics page and the crossword puzzle, that is supposed to be fun, where the idea is to escape from the cares of the daily grind. There's a reason sports is often referred to as the newspaper's toy department. If you want serious, turn to the front page.

That's why sports columnists generally try to inject some humor into their copy. They go for the sarcastic quip, the joke, the one-liner. I was no different. Frankly, it wasn't that hard to do, because the modern sports scene holds plenty of fertile material. After all, we live in a time when utility infielders who can barely hit their weight make $2 million a year . . . and then threaten to hold out because management somehow doesn't respect them. So being a sports columnist is a good job if you can get it. It will make you the envy of your block that you get into games for free, attend the Super Bowl every year, and are on a first-name basis with Charles Barkley.

But there are also some negatives, and I'm not just referring to the press-box food. The problem with writing only about sports is that it's basically meaningless and inconsequential to the human condition. Sure, people spend more time reading your stories each morning than they do, say, articles about zoning board meetings. But it's hardly life-and-death material. It's only bats and balls. Usually no great truths are revealed on the fields of play — unless, of course, you're a gambler and your house is riding on collecting the under-over bet.

I was reminded of that fact one day in June 1994. The pro basketball season had ended for the Phoenix Suns, and Kevin Johnson, the team's All-Star point guard, was talking at a restaurant about how the year had gone. When the formal interview was over, KJ, as he has become known, started talking about other things going on in his life. He had grown up in a rough section of Sacramento. Basketball, along with the support of a tight-knit family, had provided him with a way out of the mean streets. But KJ had never forgotten where he came from. After he made it big in the NBA, he went back to the same neighborhood where he had been raised and built something he christened St. Hope Academy. It's a place for kids to go to play, to learn, to grow. In Arizona, he had become active in the Boys and Girls Club. In fact, KJ was so immersed in charity causes for kids that he had long ago lost track of all the national awards and honors he had received for his involvement. He is one of those rare professional athletes who use their stature to promote something other than themselves.

KJ was traded from the Cleveland Cavaliers to the Suns in 1988, just about the same time I became a columnist at the *Tribune* newspapers in suburban Phoenix. Although typically columnists think of pro athletes as pampered jerks and jocks think of writers as pond scum, we hit it off. After KJ finished talking about some projects he was mulling over for his post-NBA days, he had a question for me.

"So what are *you* going to do to make a difference?" he asked.

"Me?"

"Sure, everybody has to do their part," he said.

I recall my answer being something along the lines of, "My job is to write about others making a difference. You know, I'm the publicity man." It was a lame response, which I think is what KJ said, duly noting that I wrote only about sports, not about "real stuff." Anyway, that conversation stuck with me. It occurred to me that at some point it might be a nice change of pace to write about something that really did matter.

A couple of months later, in August 1994, I wrote a lengthy feature article for my newspaper about the Arizona Boys Ranch, a controversial placement facility for delinquent youths. The Ranch was fielding its first-ever high school football team and Frank Kush, the former Arizona State coach, who is considered by many in the Grand Canyon State to be a living legend, was helping out. Little was expected from the squad on the field, and it was a good thing because that first team didn't do much. But as Kush pointed out later, you shouldn't assume that the Ranch had only four victories that inaugural season just because it won only four games. A real victory, Kush explained, was a kid learning something positive about himself on the football field and then applying it to his life when he got back out in the real world. There's a great story waiting to be told out there, Kush added. If you could get to know these kids and listen to them talk about what they have done and seen, you would consider it a miracle that they're even alive, let alone playing high school football.

That got the wheels turning in my head. I contacted Bob Thomas, the CEO and president of the Ranch, and in the summer of 1995 he agreed to let me follow the Ranch's football team on an up-close-and-personal basis during its second year. From the first week of August to the day after Thanksgiving, I followed. There were no ground rules. I got to write what I saw. I attended practices, went to meetings, covered games, and even sat down at dinner with the team. I spent as much time at the Ranch as the understanding editors at the *Tribune* could allow. I'm incredibly thankful for the support of this project shown by Sandy Schwartz, Jeff Bruce, and Dave Lumia. I would prefer, though, not to unfurl the long list of names of people who assisted in this undertaking out of fear that I may inadvertently forget someone. To everyone who did lend a helping hand, you have my everlasting gratitude.

I would be remiss, however, if I didn't acknowledge two groups of individuals. The coaches at the Ranch allowed me to be a fly on the wall. I can only imagine how disconcerting it must be to have someone shadowing your movements while he scribbles down your every word. Finally, the kids at the Ranch, who were boys on the way to becoming men, were gracious enough to let me spend nearly four months watching them learn not only how to play football but, more important, how to get their lives back on the right track. This is their story. Don't expect to laugh much.

THE LAST CHANCE RANCH

THE
PRESEASON

My name is Walik Smith. I'm 18 years old. I'm from San Diego. I've been here at the Ranch for about a year and a half.

I'm quiet. Most people think I am, anyway. But you should see my record. I didn't consider myself a gang member. Gang is just a name that society has put on it. I just hung out with a group of people. I guess it was kind of a social thing. I just wanted to fit in. To me, we were just a group of people who lived in the same area. I just started picking up what they were doing at a young age. My older brother, he don't bang no more, but I just hung with him. Then the next thing you know, it got out of hand.

I've lost four or five friends to street life. Yes, sir, they were shot doing gang stuff. I've seen a lot of that stuff, but I don't talk about it. But you hear about it on the news all the time. Babies. Infants. Kids. It's no big deal to hear about fifteen-year-olds getting shot.

Me, I got shot, too. The biggest thing is that I didn't listen to nobody, like my mom. Right before I walked out the door that night, she said, "Don't leave." And that night I came home bleeding. I was prying into other people's business. I got shot in the left side. When it happened, I felt a thrust. I knew I got shot. You just know when you get shot. I told somebody, and he said, "No, you didn't." But when I got to a friend's house, I pulled off my shirt, and sure enough, there it was. I didn't want to go home and tell my mom. I had disobeyed her. So I told my stepfather, and he ended up telling her anyway. The doctors said that the bullet was an inch away from my heart. So they couldn't take it out for like two weeks because it was so close. I had just turned fifteen. That should have changed me, but it didn't.

About three years ago I got caught for assault with a deadly weapon. I was with my friends. It was back home and we got drunk. I shouldn't have even been doing nothing. But a friend of mine got into a fight with another friend. A big fight erupted, and I ended up stabbing one of my friends. I told him to get off because the second friend was like my cousin. But the guy wouldn't listen to me. I just took it to the next level. I guess he ended up being OK because he was at court and everything.

Ever since then, I've been going in and out of placements. I was in a camp in San Diego and got kicked out of there. I got kicked out of another placement for fighting. I've got an injury from a gang fight there. I got hit in my right eye. When I lay down, it hurts a little. They say it's healed, but it still hurts. I can see all right to a certain extent. But when I look down a bit and look up quickly, I see double on things far away. I didn't want nobody to know about that, but I guess the word got out. The coach-

es here have told me that there would be times on the field where the foot-ball was right in front of me, and I couldn't see it. That's part of the rea-son why they're always yelling at me on the field. They're always shouting, "Walik, Walik, Walik!" And then I start dwelling on the negative stuff.

After I got kicked out of that last place, by then I was the age where they told me it was either here or CYA. That's California Youth Authority. I knew if I went there, the cycle would have kept going. That's just a peni-tentiary for youth. Some people are afraid of it.

I really don't like it here. It's all right, I guess. If you want to change, if you want to get away from that stuff, then this place is good. But when I first got here, it was hard. Real hard. But then I started letting people help me instead of being a rebel and running my own program. I started to trust adults and listen to their opinions. Before, I would just do what I thought was right. I still am, I guess. But I'm trying to do the right thing now.

I've learned to try and sit back and evaluate situations, to just think about what's going to happen. I've learned about options. Should I try to talk to the individuals, or should I turn my back and walk away? You've still got that mentality that says that you should stay because you want to fight. You always want to fight. That's me. But you have to control your-self.

I guess it took a couple of deaths for me to change. I thought that if I didn't want to end up like my friends, then I need to keep on doing what I've got to do. If I don't, then I know what's going to happen to me. So I know that I've got to do the right thing. I was hardheaded. It shouldn't take all that to see the light. But look at all the people who are locked up for gang life and thuggish behavior. Some people just have to learn the hard way.

Walik Smith was walking into the cramped, austere locker room when he stopped and turned. Practice had ended, and the sun was just beginning to set in the distance. He wanted to add one last thing he thought was important.

"I could have left," Smith said. "I don't have to be here now. My time was up in the spring. But they gave me the choice of staying if I wanted to. They said they could put me on scholarship if I wanted. Sometimes I feel like I should be somewhere else, doing something. I feel like I'm standing still. But I decided to stay because I wanted to play football.

"See, I've spent half my life being locked up," he continued. "I missed the prom, homecoming — all that kind of stuff people out in the real world get to do. I ain't had any of it. But I could play football if I stayed here. This is the one chance I had to do something like that. I grew up too fast. I never got the chance to be a kid. This is my chance."

A SNOWBALL'S CHANCE IN . . .

It was the dawn of a new day. Two weeks of hell were about to begin. Sunrise had already come, and the blinding fireball in the sky was beginning its ascent. From that perch, the sun would turn the Arizona desert floor into a griddle, cooking it to sizzling temperatures. It was August 7, a Monday morning. The weatherman on the radio said that today would be the fourteenth consecutive day of 110-plus-degree weather in the metropolitan Phoenix area.

These were the dog days. This was the time of year when lucky Arizonans headed for the mountains or the San Diego beaches. Those left behind acted like vampires, coming out only after the sun had set.

At 6:30 A.M., there was still something resembling a cool breeze in the air as Richard Gray marched purposefully around the practice field, finishing his last-minute preparations, making sure that everything was in its proper place. He wanted his tackling dummies and blocking sleds organized just so. Gray, a tall man with glasses that gave him a studious appearance, was about to begin his twenty-fifth season as a football coach. Yet he was nervous. Every coach must be at the beginning of a new season. There's optimism and excitement at the thought of getting down to business. But there also is the creeping terror that comes with the knowledge that there might be too much to do. There were so many holes to fill, and what if he didn't find those defensive backs he needed, and what was he going to do about his quarterback? The list seemed endless. "You never sleep well the night before the first practice," Gray explained as he pushed a sled toward one of the end zones. "But you always sleep well the night after the first practice."

This wasn't just any coaching job, either. Gray was about to begin his first season as head coach of the Arizona Boys Ranch. He had no idea what to expect. Nobody did. Nothing like this had ever been tried in Arizona before. There were only a few places in the entire country where such an experiment had been conducted. The Ranch was about to enter the brave new world of serious high school football. For some, the expectations were high. Others merely hoped the season wouldn't be a complete disaster.

At precisely 6:45 A.M., the season officially started. The Boys Ranch Spartans silently jogged onto the practice field. They were lined up in formation, two by two, like animals ready to board Noah's Ark. There were nearly eighty of them. They wore matching green helmets and shorts, and gray T-shirts with the words "Whatever It Takes" printed on the back. All, that is, except one: Shaune McKissic, the team's starting quarterback, wore a yellow T-shirt. Most high school, college and professional football teams have their quarterbacks wear different-colored jerseys. This is to remind the other players not to hit them in practice, because quarterbacks are too valuable to risk getting injured by teammates. But that wasn't why McKissic's shirt was a different color from the rest. Yellow was the Ranch's version of the scarlet letter. It was a sign that a guy had screwed up and was paying the price. To be a yellow shirt on the Ranch was to be in your own private purgatory.

"I've been hearing about this kid ever since I took this job, and now he's wearing yellow," Gray said, shaking his head. "Everybody keeps saying what a great leader he is, but then he has two major problems in a month. We'll have to see what kind of leader he is now."

After jogging around the field twice, the players broke down into several rows in the middle of the field. One player, a big defensive lineman named Tamar Armstrong, led the team in basic calisthenics and stretching exercises. After about fifteen minutes, the players formed a single line and counted off into eight groups. Gray and his coaches had set up different stations around the field to begin working on the most rudimentary football drills. The players would spend the next ninety minutes attempting to grasp basic concepts of the game as they rotated from area to area each time an air horn sounded.

Alvin Moore's station was simple. He held a foam blocking pad in front of him, while players lowered their heads and tried to hit him as hard as they could. The emphasis was on the word "tried." Moore had been a star running back at nearby Arizona State. He had played for six years in the NFL with the Baltimore/Indianapolis Colts and the Detroit Lions. He knew hitting. This wasn't hitting. So as one player after another gave him a love tap, the fuse on Moore's temper got shorter and shorter.

"No, no, no!" Moore finally growled at a small Hispanic player. "You don't hit a bag like that. This bag is your enemy. Your enemy isn't some make-believe thing. It's not something you made up in your mind, some other Hispanic kid in some other gang who wears different colors. He's not the enemy. This bag is the enemy! Where's that intensity you have on the streets when you're trying to kill your make-believe enemies? You have to take it all out on this bag. Now try it again."

When the boy hit the pad this time, there was a crisp pop.

If you didn't know any better, it would be easy to assume that this was just another high school football team embarking on the annual grueling three-a-day practices to get the players in shape for the upcoming season. But this was not just another prep team. This team had been organized by various juvenile courts around the country.

This morning the players wore green. Before they arrived here, their colors had been blue or red or black or white. They had fought for those colors. They were Crips and Bloods. They were members of Hispanic gangs that had yet to gain the notoriety of the black gangs. They were members of Asian gangs, which the staff would tell you were the most deadly and vicious of them all. Others were white supremacists, who hated any skin color but their own. Still other kids had come here with no gang affiliations. They didn't need six homeboys behind them to back them up on the streets. They were nasty sons of bitches who could take care of their own business without any help. They came from different parts of the country and different backgrounds. Most had known each other only a matter of months or weeks. If they had crossed paths on the street, something violent probably would have ensued. These were not Boy Scouts. On the whole, you wouldn't have wanted to meet these kids in a crowded place at high noon, let alone by yourself in a dark alley at night.

But now they were Arizona Boys Ranch Spartans. Together they were trying to play football. In another time, this place might have been called a reform school. Today, it was termed a "residential placement facility for at-risk youth." These boys had been shipped here by the juvenile court system in the hope that somehow, some way, they would be changed, that their out-of-control lives would be salvaged before it was too late.

On "the Outs," as the residents described the world beyond the Ranch's property, the boys underneath these helmets were the most dangerous of young men. "You have some guys out here that you think to yourself, 'They're not so bad,' Gray said. "Then you look at their reports and read about why they're here and see what they've done and you say to yourself, 'I'll be damned.'"

Some of the kids were relatively average teenagers who simply had made horrible mistakes. Others had been just plain bad. They were the serious, hard-core gang bangers. Virtually every crime for which somebody can be charged was represented: robberies, selling drugs, assault, sexual assaults, drive-by shootings. A handful of boys had killed people, although none of those was trying out for the football team. But then Ranch staff didn't differentiate much between kids who had killed someone and those who were here on charges of merely wounding people in drive-bys. The only difference was the killers' aim had been a little better.

So even though Ranch staff didn't like to describe the residents this way, the simple fact was that their facility housed the worst of the worst juvenile offenders that American streets had to offer. Their rap sheets were lengthy. Most of the boys had screwed up somewhere else, been kicked out of other placements, or been rejected by other facilities because they didn't handle unrepentant gang members. When all else failed, this was where they landed. Residents at the Ranch had no place else to go. This was the end of the line — the Last Chance Ranch. This was New York in reverse. If you couldn't make it here, you couldn't make it anywhere. If the boys who arrived couldn't cut it and see the error of their ways, then they surely were destined to travel one of two paths: to a long jail term or to an early grave.

The only other option was to take the opportunity offered at the Ranch. The whole point of their being here in the first place was that somebody — judges, probation officers, social workers — had sensed something in each and every one of these boys; something that indicated to them that in the right environment and with the right guidance, they possibly could change. There was slight hope for them. They had been deemed salvageable.

Later in the morning, though, Moore was coming to the conclusion that as football players, these kids were worthless. During a pass-catching drill, Moore kept shaking his head angrily as one running back after another dropped the ball. "Look," he told the backs, "you know what happens in the NFL when you drop the ball? It costs you $100. Then, pretty soon, they stop putting up with $100 drops. They drop you. Then you can read your name in the newspaper under 'Transactions.'" The boys listened to this. But judging from the blank expressions on their faces, it was unclear if any of them knew what the hell Mr. Moore was talking about . . . except that maybe it was going to start costing them 100 bucks they didn't have if they did start holding on to the ball.

A few minutes later, Alan Shofner, another one of the football coaches, ran over with a group of about twenty more players. They had not taken part in the Ranch's summer conditioning program, so Shofner would be working them separately until they were in good enough shape to join the rest of the squad. Many of them were new arrivals, and for that reason they wore red shirts, meaning they were orientation kids, newcomers still learning the system. Thus, they also were among the highest risks for going AWOL. Red shirts meant these kids had to be watched extra closely.

Shofner, a middle-aged man with close-cropped hair and a booming voice that a drill sergeant would envy, began pointing out the coaches to his group. "Right there, that's Coach Gray. He runs the football team. Over there, that's Coach Moore. He might yell at you a lot, but he's going to make you a better football player if you listen to him. Way over there, that's Coach Kush," Shofner added. "If he doesn't call you a jackass, you ain't nothing. It's an honor to be called a jackass by that man." A few moments later, as if on cue, Frank Kush threw his cap into the air in disgust and began chewing out a receiver for not running a pass route correctly. From halfway across the field, the word "jackass" boomed out distinctly. Then, with a point of his thumb, Kush commanded the offending player to take a lap around the field.

Once Kush had been the most recognizable sports figure in Arizona, a man whose reputation had grown into almost mythical proportions. He had risen to the pinnacle of his profession — coaching in the NFL. Later this month, he would be inducted into the College Football Hall of Fame. Yet this morning, still energetic at age sixty-six, he was yelling at sixteen-year-old kids who couldn't figure out how far seven yards was so they could run a pass pattern properly. "Sometimes," Kush said during a water break, "you have to take a step back and ask yourself,

'Why are they here?' The answer is they're here because they have an inability to focus, to pay attention and abide by the rules. That's what we're trying to teach here. Every day is going to be like reinventing the wheel. But they've never had to dot the I's and cross the T's. You can tell that they've had dysfunctional backgrounds."

When the break was over, he went back out on the field to call somebody else a jackass.

As the temperature soared into three digits on a day when the mercury eventually would top out at 114, Lance Michel, the Ranch's head trainer, was watching for signs that kids were wilting in the extreme heat. He was off and running, his belt full of first-aid gear, as one boy frantically began motioning to him for assistance during the second morning practice session. It was only when Michel reached the youth that he realize the source of the problem. The boy's chin strap had come unbuckled from his helmet. He was afraid that somehow he had broken it. "Sir, sir, how do I put this back on?" the boy pleaded. "I can't do it!" As Michel showed him how the strap snapped into place, relief spread across the boy's face.

The Spartans were starting at ground zero.

The previous fall, the Ranch had fielded its first football team. It had been admitted as an associate member of the Arizona Interscholastic Association. The AIA wanted a sort of trial run to see how things went. The belief at the Ranch was that state officials wanted to make sure the Spartans weren't just a bunch of street thugs who beat up the other players on the field. Burke Whitfield, the principal at the Ranch, who also served as the athletic director, said that years before there had been an institution in Arizona called the Fort Grant Industrial School for Boys that also had fielded a football squad. Over time fights during games and muggings in the stands had caused the program to be discontinued. Some folks in Arizona high school sports had long memories. So when the Ranch petitioned the AIA for admission, Whitfield said, "People thought, 'Great, here's another reform school.'"

Ranch officials had their own concerns, but not about how their kids were going to act on the football field. The first thing residents learn at the Ranch is the primary law of physics: For every action, there is an equal and opposite reaction. In other words, Spartan players knew that if they acted improperly during games, they would be held accountable for it later and the consequences would likely involve lots of manual labor and sweat. Instead, what worried the staff was whether they knew what they were getting into with a football team. The fear was that they might be setting themselves up for failure. In fact in the beginning, the Spartans were basically at a Pop Warner level understanding of football. The coaches had to explain everything. Some kids didn't even know how many yards it took to get a first down. In their first scrimmage, the opening four snaps between the center and the quarterback had been fumbled.

Not only were the players new to the game, but so were the coaches. Ray Perkins, a staff member who had been an NFL defensive lineman for the Dallas Cowboys, Tampa Bay Buccaneers, and Arizona Cardinals, was named the interim head coach. But he had never run a team before. None of the staff had, except Kush, who carried the title of director of football. Yet somehow the Ranch had managed to do all right. As an independent team in the 2A classification, the smallest division for eleven-man football in Arizona, the Ranch had been a respectable 4–5 in 1994, playing mostly against rural schools, including several Native American reservation teams. Predictably, the Spartans had been crushed by schools that were known for having good programs.

More important, though, not a single complaint had been registered against Spartan players by opponents or officials. Instead, after several games referees commented that the Ranch's players had acted in a more sportsmanlike manner than the players on the other team. Ranch staff never quite knew how to react to those kind words. On one level, they accepted the compliments in the obvious heartfelt manner in which they were given. On another level, they cringed. Everyone was always expecting the Spartans to act like the worst kind of young punks. "We don't act like hoodlums here," Shofner said defiantly. Nevertheless, the Ranch had passed the unspoken test. So this season, the Spartans had been admitted as a full-fledged member of the AIA and moved up into 3A classification. An experienced coach — Gray — had been hired to take over the program as Perkins became the defensive line coach. After a one-season trial run, everyone at the Ranch considered their second year to be their first real foray into the realm of competitive high school football.

The average stay at the Ranch is only about eighteen months, so that by 1995 virtually the entire 1994 squad was gone. The team's star linebacker was one of the few players who had been expected to be back for this season. He had done so well the previous year that his mug shot — and not one taken at a police station — graced the cover of one of the state's preseason prep football magazines. He was considered among the top returning players in Arizona. "The closest thing to Lawrence Taylor that you'll ever see on a high school field" was the way one Ranch staffer described him. Trouble was, the linebacker was no longer at the Ranch. The California county that had sent him here had determined that his time was up, and he was sent home. Ranch officials had been trying to convince him to return so he could complete his high school education and maybe get a chance to earn a college football scholarship. Unfortunately, he had other obligations: He was in a California lockup. The Lawrence Taylor clone would not be suiting up this season for the Spartans.

So the harsh reality was that Gray had a raw team with little experience. Green was a fitting team color. The week before, Gray had called a meeting of all the kids on the Ranch who were interested in playing football. Nearly one hundred had showed. Gray asked them how many had played real, organized football for youth or high school teams. Only nine raised their hands. Most had never stuck around a school long enough to play.

Gray took a deep breath.

The top two quarterbacks, McKissic and a slim fifteen-year-old boy named Todd Harris, were back from last year's squad. So was Armstrong, the Ranch's best defensive lineman. Two good running backs were returning: a quick slasher named Corey Cabell and a tough, straight-ahead runner named Tim Elliott. Gray had a good all-purpose athlete named Juan Sparkman, but he didn't have much else, and a handful of players don't make a complete team. Meanwhile, McKissic, the leader he was supposed to build his team around, was in a yellow shirt.

Gray used that first meeting to go over the basics. He showed the players how to put on the equipment. One boy was used during a show-and-tell demonstration on how to wear shoulder pads, hip pads, a helmet, and so on. Gray said all eyes were watching intently. "You know how peer pressure is with kids," he said. "Nobody wanted to look dumb and admit that they didn't know how to put the pads on. But they were all watching me real close when I was showing them how to strap them on."

Yet for all the disadvantages Gray faced, he did have a few things going in his favor. Although he had an unskilled team, he had a wealth of experience on his coaching staff. There were thirteen coaches, which was the size of a college staff, including a couple who offered their services on a part-time basis when their Ranch duties would allow. Gray himself had been the head coach at three Phoenix-area high schools as well as an assistant at Northern Arizona University, a Division I-AA school, for five years. Perkins and Moore had played in the NFL, and so had Gallen Allen, the linebacker coach. Gary Winchester, the offensive line coach, had been the head coach at nearby Queen Creek High School and also had played with British Columbia in the Canadian Football League. Most of the other coaches had played collegiately.

The only coach the Ranch had hired specifically for the football program was Gray. Everyone else had already been there. The place was brimming with ex-jocks, because Ranch officials liked to hire people with either military or sports backgrounds, people accustomed to discipline.

Few high schools had so many coaches, but the Ranch needed that many. The reality was that with one hundred juvenile offenders on the practice field, there had to be a lot of staff members around to keep matters under control. If a boy began to act in a manner deemed to be improper, he would be "addressed," an all-purpose phrase meaning a staff member would get into the kid's face and chew out his butt. The rules were that there had to be at least two staff members present when an addressing took place, in case it led to a physical confrontation and the boy had to be restrained until he calmed down. The standard tactic was to remove the boy from his peers so he wouldn't feel the need to stand up to the staff in front of his friends in order to maintain his tough-guy image. So an addressing would automatically take two staff members from the field. Hence the reason for the number of coaches. Disturbances like riots or brawls never happened at the Ranch, though, because the staff wouldn't allow them.

Gray wasn't completely pessimistic about his players, either. He had about twelve kids who weighed more than two hundred pounds. The Ranch team probably would be bigger than most schools it played. And he had speed. Gray had never coached a high school team this fast, so he wouldn't be lacking for skilled position players like running backs and receivers. Any football coach will tell you that when you have big-play speed, you can make up for a lot of other deficiencies.

But what Gray had this morning was a bunch of kids who didn't look as if they knew what they were doing. The second morning practice of the day ended with gassers — sprints from one end of the field to the other and back again. This is the kind of drill that tests players and makes them wonder if they really want to put themselves through agony to play football. After a series of sprints, the players were left doubled over in exhaustion as they struggled to regain their breath. Fountains of sweat poured off their bodies. Even the T-shirts of the student trainers were soaked as they pulled the water caddies around to the players. It was not quite noon, and the sun was beating down directly on the field. After allowing the team a brief water break, Gray pulled the players together. While he could scream and yell when the situation called for it, Gray was a patient, low-key man by nature. "The coaches have made a commitment here," he told them. "We're going to get you ready to play football by the first game." That was the extent of the season's first speech. There was no talk of victories, league championship, or state title. Gray knew better.

But before some players could head back to the locker room and get ready for lunch, several had one more task to complete. A small group of well-dressed men had gathered under the meager shade offered by a eucalyptus tree a short distance from the field. Shofner read off a roll call of names. These boys had to go meet with their probation officers.

LOST BOYS

Juan Sparkman felt good. There was a bounce to his step. He was psyched about the upcoming season. He planned to introduce himself to 3A teams all around the state. The coaches had told him he was a big part of their plans. He was going to play defensive back and wide receiver. Gray had already explained that Sparkman was going to be one of the blocks on which the rest of the team was built. At five feet ten, 170 pounds, the sinewy Sparkman had the look of an athlete. He was an outgoing teenager with a quick smile that would light up his entire face. It was impossible not to like him, and he was a favorite of most of the staff — even when he did things that made them want to wring his neck.

He also was one tough kid. As far as anyone at the Ranch could figure out, Sparkman had no home. He stayed because he had no place else to go. A seventeen-year-old native of San Diego, he had been here going on five years. This was his family. He said his parents were dead, although he spoke only vaguely about them. "My mother died of a heart attack, and my father got shot," he said during a break between practices. "With my dad, it was about three and a half years ago. I was already at the Ranch. He was really heavy into gangs. He just got caught up in them, I guess. One of his rivals shot him. That's how it goes. They shoot one of yours. You shoot one of theirs."

He talked about having a twin sister whom he hadn't seen in three years and three brothers. "But I'm really on my own," Sparkman said. "The Ranch has basically raised me. They've turned my life around here and gotten me away from those illegal things and got me to do the right things."

Sparkman had been doing the wrong things for a long time. He grew up in a rough part of San Diego, technically in an apartment with an aunt and her family. In reality, he had been reared on the streets. By the age of eight, Sparkman said he was running with a neighborhood gang called the West Coast 30s. He quickly learned the street life from his uncles, including how to sell drugs.

"It was mostly gang banging over turf, selling narcotics, a lot of pimps, all that kind of stuff," he explained casually. "I was just doing what my uncles were doing. They were the only parents I pretty much had, and they lived the wild life. One uncle is dead now. But I thought that life was OK. When you're that young, you really don't know. You just think it's cool. If your whole family is doing it, eventually you think, 'Dang, this must be the family business, and someday you get to take over.' "

Juan was hesitant to reveal details of his previous existence. But then many boys at the Ranch were like that. There are chapters in everyone's life that are not open for public viewing. That was especially the case with the boys here. In some ways, they tried to treat their days before coming to the Ranch like bad dreams, something that never really happened. They disassociated themselves from what they had seen or their specific acts. There was another reason Sparkman didn't like to talk about "the Outs." The more you talked about gang life, he believed, the better your chances were of going back to your old ways when you left here. You had to make a clean break, he said. That included forgetting about the past.

Occasionally, though, Sparkman painted a vivid picture of what it was like in the inner-city jungle. And the word he kept coming back to was "wild." In San Diego, he had slept during the day and run the streets at night. There was no time for school, or, as Sparkman called it, "books and stuff." There was too much action going on to be worried about attending classes. Besides, where was that ever going to get him?

"Every day was a party," he said. "Shooting guns. Doing drugs. All kinds of stuff. Every day you'd find out more about your family. You'd come home and see family members that you didn't even know you had — an uncle or a niece or somebody. There was stuff happening every day, but it was always negative. I started off stealing from stores and stuff. Then you go up to armed robbery and GTAs [grand theft autos]. It just added on. You think that's the right thing to do because you never seen anything else."

Once, when he was eleven, Sparkman was walking down the street with a friend, minding their own business, he said, when a car slowed down and pulled up beside them. Sparkman remembered hearing some popping noises, and instinctively he hit the pavement. So did his friend. "I ducked. I thought he ducked, too. But he didn't duck because he wanted to." His pal had been shot. Sparkman watched the boy's blood and life pour out of him right there on the sidewalk. He died before the paramedics could get him to the hospital. The police, he said, never found the shooter or determined if there even was a reason for the murder other than that somebody just felt like killing somebody else that day.

"That's the worst thing I ever saw," Sparkman said softly. "I had been standing right next to him. We was just walking. I was shocked. I had never seen that kind of stuff before. That made a big impact on me. It showed me that you could be dead in an instant, especially in that environment."

It was only a matter of time before Sparkman ended up in the juvenile court system. He was caught on a grand theft auto charge and also was accused of assault with a deadly weapon and selling drugs. After running away from another placement facility, he had ended up at the Ranch by the age of twelve. Sparkman had been at the Ranch longer than most of the staff. He didn't really like being here, yet he knew there was no place else for him to go. Deep down, he knew the Ranch had been good for him because staff had made him face his problems. For the first time in his life, he had to deal with consequences. Sparkman felt that he had changed and had no desire to take up his old habits. He hoped to stay in Arizona when he left the Ranch the following May and maybe get a football scholarship at a local junior college. But Sparkman still had a healthy temper, and sometimes an internal cauldron would boil over in a cascade of frustration.

"I don't know why," he said. "Maybe it's not liking authority. I don't like it when people tell me what to do all the time. But I realize that's life. People are always going to be telling you what to do. Sometimes staff here will test you, to see how you will react, like if you were on 'the Outs.' You fail a test out there, and you'll end up locked up."

There had been an incident a few months earlier after Gray had arrived at the Ranch and held spring workouts to introduce the kids to basic plays. Kush was there, too, and he was doing what he had always done: get on players. One day he was barking at Sparkman, and Juan didn't like it. So, in Ranchspeak, he went off. But the guy he decided to take out his anger on was a curious choice. Tunufa'i Ta'ase was a mountain of a man. An American Samoan, Ta'ase (Ta-SAY) stood six feet two and weighed 320 pounds. He had an expressionless face, but he also had piercing eyes. Ta'ase's cold stare could stop boys in their tracks. He had been an offensive lineman at the University of Utah in the late 1980s and might have gone on and played in the NFL if he had not blown out his knee in the Hula Bowl, an all-star game for seniors. Ta'ase had decided he'd rather be able to horse around with his kids and walk later in life than play pro football.

During his years at the Ranch, Sparkman had developed a bond with Ta'ase. When Juan had a problem, he knew he could go to Mr. Ta'ase and talk about it. Mr. Ta'ase understood where he was coming from. Sparkman could revert to street slang, which he fell back into when he was upset. Other staff sometimes took that as a sign of disrespect, but Ta'ase would let him express himself as best he could. The truth was, Sparkman liked Ta'ase. On that day, though, something tripped inside Sparkman's head. Mad at Kush and frustrated with being bossed around all the time, Sparkman got out of hand. He jumped Ta'ase, who, besides being the adult he was closest to, was also the biggest staff member at the Ranch.

After Sparkman was pulled off Ta'ase and had settled down some, the two had a long chat. When they were done talking, both even agreed that something positive had come out of Sparkman's explosion. When boys acted out at the Ranch, it gave staff an opportunity to find out what was really going on with them, the source of the problem.

Juan wasn't mad at him, Ta'ase would say later. He just happened to be nearby. In the wrong place at the wrong time — or maybe it was the right place at the right time. Ta'ase felt that he and Sparkman had made some progress in curbing the boy's violent tendencies. He's got to understand, Ta'ase added, that he just can't attack people like that simply because he's mad about something. "I don't care if he's a good football player," he said. "I just want him to deal with his anger in an appropriate manner."

Sparkman wasn't a dumb kid. He often talked about how he wanted to channel his aggression, but that it was sometimes hard in the heat of the moment. But this he knew: If he had popped somebody out on the streets like that, he probably would have ended up in jail — or worse. And, then he wouldn't have been able to pursue his ultimate dream: becoming an actor.

But first, Sparkman was going to play some football. "We're gonna rock some houses this year, baby," he said.

Four hundred residents between the ages of eight and eighteen called the Arizona Boys Ranch their temporary home. Counties and tribal courts from five different states — Arizona, Nevada, California, Indiana, and Illinois—sent juveniles here. The Ranch had three facilities in Arizona, but the two hundred–acre main campus was located in Queen Creek, thirty-five miles southwest of Phoenix, amid the cotton fields of central Arizona. About 240 boys lived here.

In its pastoral setting, the Ranch could have been mistaken for a small community college. The campus grounds were immaculate. The lawns were a lush green and always cut short. That's because almost every day of the week, residents and staff—work crews—could be seen pushing lawn mowers. There were classrooms, dormitory-like cottages where residents slept, a pantry (which was what the Ranch called its dining hall), barns, and a chapel, among other buildings. Two new structures had just gone up: military-style barracks to house the kids from the Civic Conservation Corps who would be playing on the football team. Civics, as it was known, was based near the town of Oracle, about ninety miles south of Queen Creek. It was a highly structured paramilitary program for boys at the Ranch ages sixteen and older. Because the Civics camp was so far away, the kids playing football lived on the main campus for the course of the season.

The Ranch had absolutely none of the trappings of a penal institution. There were no locks. No walls. No bars. No guard towers. No fences, unless you counted the ones that kept the cattle, sheep, pigs and horses. There was nothing to suggest that the people who lived here had been judged to be menaces to society. One of the Ranch's central tenets was that if you treated kids like inmates, they would act like inmates. So the kids were not locked up. What the Ranch did have was staff. They served as the boundaries.

"There's a fence here, but you just can't see it," Whitfield explained. "That's because there's always a person with you. He checks to see if you're in bed at night. We have roll calls during the day. But what's the alternative? A place with bars where your parents come to visit you in a cage for a couple hours on weekends? But because we don't have walls, the kids see me as a principal and not as a warden. They don't see staff as prison guards. The state of Arizona would rather see kids locked up. But you don't treat kids when they're locked up. The state locks 'em up and says screw 'em. The United States is already full of kids in prison. We've got some bad-ass kids here. But some kids just made bad choices. They don't deserve to be locked up."

Much of the time the boys were marched in a group, side by side, from place to place by staff. It was rare to see kids walking by themselves, because staff liked to keep an eye on everybody. Nevertheless, it wasn't that unusual for kids to go AWOL. It might have happened more often if the Ranch were in a more urban location. But the facility was in such a remote spot, on the edge of the Sonoran Desert, that the natural terrain offered a strong deterrent. More than one resident would say that when he first arrived here, he thought he was being dropped off in a land-locked Alcatraz. The area around the Ranch was completely flat. Directly to the north was Williams Air Force Base, which the federal government had closed a few years earlier as a military facility. To the east was the small farming town of Queen Creek, which was the kind of sleepy place where dogs meander across the street and pickup trucks slow to let the critters pass unscathed. To the west and south were miles of farmland. Several miles to the south, the San Tan Mountains rose from the desert. There wasn't anyplace to run if residents decided to try their luck, although some kids still liked to roll the dice.

Of all the residential placement facilities for juveniles in Arizona, the Ranch was by far the most controversial. Some might even say it was the most notorious. The Ranch had been in the headlines, for both good and bad reasons, for most of its existence. Four times the Ranch had endured major investigations into abuse charges leveled at staff by residents. The latest investigation had been in 1994. That had been a hellish year for the Ranch. A resident had drowned in a canal and Alameda County in California had pulled the boys it placed at the Ranch when allegations of abuse surfaced. State investigators later said they had substantiated numerous charges of physical abuse. A series of newspaper articles had painted the Ranch as a place where street kids were no longer the predators but the prey of out-of-control staff. Or as an editorial in the state's largest paper, *The Arizona Republic,* charged: "If only a portion of the allegations are true, they raise disturbing questions about ranch operations and the methods employed to try and show wayward juveniles the road back."

It wasn't the first time the Ranch had to defend itself.

In the beginning, it had been an orphanage, a place for lost boys with no place else to turn. It was incorporated as a private, nonprofit organization in 1949 by the Phoenix Rotary Club. Civic leaders, including a man named Howard Pyle, who would soon go on to become governor of Arizona, thought there ought to be some kind of facility besides Fort Grant juvenile prison where not-so-bad kids could be sent. Two ranchers offered 188 acres in the isolated community of Queen Creek, and donations were solicited. The first cottage was opened in 1951, and the first boy was accepted. Back then, the Ranch was designed primarily for kids whose sole crime was homelessness or running away from broken homes. Kids with records of hard crime weren't taken.

Arizona's leading citizens and civic organizations quickly accepted the Ranch as a worthy cause that deserved special attention. A Presbyterian minister named Wendell Newell, who favored cowboy hats and boots, was hired in 1954 to become the superintendent, a job he would hold for seventeen years. Newell would become a well-known figure in the state. He was quick to chastise anyone who labeled Ranch residents "problem boys." Rather, they were "boys with problems." He also liked to call his wards "less-chance boys." During his tenure, the Ranch grew in size and numbers. By 1971, 110 residents lived there. It seemed to be the model facility for troubled youth.

In 1971, the Ranch also had its first brush with bad publicity. Critics charged that Newell's spare-the-rod-and-spoil-the-child methods were outdated. Newell never denied that he struck boys from time to time, but he maintained that he always did so in moderation. He declared that he had never beaten boys, and ardent supporters of the Ranch defended him. Still, there were concerns that he had stepped beyond acceptable boundaries, and later the allegations became uncomfortably specific. He was accused of hitting boys and making kids walk barefoot in hot sand. The same society people who had been writing checks and helping raise funds for the Ranch turned away. A probe was launched, and the next year Newell was dismissed. There was a general sense that the kids housed at the Ranch were getting tougher and that Newell just didn't know how to handle them.

A new director took over and promised that there would be no more physical punishment. But stung by the bad press, the Ranch had already lost its favorite-cause status. Funding and the number of residents were dwindling. The facility seemed to have lost its effectiveness. The day thirty-three-year-old Bob Thomas arrived in 1977 to become executive director, the Ranch had only forty residents. The place was in shambles.

During the years that followed, everything the Ranch became could be attributed to Thomas. By the fall of 1994, there were almost four hundred boys in the Ranch system. Administrators now claimed a 68 percent success rate. In other words, that percentage of boys left the Ranch and never ended up back in the judicial system. Now those same officials also were honest enough to admit that figure probably included boys who had gone back to their delinquent ways and simply hadn't been caught. Still, the Ranch seemed to have a successful formula.

But something else also had increased over the years: the number of state inquiries into the Ranch's methods. In 1982, 1987, and finally 1994, the state had looked into charges of abuse of residents by staff. Over the years, a pattern had developed. Investigators from the Department of Economic Security's Child Protective Services agency would substantiate charges of physical abuse. Then Thomas would launch a verbal counterattack, lambasting state officials for being incompetent as well as horribly naive about the Ranch's residents. Thomas maintained that the easiest way for boys to get out of the Ranch was to cry abuse and then tell investigators exactly what they wanted to hear. CPS might be trained to deal with three-year-olds with cigarette burns on their bodies, Thomas said, but they didn't know a damned thing about dealing with hard-core gang bangers who had survived on the streets by manipulating people.

By 1995, what had begun as a difference in philosophy between a stubborn state agency that saw its duty as protecting children and an equally stubborn placement facility whose mission was changing the behavior of young thugs had erupted into an all-out war. The battle would be waged on the front pages of Phoenix-area newspapers before eventually, and probably inevitably, spilling over into court.

———

The questions being raised were obvious: Why were these kids playing football? Why would a place designed to correct the deviant behaviors of seriously troubled and delinquent youth concern itself with teaching proper blocking and tackling techniques? Why would Kush, of all people, be out here working with these gang kids? Running the Ranch football program certainly wasn't cheap. The estimate was that the Ranch had sunk about $100,000 in donations into starting the program.

And teaching these boys how to play an inherently violent game like football seemed to fly in the face of the Ranch's main objective, which was to control aggressive tendencies. But, the goal of the program was to channel that aggression in a way that was socially acceptable. It was all right to beat the everlasting stuffing out of somebody on the football field — as long as you did it within the context of the rules.

It is often said that high school football builds character; that the game teaches kids fundamental lessons about life, such as teamwork and how to overcome adversity. Often those phrases are mumbled by coaches more intent on wins and losses than on molding America's youth. At the Ranch, though, those words were more than clichés. The football program here wasn't launched to win trophies. Oh, sure everyone hoped the team would win, but the true goal was to use football as a tool to reach these boys.

These kids basically were losers. That was what they had been told their entire lives. They were even losers as criminals, because they had been caught. They arrived at the Ranch wild and untamed. They generally had never worked for anything their entire short lives. They would rather have stolen what they wanted. They had no respect for authority. They didn't listen to their parents (if they were around) or to teachers or cops or judges. They had no discipline.

Football, perhaps more than any other sport, required discipline. It demanded hard work, cooperation, a willingness to follow directions. Ranch staff hoped that whatever lessons the boys learned on the field could be put to use in real life. This idea was based on a theory called transfer. The Ranch used its livestock program in much the same way. By taking care of cows, horses, pigs, and other animals, the boys learned responsibility. They developed empathy. If they could have feelings of compassion for four-legged creatures, maybe eventually they could have it toward two-legged animals, too.

Should the Ranch be fortunate enough to win some football games, then it would also show its kids that if they played by the rules and did things the right way, they could achieve some success. That could only help build self-esteem. The other goal of the football program was to teach kids the true meaning of toughness. The game was a way to show the boys that they weren't nearly as macho as they thought they were.

"They come here thinking tough is pulling a gun or a knife," Whitfield said. "They don't know what tough is until they come out here, get knocked down, and then have to pat the guy who knocked them down on their butt." Whitfield had come out to watch part of a practice. A huge man with gray hair and a blunt way of speaking, Whitfield knew a little bit about successful child-rearing. He had a son who was a freshman at Duke on a soccer scholarship. His belief was that even if a kid didn't change at the Ranch, at least for those months he was here he wasn't out on the streets terrorizing others.

"We've had kids leave here and kill people," he said. "We've had people leave here and get killed. But they already were heading down that path. Most of these kids just want the same things we do. They want a life, and if they don't get that, then they're going to take a life. We have some kids out here at the Ranch who have murdered. They have killed. But there are worse things."

Whitfield allowed that to linger in the air for a moment.

"For instance, how about a fourteen-year-old taking a ten-year-old out back of a building, pulling down his pants and, saying, "'Suck my dick,'" he continued. "Maybe he doesn't like having his dick sucked, but it makes him feel good to make someone else feel real bad. That's the way it is on the streets."

My name is Jerrold Smith. I'm from San Francisco. I'm sixteen. I've been here twenty-three months.

How do I like it here? It all depends. Sometimes you like it, and sometimes you want to get away. Sometimes you don't want to do nothing. You think about home, and you want to go. You want to be with your friends. After a while, you know what you need to do and you get on with it. You learn what not to do, like talking back to staff and not listening. When you do that, you're gonna fail.

What's it like back where I'm from? In San Francisco? It's rough. People selling drugs and gang banging. I'm from the Fillmore district. It's in the central area. It's tough where I grew up. Then I came here and you see the opportunities. You see the potential.

Dope selling got me here. That and robbing and stealing money. I just did what I had to do. Before I came here, that's how I was. If you want something and your family can't get it for you, you had to get it. It's like those T-shirts that we wear. They say, "Whatever It Takes." That can mean something good or it can mean something bad. I did whatever I needed to do to buy drugs. There's peer pressure on the streets. You try to stay away from it. That's all you can do; be your own man, be a leader and not a follower. But that's hard. That's why I'm happy to be here. I know that if I wasn't here, I'd probably be dead. But staff is always yelling here. Sometimes they be yelling for nothing. You go to football practice tired and you don't want to hear all that yelling. You know what I mean? But I take it.

When I leave here, I won't be going back to San Francisco. I be going to New Orleans. That's where my mom and my grandmother are. It's just another chance there for me. If I go back to San Francisco, I might end up locked up for the rest of my life.

I had played in Pop Warner before, so I knew that I could play football. But I never really got the chance to play beyond that. Football is good for me. I like it. See today, I was feeling down. Then I went into the locker room and saw my name on the list of players who coaches said are doing well. Now I feel good. I'm excited. They call me "the Hitman" on the football field. Back home, I like hitting people hard. I always felt like I had to prove myself. If you called out my name or something, I wanted to fight you. I had a short temper. That's what I need to work on here.

I really don't want to say what I did to get in here. I don't like to talk about what I did. I'm away from that stuff now. It's the kind of stuff that you don't talk to nobody about. They say they've got a priest here who will come and talk to me. They say I can talk to him about things that I've *never told nobody. They say you can tell a priest anything. But I don't know if I can even tell him. I really don't believe that. You can tell people certain things, but not all things.*

————

A few weeks later, before a game one Friday night, Bob Thomas and Father William Mitchell, an older Catholic priest with snow-white hair who served as the Ranch's chaplain, saw Jerrold Smith sitting with the junior varsity players. Smith had been sent down to the JV before the start of the season. Thomas encouraged Father Mitchell to pass along a story about Smith. It seemed that the priest and Smith had been talking, and when they were finished, Father Mitchell gave the boy the sign of the cross on his forehead. Smith looked at the priest skeptically.

"What you just did for me, that's good?" Smith asked.

Father Mitchell assured him that it was.

So then the boy said, "Well, Father, I would like to do something for you now."

Then he made the sign of the cross on the priest's forehead.

"I've never had that happen to me before," Father Mitchell said. The priest chuckled softly at the memory.

THE LAND OF OPPORTUNITY

The football field was like a second home for Mike Smith. A former wide receiver at Arizona State, he was a volunteer assistant with the Spartans. Smith had a jaw that looked as if it were chiseled out of granite, and it was symbolic of the rest of the man. Smith, who was one of the program coordinators on the main campus, related well to the boys. But he did not put up with the slightest bit of trouble, either. That's why most residents didn't care much for Mr. Smith when they first met him. Smith used to be the Ranch's intake director. That meant he would "greet" new arrivals. Over the years, he had perfected his speech: *Welcome to the Arizona Boys Ranch. This is the land of opportunity. This is like no place you've ever been before.* Then the adventure would begin.

Not every boy was suited for the Ranch. That's why staff would conduct interviews in juvenile halls with prospective residents after they had been recommended by judges, lawyers, or probation officers. There were kids that the Ranch just couldn't take. Because it was an open setting, high AWOL risks weren't accepted because they would run the first time staff turned their backs. Kids diagnosed with severe psychological problems or who were high suicide risks weren't taken either. Nor were boys who had truly violent tendencies — those who would reach for a knife or a shovel every time they got angry. Kids also had to be physically capable of doing the program. Everyone else, though, was fair game.

The Ranch's reputation as being a tough place was known in juvenile halls. So it wouldn't come as much of a surprise when Smith, after he had made his introduction to the new residents, would begin to lay down the law. The boys called it "setting the tone." Here are the rules.

You will follow them. You will act in an appropriate manner at all times. You will practice good hygiene. You will address all adults with respect; that includes saying "yes, sir" and "no, sir." There is no fighting. No swearing. No use of gang talk or gang signs. Gangs are not tolerated here. You will keep your shirt tucked in. You will keep your shoelaces tied. There is no smoking. No alcohol. No drugs. No weapons of any kind. You will be attentive in the classroom. When you are told to stand straight at attention, you will. When you are told to march in an orderly manner, you will. When you are told to perform your daily chores, you will. When you are told that it's lights out and time to go to bed, you will. When you eat at the pantry, you will finish all the food on your plate, including veggies, or you will not receive dessert. And on and on.

The boys would then be taken to get a close-cropped haircut and to receive their Ranch clothing, including the red T-shirts that indicated they were newcomers. Later they would be brought to their temporary home: the orientation cottage. After they had completed orientation, they would be moved to other cottages that were run by husband-and-wife houseparents. The idea was to create a family environment, something most of these boys had never experienced.

There may have been no tougher job on the Ranch than being a houseparent. They were on the front lines, living with the boys on a daily basis. Greg Milbrandt, who was the football team's quarterbacks coach, liked working at the Ranch, but he conceded that he had once considered finding a new line of work. When he first came to the Ranch, Milbrandt said, he would fill in for the regular houseparents. One night, a boy in his cottage stole his car and went AWOL. The next morning, the other residents told him that the boy's original plan had been to knock out Milbrandt with a length of chain that had a padlock on the end while he was sleeping. That way he could look for the car keys unobstructed. Luckily for Milbrandt, the boy found the keys without having to whack him on the head. Maybe that's why Milbrandt was happy with his current job as the Ranch's P.E. instructor.

A regular day at the Ranch began about 5:30 A.M. Boys were expected to perform basic chores like making their beds and cleaning up the cottages. Breakfast was at 7:00 A.M. School began at 7:30 A.M. Boys didn't have to march to class, but they were expected to line up outside each classroom at parade rest attention with their books in their right hands. When they were allowed to enter the classroom, they had to stand next to their desks until the teacher told them to sit. When class was over, they had to stand quietly again until they were dismissed.

Classes would run through the middle of the afternoon, just like at any school. Unlike other schools, though, there were roll calls during the day to make sure no one had slipped away. After dinner, there was quiet time and meetings. Sometimes the residents of cottages would get together just to talk. There were counseling sessions to deal with specific problems for kids who had abused alcohol, drugs, and so on. There were also treatment team meetings. Each boy had a team, consisting of teachers, social workers, houseparents, maybe even a coach. The team would meet on a regular basis with each boy to discuss his progress and what he needed to work on.

The hole in the schedule was the afternoon. That's when kids worked on activities. Maybe they were on the football team. Maybe they took part in the Ranch's farm program. Or maybe they were on work crew. There was a lot of the old Puritan work ethic at the Ranch. The belief was that hard work well done would lead to a positive self-image. This was a new experience for most of the boys, whose previous idea of "work" was hanging out on street corners and selling drugs. There was a shed located next to the football practice field where equipment like lawn mowers, weed cutters, shovels, and wheelbarrows was stored. Every day a parade of boys would march over, get their gear, then march away with it to their work sites. Later they would be seen marching back.

For boys who misbehaved, there were consequences. The Ranch had created a new verb, "consequencing," as in, we are now consequencing this boy for his inappropriate behavior. Punishment might mean performing manual labor, such as digging ditches or clearing out irrigation canals or maybe cleaning the pigpens with a staff member. Every resident at the Ranch went through consequences. It was inevitable. Nobody's perfect, or they wouldn't have been here. The staff actually took it as a good sign when kids acted up. Every mistake gave them an opportunity to get inside the boy's head and find out what made him tick.

The kids who really bothered the staff were the "creamers," the ones who went with the flow. They quickly figured out the system and how to skate by with minimum trouble. Only they weren't dealing with their problems, and when they would leave the Ranch they wouldn't have changed one bit. That's why staff wouldn't let those kids get too comfortable. They would create some adversity, just to see how they would react. Boys called it being "tested." It might be something as simple as not allowing a boy to have dessert. Or maybe it would mean being sent down to Civics, where there was a boot camp mentality. Anything that might bring forth a reaction and make the boy open up and spill out his frustrations. The idea was not just to pacify the boys, but to treat their problems.

The Ranch environment was confrontational. It never took long for kids fresh off the van to figure out that this wasn't Camp Sunshine.

The calendar said it was 1995, but at the Ranch it seemed like it was 1984. Big Brother was always watching. He had many eyes. To make up for the lack of bars, fences, and locks, staff kept close tabs on the residents. When players walked to the field from the locker room, somebody was with them. When they walked back, somebody accompanied them. When they ate dinner, staff sat with them. When the players were showering and dressing in the locker room, several staff members would stand at strategic locations to view the entire area. While this meant a lack of privacy, the kids seemed to accept it as a necessary trade-off for not being in a real jail.

Alvin Moore was one of the football coaches who would usually take up a position in the locker room. This would unnerve many of the kids because of all the coaches, Moore probably was the toughest and the hardest to please. A word from him was enough to send a chill down their spines. He delivered the constant message that they were here for a reason, so let's work on it. He refused to let them slide through the program as he played the role of "bad cop" to the "good cops" on the coaching staff, such as Perkins, Milbrandt, and Winchester. He was always needling kids. One day Moore loudly addressed a JV player on the field after he almost got into a fight with a teammate. Later, in the locker room, long after the youth had calmed down, Moore called him over. The boy explained that he had been locked up much of his life and he was just tired of it. "Well, whose fault is that?" Moore countered. "Don't blame somebody else. Change your ways and you won't be back in the system." That was the essence of Moore: no nonsense.

Milbrandt walked out of the coaches' office holding a Minnesota Vikings trash can. He was a fan of the team and was heading to dump the contents in a garbage bag in the main locker room. "I've got something from the Vikings, too," Moore said. "It's a game ball. I've got it on my mantel. I got it for running all over them one game." Moore had been a star schoolboy running back in Arizona. He had played for Kush at ASU and later spent six years in the NFL before retiring in 1988. "If I wanted to bounce around, I could have for a couple more years," said Moore, who still limped slightly from an old ankle injury. "But politics drove me out. It wasn't fun anymore. When I said it was a game, they said it was a business. Then when I said it was a business, they said it was a game." That was a famous line from the football film *North Dallas Forty.* "I saw it in about my third year in the league, and that movie was dead on target," Moore added. "They don't play who's the best. They play who makes the most money. I never saw the parties and the drugs. But sometimes you'd see a guy who hadn't been around in a while and you'd ask, 'Where you been?' And then he'd say, 'Drug rehab.'"

Moore had had a different childhood than most kids at the Ranch. Moore spent his free time playing football or basketball at the park. He had also worked hard in school. If he didn't, Moore knew his daddy was going to whip his butt. What Moore left unsaid was that he acted as an authority figure to the Ranch boys much the way his father had done for him. Moore would let boys know that he cared, or he wouldn't be wasting his time with them. But he never coddled them, either.

"I don't tell them that life is going to be easy when they get back out there, because it's not," he said. "You either learn to make the right decisions or you're going to go back and hang with your old friends, getting high every day and robbing somebody. They've really only got three choices. They're either going to be dead, in prison, or on the right path. Those friends of theirs, they need to leave them at the fork in the road. They go left and you go right. You leave them behind. Those people don't want nothing in life except to bring everybody around them down with them. I can talk until I'm blue in the face, but they've got to go out and do it themselves."

But talking—and sometimes yelling—was what Moore did best. Another afternoon, a resident was showing disrespect to a Civics staff member in the locker room. Moore got in the boy's face. He said, "You know what's gonna happen if you argue with your boss like this? I'll tell you. He's gonna fire your black ass." When the boy gave the obligatory I-don't-care blank stare, Moore really got angry. "OK, then what are you gonna do about your family when you ain't got no job? How you gonna feed your wife and babies? What are you gonna do, rob somebody, then get thrown in jail? How are you gonna take care of your babies in there?"

For Moore, everything that happened at the Ranch had a practical application. There was a lesson to be taught in every situation. Heaven help a player if he caught him rounding off the end zone corners instead of running all the way around the field when the team did laps. That would lead to a loud lecture about how cutting corners in life had gotten the boy here in the first place.

After Milbrandt walked back into the coaches' office with his Vikings' trash can, Moore put his hand on a passing JV player's shoulder and the boy stopped dead in his tracks. "Do you know the difference between pain and injuries?" Moore asked, his eyes boring holes into the back of the boy's skull. The youth was doing his best to act as if he wasn't intimidated and was failing miserably as he started to fidget. The player had sat out that day's practice, and Moore had been riding him for dogging it. "You're sixteen," Moore told him. "You're almost a grown man. You know what your problem is? You're not serious in life. That's why you're here. Now this football team ain't about us coaches. It's about you. You can get something out of this that can help you in life. This should be the greatest time in your life, playing football. After this, it's all business in the real world. You can't just walk around looking down in the dumps because you're having a bad day. Are you gonna mope around after your boss chews you out in his office, or are you gonna stand up like a man, accept some responsibility, and say, 'Yes, sir, but I can do better tomorrow and I will?' That's why I throw a little adversity at you. I thought you would mope around, and you did. But you're better than that. Now get out of here."

Moore watched the boy make a hasty retreat out the door.

"These guys all think they're tough," he said. "They think they're tough on the streets when they're playing with twenty-to-one odds, when they're hanging out with a gang. But on the football field, it's just one-on-one. You strap on the pads and you're going to find out what tough is real quick."

———

There was something else instantly noticeable in the locker room besides the constant presence of coaches' tattoos. There were more tattoos here than in the merchant marine. As players would walk through the locker room with towels wrapped around their waists, many of their upper bodies looked like canvas because they were adorned with so much artwork. There were tattoos on their arms, shoulders, backs, chests, and even ankles. Some were crudely designed, suggesting that they had been done by amateurs behind bars. Others were drawings that seemed worthy of being hung in a gallery. But if you looked closely, the tattoos were for more than mere style. Every picture told a story. The tattoo contained the boy's name, his street name, or sometimes the identity of his gang. For instance, Lono Hill, the team's tight end, had a tattoo on his upper arm that read "Laie Boy." That referred to the town in Hawaii where he was born.

Ailepata Suiaunoa's tattoos were typical of the body art worn by many boys on the Ranch. "Ali," as he was called by the coaches, was a starting linebacker from Oceanside, California. He and Derrick Letua formed the Ranch's Samoan linebacker combination. At age seventeen, Ali had been at the Ranch for about three months. He didn't mind being called Ali, but his friends on the street had called him something else: Psycho. "If anybody made me mad, I would do something to hurt them," Ali explained. "I liked hurting them." On his forearm was a skeleton figure rolling dice. There also were the initials DVB for his gang, Deep Valley Bloods. He was working on controlling his anger but didn't know if he was making any progress. "I liked the name Psycho," he added. "It fit me."

The only thing Obediah Breer knew about the origin of his first name was that his dad had picked it out of the Bible. Obediah was a minor Hebrew prophet. This Obediah was an eighteen-year-old offensive lineman from Oceanside who had been at the Ranch for about sixteen months. When a Ranch staff member interviewed Breer in juvenile hall, he discovered that a psychologist had written this conclusion after evaluating him: "Unmotivated lump of flesh." Now Breer was only a few months away from leaving the Ranch with a high school degree, which wasn't bad for an alleged unmotivated lump of flesh.

When he arrived, Breer had been a skinhead and claimed that his family had biker roots and ties to the Hell's Angels. "I didn't have any respect for black people," Breer said. "I thought my race was superior over everyone's." Breer was one of the few white kids on the football team. And with the resident population being about 70 percent minority, he was one of the few white kids at the Ranch, period. That was a problem for Breer when he first arrived at the Ranch. But Breer said that with the help of two black staff members, he had learned to respect people of other races. He felt bad about a lot of things he had done in life, like selling drugs. But what he regretted most was his bigotry. There was something else he was remorseful about: a particularly strange tattoo on his upper-right arm. It was the head of a menacing figure wearing a hat. On the cap were three letters: F.T.P.

When asked what they meant Breer answered. "Fuck the police," he said.

Staff usually took it as a good sign when boys would come to them and ask how they could get their tattoos removed.

————

At more than 113,000 square miles, Arizona is the sixth-largest state in the Union. But although this Sunbelt state is one of the nation's fastest growing — the invention of air conditioning was like the discovery of gold when it came to luring people here — with only 4.5 million residents, Arizona ranks near the middle of the fifty states in population. Of those people, nearly 2.5 million live in the booming central Arizona metropolis of Phoenix and its surrounding Maricopa County suburbs, known collectively as the Valley of the Sun. Locals just call it the Valley for short.

Another half million or so people live in the state's other major city, Tucson, which is 110 miles to the south. The rest of the state's residents are scattered hither and yon. There are some smaller cities, such as Flagstaff and Kingman to the north, Yuma to the west, and Nogales to the south. But beyond that, Arizona becomes the domain of the small town. Look at a map of the state and you will see small dots in the middle of nowhere in the vast, empty expanse of land. You often have to travel long distances to get from one town to another. Some are mining towns. Some are farming and ranching centers. Some are reservation towns. Some towns situated in the high country rely on timber or tourism for their existence. But as diverse as they are, most have something in common. High school football is a main thread in each community's fabric.

Football in Arizona is divided into five classifications. The largest high schools are in the 5A and 4A classes, and all of them are located in the state's cities, mostly in Phoenix and Tucson. The 1A level is reserved for eight-man football, which is played in the smallest communities. The rest of the state — all those small towns — make up the bulk of the 2A and 3A levels.

Up until 1994, the boys at the Ranch were working toward high school equivalency degrees. But that year, the facility was accredited by the North Central Association. Now the Ranch was considered a full-fledged high school. That meant the school also met the requirements of the AIA. Fielding high school sports, long one of Thomas's dreams, now was a possibility. It was an idea Thomas had to sell hard to the Ranch's board of directors because it was expensive to buy equipment and build facilities. But after a successful test run the first season in 1994, the Spartans were upgraded to full AIA membership as a 3A school.

At a meeting with AIA administrators, it was decided that the Ranch would be placed in the 3A South Region. That meant that the Spartans would compete mostly with towns in the central and southern Arizona desert that were within reasonable driving distance. From a strictly geographical standpoint, playing in this league made sense. Although the South Region traditionally was considered to be a good football conference, Thomas was pleased because he believed the Spartans could at least be competitive right from the start.

The official announcement that the Ranch would play in the South Region even appeared in the AIA's newsletter. Then suddenly, for reasons that were never explained to the Ranch, it was moved to the 3A East Region. "I don't know how I left the meeting and we were in the 3A South and then we ended up in the 3A East," Thomas said. "Now I don't mind. I like competition because that makes you better. But just let me know what happened."

Competition.

That word didn't quite describe the 3A East Region. It was known throughout the state as the Mountain League, since most of the schools in the East were located in the White Mountains near the Arizona–New Mexico border. Most were in predominately tight-knit Mormon towns. Also, it was the home of the state's best small-school football.

Football in the White Mountains was taken no less seriously than it was in West Texas, Oklahoma, Florida, or any other section of the country that had a reputation for its communities living and dying with the local high school gridiron squad. Football was the lifeblood of these towns. It was a source of both civic pride and identity. Games became town hall meetings as people gathered under the lights that illuminated their football fields on Friday nights. It was more than just a game for these people. There was nothing quite like the 3A East in the rest of the state, or maybe the rest of the country. For instance, a town whose team was in this league was the home of the only dome built specifically for a high school in the entire United States.

Almost every year the 3A East sent players off to Division I schools like Arizona, Arizona State and Brigham Young. And every single year for the previous decade, the 3A state champion had come from that region. In five of those years, the state final matched two East Region teams against one another. That had been the case the year before, when Blue Ridge had defeated Winslow in the championship game. During that decade, Snowflake had won five state crowns and Blue Ridge four, and in one year Snowflake and Round Valley had tied for the title. They were the kings of the 3A mountain. Prior to that, schools from the White Mountains had been beating up 2A competition in similar fashion. But over the years the towns had grown in size, so they simply began whipping the bigger boys.

Now the region had a new welcome mat: the Ranch.

It simply made no sense. The Ranch wasn't within a four-hour bus drive of any school in the league. The Spartans would be traveling two hundred miles, one way, for some games. It was hard traveling, too, on winding, two-lane highways that passed through deep gorges and up mountains that were guaranteed to push any bus past its engine's red line. The decision guaranteed that the Spartans would sometimes be on the road past 2:00 A.M. Saturday returning from games. That obviously was a dangerous proposition.

"Everybody knows that they set us up," Gray said simply.

The 3A East was the meat grinder, and the Ranch was supposed to be the hamburger. The Spartans would be at the low end of the football food chain. Officials at the Ranch, which was long accustomed to being an outcast and a pariah, figured that this was the state's high school sports bureaucracy's way of keeping these boys down. They suspected that the AIA wasn't all that thrilled about admitting a school consisting solely of kids who were troubled at best and flat-out delinquents at worst. But what the AIA could do was make life as difficult as possible for the Ranch. So, you want to play football? OK, we'll let you play. Let's see how you handle a few good old-fashioned butt-kickings. The Ranch, of course, was in no position to complain. The Spartans simply had to go where they were told and then take their medicine on the field.

"They don't want us to win because they think it sends the wrong message to have us beating on public schools," Whitfield said.

That only fed into the already prevalent us-against-the-world complex that flourished at the Ranch. The coaching staff then furthered that attitude. For instance, Gray had received a letter from a man who used a computer formula to rank the state's high school football teams. His computer had rated the Spartans No. 32 among the state's 3A schools. Since there were only thirty-two teams in the 3A classification, that meant the Spartans were being ranked as the worst football team in the entire state. Also, the two preseason high school football magazines were published in Arizona. Each examined every conference in the state, offered an analysis of the schools, and made projections about which teams would make the playoffs. The Ranch received the smallest amount of space in both magazines. The Spartans were an afterthought.

The reality was that people in the area expected nothing from the Ranch. Why would they? There were only a handful of players back from the previous year. Fewer than ten had ever played serious, competitive football. Now, like lambs being led to slaughter, they had been shipped into the toughest 3A conference in the state. There they would play kids who had been lining up next to one another since youth football. They would be competing against towns where a strong Mormon church influence emphasized the importance of athletics.

Qualifying for the play-offs—which meant placing among the top four of the league's eight teams—would require a minor miracle. Gray leaned back in his chair in the small coaches' office, stared at the team's schedule tacked to the wall, and let loose with a heavy sigh. Blue Ridge. Snowflake. Round Valley. Winslow. Show Low. All were traditionally powerhouses. Then again, even the supposedly bad teams in this league were pretty good. It was enough to make a coach lay awake at night.

"Our kids are from Indiana, from Illinois, from California," Gray said. "They're from rival gangs, rival races, rival religions. And now they've got to forget about all that and work together. The question is,

How are they going to react when that first real adversity hits and they experience everything they've been fighting their entire lives? Will we come back and continue to work hard, or will one good ass-whipping make them start blaming each other and deciding that this is not worth it? We're going to get our ass whipped sometime. The only question is, How are we going to come out of it? We can be pretty good or we can just be terrible. We have a slim margin for error."

The games that Gray had circled in his mind's eye were the first two. They were the only nonleague games on the schedule: Ray, which was one of the state's top 2A programs, and Globe, which was expected to be one of the better teams in the 3A South. Win those and the Ranch would have a chance this season. Lose them and . . . Gray didn't want to think about that possibility.

But while Gray played the role of grim realist, others at the Ranch thought the 3A East was in for the shock of its life. They thought those mountain boys wouldn't know what hit them after the Spartans were finished with them. Both Whitfield and Thomas were openly predicting a berth in state. Even some of the coaches agreed. "I'd bet my little eighteen-month-old that we're going to make the play-offs," Shofner said.

Gray would have told him to hold off on taking that bet just yet.

BLOODS, SWEAT, TEARS

When Shaune McKissic would introduce himself and shake someone's hand, he always was quick to identify himself as the Ranch's starting quarterback. For McKissic, it was an obvious source of pride. But he was slow to reveal much else about himself. A handsome boy of seventeen with a slight build, McKissic had constructed a well-guarded fortress around himself. Although he clearly was one of the most popular kids on the Ranch, he often could be seen walking on the grounds — like after practice between the locker room and the pantry and then from the pantry to his cottage — by himself at a brisk pace. He was moving at a hurried schedule known only to him.

"Maybe that's because I've been thinking lately," he explained. "I've been trying to think about myself and where I'm at and what I want to do. I'm going to be eighteen. I'm going to be getting my high school diploma. In this next year, I'm going to make some of the biggest decisions of my life."

If there was a big man on campus, McKissic was it. The Ranch's star resident, he was bright, articulate, and eager to please staff. For the majority of the two years he had been here, McKissic hadn't caused the least bit of trouble. At five feet ten and 165 pounds, he didn't look especially athletic. But it was a mistake to judge this book by its cover. McKissic was one of those rare individuals who excel at any sport they try. It wasn't just that he was physically gifted. He also was jock smart. He understood how the games were played. He had an innate awareness of what was happening on the field and an almost instinctive sixth sense about when danger was approaching, such as a defensive lineman barreling down on him from his blind side. Maybe most important, though, he was a natural-born leader. Others gravitated toward him.

They followed him. That had as much to do with his being the starting point guard on the Ranch's basketball team and the football team's quarterback as his natural ability.

McKissic loved having the ball in his hands. He had never played football before arriving at the Ranch, yet he wanted to master perhaps the toughest position in any sport: quarterback. He wanted to be in the middle of the action and to have people depend on him to get the job done. Before the first game he had ever played last season, a flock of butterflies flapped in his stomach. When he reached his hands under center to take his first snap, he looked out over the defense and saw all those big ol' guys getting ready to try to hit him. He was scared to death. But what made McKissic different from most kids was that he never let anyone know that he was shaking with terror. He never let anyone see him sweat.

Yet, although in many ways McKissic represented the Ranch's best and brightest, during the summer passing league, in which the Ranch played flag football against other area schools, McKissic had been left behind at Butler Cottage, where the reorientation boys were housed. Todd Harris, his backup, was playing quarterback, and by all accounts doing a good job. Figuratively, McKissic had been given the keys to the Ranch and hadn't handled the freedom well.

The Ranch operated two transition homes: one in Tucson for the Civics program and one in Mesa, a suburb of Phoenix, for boys from the main campus. The Mesa home was called Robson House. Only the top residents got the chance to live there. Robson was a nice house in a normal residential neighborhood. Living there helped boys readjust to life in the real world, away from the structure on the Ranch. It also offered staff an opportunity to see just how far kids had come and if they really were ready for the challenges and temptations beyond the Ranch. That's where McKissic had been . . . until he turned up dirty in a drug test for marijuana just weeks after arriving there.

That was strike one. So, McKissic, was brought back to the main campus as punishment, shown his way to Butler and given his a yellow shirt. Staff then basically set about making his life miserable. The idea was to make a resident hate being a yellow shirt so much that he never wanted to wear it again. But there wasn't much worse they could do than prevent McKissic from playing in the passing league.

Strike two occurred on the Saturday before fall practice started, when McKissic was caught smoking cigarettes, which is taboo at the

Ranch. Even veterans who through years of experience had learned to expect the unexpected were shocked by McKissic's behavior. He was the absolute last person they thought would crash and burn like that.

"I've been out here five years and he's the one kid who I would have bet my bottom buck that he'd go straight," said Kush, who had gotten to know McKissic well because he helped tutor the quarterbacks. "He's got a lot of character. He's a good kid. Now maybe if I didn't know him and found out that he had trouble with marijuana, I might say screw him. But I know him. He's got maybe an 80–20 ratio of positive values to negative values. When he got here, maybe he only had a 20–80 ratio. If he were an adult, you might say forget him. But he's only a kid. He's still got a chance. You have to remember why he's here. Nobody ever made him accountable. But, sure, it bothers me. I was surprised, disappointed, and irritated. It bothers me that this kid has all this talent and he's not using it."

The thing that had surprised the staff the most was that McKissic had given in to peer pressure. On the Ranch he always seemed to be the one blazing the trail for everyone else. But McKissic said he hadn't always been like that. "When I was at home, I was a follower," he said. "Before, I was following the wrong people. I was following them into negativity. I wasn't trying to stay in school. It's easy to do bad. There's nothing to it, especially if you're not thinking about what you're doing and not thinking about everything you're putting into jeopardy when you're doing it."

McKissic was an only child. He had been born in Nuremberg, Germany, where his mother was stationed in the Army during what eventually would be a twenty-year hitch in the service. His parents didn't marry, and Shaune never knew his dad and had no idea where he was now. His mom was discharged from the Army when Shaune was seven. She would later marry briefly, but that marriage would end in divorce. So it was Shaune and his mom, together against the world. They developed an extremely close relationship. They lived in North Carolina for a few years. Then, in the late 1980s, they moved to Stockton, California, where they had family. They stayed for a while with his mom's great-aunt in what McKissic quickly would discover was a rough neighborhood. "There were shootings going on," he remembered. "Robberies. Gangs. Fighting. People getting killed. Drugs floating around. Anything you can think of."

That was where life began to deteriorate for both Shaune and his mother. McKissic, who was still in elementary school when they arrived in Stockton, was enrolled in an accelerated program for academically gifted students. He had fit right in at school. But as he sought out new friends, he hooked up with the wrong crowd. "I had some good friends, who weren't in gangs or selling drugs or hanging out all night," he said. "But I just chose not to hang around with them. I chose the negative."

McKissic lost interest in schoolwork and started going downhill fast after that. He stopped going to class. Then he began stealing cars with friends. He was staying out late and missing curfew. He got in serious trouble once when he was caught in a burglary attempt at a middle school.

"I remember there was one time where I was at a party and I was dancing," he said. "All of a sudden, the lights came on and people were yelling. There was this guy right next to me who was shooting up in the air with a gun. It blew my ears out. I started ducking, and I ran outside. That scared me really bad. I thought I was going to get shot or something. That's one thing that sticks in my mind about being at the wrong place at the wrong time. I wasn't supposed to be there anyway. I was supposed to be home. Heck, I was only fifteen."

McKissic didn't like guns. He was afraid of them. He said he was glad he never got into the typical gun play of the streets because he was sure he would have come to a bad end. But one thing he did do was sell drugs. McKissic said he started because his mother wouldn't give him any money, because she knew her son would just turn around and buy drugs and alcohol with it. Fine, Shaune thought, I'll just start my own business and create my own cash flow. Meanwhile, part of the reason McKissic's mother was having trouble dealing with her son's wild behavior was that she was wrestling with her own demons.

"My mom had a drug problem," McKissic said. "She's a cocaine addict. She tried real hard to beat it. I tried to help her, too. But how much could I do when I was doing drugs, too? How could I help somebody when I wasn't even trying to help myself? That just made it worse. Me and her, we would move around a lot in the city. We'd move to different places to try and get away. My mom was in and out of rehab houses, dealing with her addiction. When she was in those rehab houses, I was in there with her. I'd see the changes in her. I already knew how she was before she started using cocaine. She was a good mother to me. She taught me a lot of things about how to be a good person, or I wouldn't be the way I am today. Those values had to come from somewhere. You just don't pick up that kind of stuff from anywhere. It started with my mom."

But at age fifteen, McKissic's time on the streets came to an abrupt end. He was arrested and charged with possession of cocaine for sale. He was sitting in juvenile hall in Stockton when the court decided that it was time to do something with young Mr. McKissic. The judge who reviewed his case thought that Shaune would be a prime candidate for an alternative placement facility because he was obviously intelligent and had not been involved in any violent crimes. So while McKissic was languishing in a lockup, he began receiving visitors from various facilities that deal with delinquent youth. They would show him a video and give him a book of rules and other informational materials about their programs. Then they would interview him.

The first person who interviewed him was a worker with the Glen Mills School in Pennsylvania. The Stockton judge had thought its program would be ideal for McKissic. Another residential placement institution, Glen Mills is renowned for its sports programs. Even in California, kids knew about Glen Mills, and McKissic was excited about the prospect of going there. "But during the interview, they ask you certain questions, like, 'What kind of crimes did you commit?' and 'Have you ever started a fire?'" McKissic said. "Glen Mills didn't accept me because I started a fire when I was about five when I was in Germany. They don't want no arsonists. I told them it was just an accident, but it didn't matter."

After that, McKissic was visited by people from a couple of other programs, including the Arizona Boys Ranch. Ultimately McKissic decided on the Ranch because a friend of his was already there. McKissic arrived on December 23, 1993, and he wasn't the least bit happy about it. He was a long way from home and his mother. He was wearing a red shirt, and all these adults were telling him what to do. Merry Christmas, Shaune. "But then they gave us presents," McKissic recalled. "I said to myself, 'Whoa, look at that. Christmas presents for me and I just came here?' " That was McKissic's first indication that maybe the Ranch actually cared about the kids it treated.

McKissic decided to give the place a chance and ended up having relatively few of the problems most newcomers experience. He did well in the classroom. On the football field and basketball court, he stood out. What made McKissic unusual in the Ranch population was that he thrived on pressure. He liked having everyone watch him with the ball in his hands as the clock ticked down. Still, some staff wondered about McKissic. He had been doing all the right things, at least until recently. Yet, he hadn't really opened up to anyone. Precious little light had been cast on why such a clearly talented young man had gotten himself on the path that had landed him here. "You try to reach these kids," said Gary Winchester, one of the coaches. "You try to get inside their heads. But Shaune hasn't let me inside yet."

Winchester didn't claim to know McKissic well. But Winchester might have known McKissic as well as any staff member did. He had even accompanied McKissic to California for a home visit about a year earlier. Every several months or so, the Ranch takes kids back to their families for supervised visits. Or their parents come to Arizona. The plan on this particular home visit was for staff and residents to arrive at a hotel and for the families to come and pick up the kids. One family after another came to collect a boy until only Shaune was left. For some unknown reason, his mother hadn't been able to pick him up. Shaune thought his mom didn't have a car and couldn't get to the hotel. But Winchester wasn't able to locate his mother, either. The longer this went on, the more upset McKissic became. He was the only boy who had to stay at the hotel that night, and Winchester ended up consoling a tearful McKissic. He said it was one of those times when your heart just breaks for a kid. Finally, Winchester and another staff member tracked down Shaune's mother by phone. "We said, 'Look, your son is here from Arizona and he desperately wants to see you,' " Winchester recalled. "She finally came." Then they had a great couple of days together.

McKissic said he used to try to control his mother, gathering up her drugs and telling her that she couldn't have them. But through group meetings at the Ranch, McKissic said he slowly had figured out that you can't help someone until they're ready to be helped. All he can do, he said, was tell her what he felt and hope she accepted it. He had to worry about getting his own life straight right now. "I haven't heard from her in a few weeks," he said. "Since I've been here, I really can't stay in touch with her like I want to because she doesn't have her own phone. But I can write letters to her. She's still struggling a little bit, but she's doing much better."

McKissic had been struggling a bit, too. Hence the yellow shirt he was wearing. When a boy was clothed in that color, he lost privileges.

He had to do extra work, to stand during cottage meetings, to do P.T. — physical training — even after football practice. But McKissic said not to be fooled by the temporary setback. He had changed his entire outlook on life. Before, he said, he never took anything seriously. School, sports, nothing. Life was just one big party while he hung out with friends. When he was doing that, it didn't take long to find trouble, either. But he wasn't like that anymore.

"I most definitely feel I've changed," he said. "If I didn't come here, I probably would have ended up dead or something. Or I'd just be out on the streets. I made some bad mistakes out there. I wasn't thinking straight. I wasn't using my head. I've made some wrong decisions here, but I think I've gotten a lot better. What's good is that when you mess up here, the consequences aren't sending you to another jail. The staff continues to help you out, trying to get your head straight. Wearing the yellow shirt isn't fun. But it makes you not want to wear it again."

Even though McKissic was technically a junior, he was scheduled to get his high school diploma in May. In the classroom, he once again was demonstrating that he was a sharp kid. He intended to stay at the Ranch through the summer so he could work and save money for college. He realized that any hopes of playing in the NFL were a pipe dream, but football might get him a scholarship somewhere. He also studied hard because he understood the importance of getting a college degree someday. The one thing he did not want to do was go back to Stockton. Instead, McKissic said he had considered following in his mother's footsteps in one way and eventually serving in the military. He had set his sights high at the Ranch.

"I want to attend the Air Force Academy," he said. "I'm working on my application right now. You basically have to be perfect to get in. I asked Mr. Whitfield to write a letter of recommendation. I sent two letters to [Arizona] Senator [John] McCain, asking for an appointment to the Academy. So I'm waiting for an answer right now."

Earlier in the year, McKissic had visited his aunt in Colorado Springs, Colorado. There, they had toured the Academy and attended the graduation ceremony. President Bill Clinton had given the commencement speech that day. McKissic had wanted to shake the president's hand, but the Secret Service wasn't letting anyone near him. Still, the experience had left a big impression on the boy. He could envision himself at the Academy. McKissic knew it was a long shot and added that he probably would be happy enlisting in any branch of the service. He was realistic enough to know that some of the things he had done would disqualify him from consideration. But he added that a person needed goals in life. "I want to fly," he said. Maybe that was why, during breaks on the practice field, McKissic could sometimes be seen watching the planes overhead as they approached or took off from Williams Air Force Base, which still had a mix of civilian and military air traffic.

And soon McKissic was out of a yellow shirt and back into a green one.

———

For two weeks the Ranch practices had looked like a scene from the movie *Groundhog Day,* in which Bill Murray keeps reliving the same day over and over. Each day was like the last. Three practices. Eight stations. Hitting the blocking sled. Running gassers. Lots of sweat and pain. The workouts seemed to melt together under the unrelenting sun. The boys showed the same kind of enthusiasm they would have exhibited if heading for the dentist's office. The only thing missing was the shot of Novocain. After several players had decided that they did not want to play football after all, Gray had called the team together and explained that these brutal workouts weren't punishment. They hadn't done anything wrong. Every team in Arizona was going through them. This simply was what they had to do to prepare for the coming season, unless they wanted to get their butts kicked all over the field come September. While they didn't want to lose any players, the coaches were forced to weed out a couple of orientation kids. They had been smart-mouthing staff as well as talking gang smack with team-mates. That had earned them one-way trips to the Civics program in Oracle, where they would be, as Ta'ase described it, refocused.

A couple of days stood out, though, like the morning a film crew from ESPN showed up. It was at the Ranch to do a piece on Kush's entry in the College Football Hall of Fame. As the camera followed Kush around the practice field, some players could be seen gravitating toward the old coach so they could become part of the background scenery on tape. It was one of the rare times that the kids actually sought out Kush, who could inspire sheer panic in a heartbeat with one angry outburst.

The next morning was memorable, too. It was the players' first day in pads. After the opening workout in shorts and T-shirts, the team jogged back to the locker room in formation so everyone could collect his gear. The first boy to bound out of the equipment room with his bundle was a Hispanic youth. As he examined the various pads, jersey, pants, and so on, he looked very much looked like a young child opening a birthday present. But as the locker room filled with players, others looked apprehensive. For most of them, pads were foreign objects. They had never worn them before. They might as well have been asked to don suits of armor. The inevitable questions came fast and furious. "Do we wear T-shirts under the shoulder pads?" "Do we put our knee braces on first?" "What's this thing for?" As they dressed in the confining space, they began exchanging furtive glances to make sure they were putting on the stuff correctly. Nobody wanted to look stupid.

"Who's No. 7 in here?" one boy asked.

"John Elway," some joker answered.

"No, seriously," the first boy said. "Somebody's got my girdle thing and I've got theirs."

One player had his shoulder pads on backward. Another was somehow trying to convert his hip pads into a protective cup device. Ta'ase had been walking around the weight-equipment room helping kids who were too proud to ask for assistance and yet hopelessly confused about how to strap on the gear. Finally, the players dropped the facade of knowing what the hell they were doing and formed a line in front of him as he made sure that everything had been put on correctly. "They're just like babies," Ta'ase announced. "Gotta help them on with their diapers."

Even the boys who had played the year before looked uncomfortable. "It feels weird, sir," Corey Cabell said to Milbrandt.

"That's OK, you look weird, too," Milbrandt answered.

When the players were finally dressed and lined up outside the locker room to return to the field for the day's second practice, they at least looked like a football team. "Yesterday it was ESPN, today it's the Cartoon Network," Milbrandt said.

Another incident stood out. One afternoon while the team was being marched to the pantry for lunch, the boys were walking in one direction and an attractive young woman—the daughter of a staff member — was walking in the other direction. When heads turned and long, wolfish stares were delivered, Shofner went crazy. He diverted the team to the practice field. By the time the players reached it,

Shofner's face was beet red from rage. There, he unleashed a wicked tongue-lashing. "That's not the way you look at a girl!" he thundered. "You don't look at her like you own her. You embarrass yourself and us when you do that. Have some pride. You don't look at women like they're objects. They're people, too. Now, do you hear me?"

"Yes, sir!" came the automatic response.

"I said, do you hear me?" Shofner repeated.

"YES, SIR!"

The team then marched to lunch.

———

The Spartans would celebrate the end of three-a-day practice hell with a controlled intrasquad scrimmage. The coaches would put the offensive and defensive units in different situations and run various plays to see what happened. No score would be kept. They were still trying to get a handle on who could play and who couldn't. Gray had discovered that he had a lot of players with God-given ability. He also had learned that most of them either didn't know they had it or didn't know what to do with it. A scrimmage would be a good test to see how far they had come in two weeks. They would even get to perform in front of a crowd. At 7:00 A.M. Saturday, boys from the main campus cottages were marched out to the edge of the practice field. When they were all seated on the grass, there were probably two hundred boys and staff members present to watch the team make its unofficial debut.

Nobody took more pleasure from this scene than Bob Thomas. The Ranch football team was his baby, and he was the epitome of a proud father as he watched the squad do its stretching exercises. There was no more controversial figure in Arizona in the field of rehabilitating juvenile offenders. Thomas did things his way. He made waves, and he did not suffer fools gladly. He challenged state officials, and he made no apologies afterward. There was a self-assured, confident, cocky attitude among staff at the Ranch. That all began with the man at the top.

The irony was that Thomas had never intended to become a child-care worker. It just sort of happened. A native of St. Louis, he had taken a job as a sporting goods company sales representative after college. But he quickly became bored. So Thomas did something his friends thought was insane. He took a pay cut and went to work for a juvenile correctional facility. Twenty-six years and a couple of master's degrees later, he was still in the field. Thomas landed at a placement facility for youth called Camp Highfields, in Onondaga, Michigan. He rose to the position of assistant director before he was hired away as executive director of the floundering Boys Ranch program in 1977.

Everything the Ranch had become was designed in Thomas's vision. To his critics, including the writers of the editorial page of *The Arizona Republic,* which had called for his ouster, the Ranch achieved results through fear and intimidation of the very boys he claimed to help. To the people who believed in him, Thomas had developed a unique program that would go a long way in solving this nation's juvenile crime problem if only it were expanded around the country. "When he got here, this place was a mess," Shofner said. "He completely turned it around and made Boys Ranch what it is now."

There was no middle ground in people's opinions of Thomas. Either they approved of the job he did, or they didn't. He wasn't particularly interested in making friends. He was absolutely convinced that he was making a difference in the lives of troubled boys. If someone didn't care for his tough, disciplined approach, he respected his opinion. He asked only that he stay the hell out of his way. Despite countless run-ins with the state regulatory agency and amid a small forest of negative newspaper stories about his style, the Ranch's board of directors had stood by him.

"I could double the population here," Thomas said. "That's not bragging. It's just the way it is. We've got a waiting list. This program works, and these kids are supposed to be the toughest of the tough. These are kids who have failed everywhere else. They failed because there was no structure. They didn't have anyone who cared enough about them to get them in line. All we do is take charge of kids. This is probably the first time in their lives that they've been held accountable. These kids can be anything you want them to be. If you have low expectations for them, then they won't disappoint you. But we have high expectations for them."

Thomas could sound like a candidate on the campaign trail as he preached the way of the Ranch. As the scrimmage got under way on the field, he had launched into a tirade about why this program could change lives and the juvenile prison system couldn't. All of these boys have been accused of being abnormal all their lives, Thomas continued. Each and every one of them is a tragedy. None of the kids on the field would be on a normal high school team. They've been told they can't compete. They've all been put in a box and had a label slapped on top. What the Ranch does, he said, is normalize boys and show them that they can compete if only they try.

Just then, Cabell took a handoff from McKissic. He faked a move left to freeze a defender and then bolted right, ripping off a nice gain before he was brought down. The crowd erupted in a spontaneous cheer, and Thomas's voice was among them. "He's looking pretty good," Thomas shouted to Moore, the running backs coach. But Moore shook his head. "That's still not good enough," he responded. Of all the residents at the Ranch, Thomas probably was closest to Cabell. He even would be taking the boy to an Arizona Cardinals game the following week. There were several reasons for their bond, but the strongest link probably was football.

If there was anything that Thomas enjoyed talking about more than the Ranch program, incompetent bureaucrats, or this country's fouled-up juvenile justice system, it was football. With a neatly trimmed white beard, he somewhat resembled a billy goat. Sometimes Thomas would refer to himself as "this old goat." But the football coaches had good-naturedly hung another name on Thomas: Jerry Jones. There were obvious comparisons to be made between Thomas and the flamboyant owner of the Dallas Cowboys. Both took a fervent interest in their teams. Both loved to roam the sidelines during games, loudly encouraging their players. There was, of course, one major difference. "I don't have Jerry Jones's money," Thomas said, laughing.

The Corey Cabell Show continued. He scored a touchdown from about 20 yards out, shredding the Ranch's first-team defense. Then he went for 60 yards as he cracked the defensive unit like a walnut in a nutcracker. He bounced off defenders as he refused to be tackled. At only five feet six and 165 pounds, Cabell wasn't big. But he could twist and turn his body so that nobody could get a clean shot at him. Even Derrick Letua, who had already established himself as the team's biggest hitter and starting middle linebacker, couldn't unload on him. When he broke into the open field, Cabell simply would outrun everyone. As he again reached the end zone, Thomas yelled: "Be humble, son. Act like you been there before. Don't be like Neon Deion Sanders and act like a fool." Another staff member added, "That's Eric Dickerson out there!"

You know, Thomas said, we don't have many Arizona kids here. In fact the Ranch currently had only about thirty in-state boys and most of them either were sent by Native American tribal courts or were private placements by concerned parents who were trying to cut off trouble at the pass. The state didn't send kids here for a variety of reasons. One was the bad publicity the Ranch had received in Arizona. It never ceased to amaze Thomas that reporters from around the country would visit and end up writing positive articles about the program while locally he was perceived as running Stalag 17. There also was a difference in philosophy. The state wanted placement facilities to have medically and psychologically trained experts on staff to treat kids with emotional problems. But Thomas had no patience for programs that relied on heavy doses of therapy and psychotropic drugs. He believed in a "reality model" whereby a boy's problems were dealt with in one-on-one counseling with staff with whom he had developed a relationship and trust. Thomas felt that the vast majority of troubled boys did not need to be medicated. His theory was that if you treated a kid like he was a manic-depressive, he would act that way. Treat a kid like he was normal, and he would act that way, too.

In the late 1980s, the Ranch received 60 to 70 percent of the boys in Arizona who were sent into placement by the juvenile courts, Thomas said. Now the percentage was zero. That was why Thomas had been forced to hit the road and sell the Ranch to out-of-state courts as a facility that was willing to take kids nobody else would. Yet each day his office would receive an average of ten to twelve calls from Arizona parents who had heard about the Ranch and wanted desperately to send their boys there because they had rebelled against every other program.

There was one other factor: money. The Arizona juvenile courts were inadequately funded, Thomas said, and it wasn't cheap to send an offender to a placement facility. The Ranch's fee was $121 a day per boy, which worked out to about $3,700 a month. Thomas claimed that figure actually was cheap compared with the going rate in the rehabilitation industry. Still, he had heard all the snide remarks about how it cost more to send a kid to Boys Ranch than it did to Harvard. But Thomas viewed it as a pay-now or pay-more-later venture. Eighteen months at the Ranch might be expensive, but it was far more cost-effective than incarcerating a boy for life, at taxpayer expense, after he had killed someone.

"Besides, why would Arizona kids want to come here?" Thomas asked. "They'd have to work on their problems here. At a corrections facility, they can smoke, sit on their butt, kick back, have fun, not deal with any of their problems, and then maybe be out in four weeks. We're a tough program. We probably should be tougher. But our structure makes this the safest environment they've probably ever been in. We won't allow boys to intimidate one another. They can't gang-bang here."

On the field, a McKissic pass had just slipped through the hands of Sparkman. It had been a beautiful spiral. Sparkman was wide open. He just dropped the ball. Technically, Sparkman should not even have been at the Ranch. His county no longer was paying his way. But Thomas had put him on scholarship. The Ranch was paying his tab. There were about thirty kids like Juan who remained even though their courts had decided that they had been treated long enough. Some stayed because they were close to getting their high school degrees. Some didn't want to go home because a gang had a contract out on their life. Or maybe, like Sparkman, they simply had nowhere else to go. "It costs us over $1 million a year to keep them," Thomas said. "But what are we going to do, turn them down and just throw them back on the streets?"

A few minutes later, Thomas pointed across the practice field to where two staff members were escorting a red shirt away. One adult had the boy by the arm while the other followed close behind. "That kid did something wrong," Thomas said. "He somehow acted like a dad-gum fool. They're not going to take him out back and beat him. They're going to confront him and make him deal with his problem. We don't hit kids here. We control them." A few minutes later, the red shirt came walking back to the field. Neither adult had his hands on him.

As the scrimmage wound down, Cabell capped off a dazzling morning with a 30-yard burst up the middle for yet another touchdown. "Herschel Walker!" somebody shouted. Here was evidence why people at the Ranch thought the Spartans would go as far this season as Cabell would carry them. A coach can teach someone how to tackle, to block, to throw, to catch. But there is one thing that cannot be taught: Either someone can run with a football or he can't. It is an inborn gift bestowed upon only a blessed few. Cabell was one of those individuals. He was a natural running back.

When Gray blew his whistle and brought the team together, he told the boys that he had been coaching for a long time and that they had

had a pretty good intrasquad scrimmage. There had been some solid hitting that they could build on. Now they were ready to pop some guys they didn't recognize: namely the players from Wickenburg High. The Spartans would be traveling to that school for a scrimmage the following Friday for their dress rehearsal for the regular season. Gray added one last thought: "You guys probably are going to hear things said about you this season. Things are going to be shouted from the stands. They may talk about your skin color. They may talk about your past. But you take it. The only time you talk to your opponent is when you're complimenting him, like, 'Hey, you did a great job of chasing me into the end zone.' You have to be tough on the field, and part of that is being a man who can rise above the garbage spewed by others."

As the team headed for the locker room and the other residents returned to their cottages, Thomas nodded in the direction of a small boy who was walking with a female houseparent. "See that little guy," he said. "He's twelve. He was involved in a drive-by murder." Thomas shook his head. "It's unbelievable out there."

———

After the scrimmage, a backup player who hadn't seen much time on the field went up to Moore in the locker room and asked, "Why doesn't Coach like me?"

"Which coach?" Moore responded.

"Coach Kush."

"Why do you say that?"

"Well, today he called me the king of the jackasses," the boy explained.

Moore just rolled his eyes.

"These kids don't understand," Moore said. "Coach Kush has been calling people that since long before they were born."

THE MAN, THE MYTH, THE LEGEND

Arizona is home to several natural wonders, including the Grand Canyon, Meteor Crater, the Painted Desert, and the Petrified Forest. Yet there were people who believed that the state's greatest treasure was Frank Kush. Differing from other legendary Arizona figures, like Wyatt Earp, Kush wasn't reputed to have killed anyone. But former players sometimes claimed that it wasn't because he hadn't tried.

Kush had one thing in common with most of the kids at the Ranch: He had grown up with next to nothing. The son of a Polish coal miner, he had been born on January 20, 1929, in the company town of Windber, Pennsylvania. Kush remembered Windber as a bleak place where all the houses were painted either yellow, green, or gray. To this day he could still recall that the town had thirteen churches and fifty bars while he was growing up.

The fifth of fifteen kids, he lived in a house located above Mine No. 35. The place had no hot water and no telephone. There were six children sleeping in his bed. Kush said the biggest paycheck he could ever remember his dad bringing home, after food and rent had been deducted, was $2.62 for two weeks' work. Such was life in the Depression. While Kush never lacked for discipline, most everything else was in short supply. He never used a fork, knife, or spoon until he went to college. There, he would watch other students closely out of the corner of his eyes to see how they used them. He claimed never to have seen a napkin until he left home, either. College also was the first time he ever got three meals a day or was introduced to steak. But if there was a saving grace for the Kush clan, it was that ignorance was bliss. The Kush kids just assumed that everybody lived as they did. "There was no TV," Kush said. "You didn't know what other people had, and thank God for that."

Life would get even harder for the Kush family. Their father died in 1944 of black lung disease at the age of fifty-one, when Frank was just fifteen. The family immediately was cut off from the town's company store. Kush said all they had to eat for three months was bread and the milk that came from the cow the family had out back. When his mother wrote to the Red Cross and explained the family's plight, the wages of three Kush sons who were fighting in World War II were garnisheed to support the family back home.

"We were as poor as some of these kids at the Ranch," Kush said. "We didn't have a pot to piss in when my dad died. But the difference was my family, my teachers, my community. They wouldn't give up on me." And he had football. In the coal-mining towns of western Pennsylvania, the game is a way of life. "I'd be dead by now if it weren't for football," Kush said. "I'd be a dead coal miner. Football saved me. The game gave me opportunities that I never thought I would have, and I took advantage of those opportunities."

Kush knew that the game was his boarding pass out of the Windber coal mines and the limited future they promised. He also knew that he didn't want to end up like Kaiser Bussick or Gump Polansky. One summer during the war, Kush took a job working on a railroad. He and Bussick, a neighbor in his thirties, would walk to the bus station together, go to the site, take up their positions, and work all day, side by side. "Kaiser had been doing that his entire life," Kush recalled. "What I asked myself was, 'Can you imagine doing this your whole life?'" The answer was no.

Then there was Gump, who was not to be confused with a fellow by the first name of Forrest. This Gump had been named to the Pennsylvania all-state football team at a time when only eleven players made the squad. But after high school, Gump had become a janitor and helped out with the freshman football team at Windber. The questions Kush asked himself this time were: (1) do I want to be a star football player like Gump and (2) do I want to work as a janitor? Yes and no. Kush was determined to be different and get out of Windber. He wasn't going to allow anything to get in his way.

Windber revolved around the high school football team during the fall. On Saturday afternoons, the town literally would close down. Before home games, a band would march through the main street, leading a parade to the high school stadium. Kush was one of the town's Saturday heroes. Despite his small size — five foot nine, 180 pounds — Kush was a demon on the field. He was a star lineman who routinely put much bigger players flat on their backs. He followed in Gump's footsteps and was named to Pennsylvania's all-state team and ended up receiving about fifteen scholarship offers. Many schools, though, weren't aware of his small stature. For instance, Kush took a recruiting trip to the University of Georgia. The Bulldog coaches had read about him in the newspapers, so they invited him down for a look, sight unseen. When Kush got off the plane, the assistant coach who was there to meet him didn't recognize him because he was looking for a big, strapping fellow. When they finally did hook up, the assistant took him to meet the head coach, Wally Butts. Butts took one look at Kush and, with a deep southern drawl, offered Kush some free advice. "Son, I think you're kinda small to be playing college football, especially at Georgia," he said.

That got Kush to thinking that maybe he *was* too little, although he was still determined to use the game as his escape hatch from the coal mines. He decided to attend Washington Lee, a private school in Virginia, but in only a matter of days Kush wondered if he had made a mistake. This was a school where a student was expected to wear a tie and jacket to class. Kush had neither. Luckily, an assistant football coach let him borrow one tie, one jacket and two white shirts. Kush wore them all year. But if Kush felt out of place on the campus, he was still at home on the football field. Kush did so well on the school's freshman football squad that he realized that he had sold himself, well, short as a player.

So Kush transferred to Michigan State. During his three years in a Spartan uniform, he was a two-way starter, the team lost one game, the school won a national title, and Kush was named All-America as a guard. After his final year, he was invited to several postseason all-star games, including the Senior Bowl, where his team was coached by Paul Brown, who was on his way to becoming a pro football giant. Although Brown told Kush that he admired his tenacity, he just didn't have the size to play professionally. He recommended that Kush pursue another career. And for awhile, Kush did try something else: the Army. And, once again, football saved him. The way he remembered it, his class of second lieutenants was about to be shipped out of Fort Benning, Georgia, to the conflict in Korea. Instead, he was told to stay and coach one of the base's football squads. Kush said he later learned that thirty-nine of his seventy classmates were killed in the fighting.

A coaching career also was born. When Kush left the service, a young Michigan State assistant named Dan Devine was taking over the football program out in the desert at a place in Tempe that was then called Arizona State College. In 1955, he took Kush with him. Three years later, Devine had moved on to the University of Missouri. At age twenty-eight, Kush found himself running his own college program. For the next twenty-two seasons, Arizona State teams, mirroring their coach, would be small, quick, tough and would usually carry a sizable chip on their shoulders. Kush liked players who had something to prove. The Sun Devils would post a 176–54–1 record under him. During a six-season run from 1970 to 1975, the Sun Devils were a national powerhouse, going 62–9 with five bowl victories, including a 17–14 win over Nebraska in the Fiesta Bowl that gave ASU an unbeaten season and a No. 2 national ranking. Kush sent player after player into the NFL, including Charley Taylor, Danny White, Michael Haynes, and John Jefferson.

Although it made the academic side of the campus wince when it was said, Kush put Arizona State on the map. The football stadium was enlarged from about thirty thousand seats to over seventy thousand during the Kush era. When he arrived with Devine, the school was fighting a deep-rooted inferiority complex because ASU had second-class status behind the University of Arizona in Tucson as a scholarly institution. But then Kush's teams began to routinely whack Arizona on the field, and that gave ASU faithful a chance to swell their chests with pride. But most of all, those in the booming Phoenix area desperately craved major league status. Kush's program provided people with that identity. In return, Kush, the self-described Polack from Pennsylvania, was granted deity-like status. He could do most anything he wanted and get away with it because he was the revered Frank Kush.

For instance, one day the team bus pulled up to the stadium only to discover that the gate was padlocked. But not for long. Kush told the bus driver to get out of his seat. From then, it took only a minute for Kush to figure out how to get the bus into first gear. "I drove it right through the damned thing," Kush said. "The fence bent. The bus bent. But we got through."

The way he created Camp Tontozona, a mountain retreat that he had carved out of a wilderness site one hundred miles north of Phoenix as a preseason training camp, was also typical of the way Kush ran his program. He just did it, then asked for permission. He had discovered the area, which was located on school property, during a fishing trip. He decided that this secluded location with no distractions would be a perfect place for the football team to prepare for the season. So he got a man that he knew who did construction work to level off an open field near the small Tonto Creek. Only after it was completed did Kush go to the school president. Fortunately for Kush, the president thought the retreat was a swell idea, too.

Rustic might be the best way to describe the early Camp Tontozona experiences. The team traveled a dirt road to get there and players slept in lean-tos. Part of practice would consist of the players dragging around a utility pole to keep leveling the ground. Then after each workout, they would line up and slowly walk across the field, picking up rocks and putting them in their helmets.

As the years passed, a mythology grew up around Kush's rugged Tontozona practices. Like many myths, these had a basis in truth. Former players said that Kush used the camp to find out who really wanted to play for him and who didn't. If you could survive Tontozona, you were one of his guys. If you couldn't, then you found your own way back home. The stories of players hitchhiking down "the Hill" to Phoenix became legendary. The truth was that Kush would lose only a handful of players each year. It only seemed like a row of tired football players were stretched on Arizona roads from Tontozona to the Valley with thumbs pointing toward the sky.

Under Kush, ASU came to be regarded as a football factory. If a player wanted to get an education, fine. But academics certainly weren't stressed. For instance, Gray, who had been a defensive lineman for the Sun Devils from 1969 to 1971, said he was the oddball ASU football player because he was at school to get a degree. "I knew I wasn't going pro, so I got up every morning and went to class," Gray said. "There weren't very many of us at that time. Those were the good old days. You were there to play football, just fill the stadium, and win games."

The Sun Devils didn't adhere strictly to NCAA guidelines, either. It was a different time. The NCAA manual wasn't yet the size of a city phone book. Or, as Kush would say, there weren't any rules — or at least none that couldn't be easily circumvented. Kush flourished in that free-wheeling era when college coaches worked the recruiting trail like cattle rustlers, stealing off with prized players in the night. It wasn't cheating if a coach didn't get caught. In those days, many coaches were known to "stash" blue-chip recruits on the eve of signing day. They would hide the players in motels to make sure other coaches wouldn't get a last chance to change the kids' minds. ASU wasn't any different from other places when it came to such chicanery.

But above all, Kush was known for running a tight ship. As the years passed, he gained a reputation for being one of the leading taskmasters in college football. He was considered to be without peers when it came to demanding discipline from his players. They either did things his way or hit the highway. Players had two beliefs about Kush. First, if they could play for that man, they could play for anybody. Second, hell would be a piece of cake after surviving four years with him. As Winchester, who had been an offensive lineman at ASU from 1973 to 1977, said: "On the football field, you feared the man. There's no other way to put it."

Kush would slap helmets. He would grab face masks because he wanted players to look him in the eye when he was lecturing them. He would yell at his players. He would conduct practices after games if he didn't like what he had just seen. There was nothing subtle about Kush the coach. His temper could quickly rise to the boiling point. Winchester said the coach would get behind offensive linemen on the practice field and start swinging a thick ship rope around like a bat, threatening to slap the linemen in the butt with it if they didn't explode off the line of scrimmage. Winchester said Kush never actually hit anyone with it because he didn't have to: Everyone moved instantly when the ball was snapped. He also would conduct "hamburger" drills, in which a player would get hit by one teammate after another until he was pummeled into exhaustion. A variation of the hamburger drill was used as punishment for an offensive lineman if he allowed the quarterback to get sacked. Kush would give the lineman the ball and tell him to pull his arm back and pretend to be ready to throw it, just the way a quarterback might be positioned when he was sacked by a defender. Then Kush would rush a defensive player to hit the poor, unprotected lineman. That way he would know how the quarterback felt.

Winchester managed to avoid that fate. And he also never told Kush that he had been a long snapper for special teams in high school. That was because Kush's stock line about long snappers was that if you botched the snap, you might as well go home with the other team because you had a better chance of surviving that way. What Winchester couldn't avoid, though, was a serious injury to his right knee during a Camp Tontozona intrasquad scrimmage. As he rolled on the ground in agony, he knew right away that he had torn ligaments in his knee. Kush came over and kicked Winchester in the butt gently and told him to get up. When Winchester tried and the knee wobbled all over the place, Kush told him to get back down on the ground. "So he moves the huddle over a few yards and continues with the scrimmage while I'm still lying there," Winchester recalled. "A little later he comes over while the medical staff is still working on me and tells me, 'I just want you to know that real football players don't get hurt.'"

Then there was the mountain. It was the source of the most enduring stories about Kush. At Tontozona, there was a hill that overlooked the practice field. It was too steep to run up it, so players would sort of climb and pull themselves up at the same time. Former players had become quite familiar with the scenic view at the top of what became known as Mount Kush. Once, Winchester had done something to earn a trip up the hill. About halfway up, Winchester realized that from his vantage point at the bottom, Kush couldn't possibly see him. So Winchester stopped and took a break. After about ten minutes, he started walking back down. When he got to the bottom, Kush was waiting. He held out his hand. "I slapped him five," Winchester recalled. "And he said, 'What the hell are you doing? Where's my stick?'" It turned out that at the top of the hill was a box and inside it were popsicle sticks. Players had to bring one back down, just to prove they had gone all the way up." Winchester went up the hill again.

Folklore about Kush had been handed down from one generation of ASU players to the next, some of which couldn't possibly seem true. Yet knowing their coach as they did, the players would figure that if any coach could have done these things, it had to be Kush. For example, there was the story about the star defensive lineman. Winchester said he first heard it on his recruiting visit but that Kush would never talk to him about it.

Supposedly, there was a standout defensive player who was getting into it with an offensive lineman one day in practice. Finally, after a series of minor skirmishes, the two players really started fighting. Kush eventually broke it up and demanded an explanation. The defensive player, who was still upset, demonstrated what the offensive lineman had been doing by popping Kush in the chest with open hands, knocking the coach to the ground. Winchester said he was told that the practice field turned deathly quiet. Kush didn't utter a word other than to say calmly that he wanted to see the player after practice. Later, Kush pulled him aside and they went into a storage shed next to the locker room. The players all hustled into the locker room and put their ears to the wall to hear what was happening. They could hear things being thrown around. The players, Winchester said, were saying things like "He's killing Frank!" Then the noise stopped.

"About a minute later," Winchester said, "Kush stuck his head in the locker room and told the team when practice would be the next day. Then the palyer walked into the locker room. Blood was trickling down from his nose."

Winchester said that the lineman himself confirmed the story. But Kush just shook his head one day after a Ranch practice when asked about the incident. "Where do they get that stuff?" he said, his eyes squinting from the sun. That's just a bunch of bullshit. I never punched a kid. I only slapped headgear. But the stories just get embell-ished. It's just like the Mount Kush stories. People got the impression that we just tortured people every day running up that hill. The truth is we hardly ever went up there. I bet 90 percent of these stories about me are myth. The other 10 percent are true. But I was tough on them. I don't deny that."

Kush's denial that he ever hit one of his players would take on great significance in the autumn of 1979. The times had changed. The pre-vious football season, Ohio State's Woody Hayes, another coach from the old school, had lost his job after striking a player from Clemson in front of a national television audience. The TV cameras at Camp Ton-tozona were paying close attention to Kush. He was doing what he had always done: grabbing face masks and rapping players on their helmets with his whistle. But the climate was different. That September, a punter named Kevin Rutledge accused Kush of punching him in the mouth during a game the year before after he had shanked a punt. What followed was a storm that divided the state. There was a hurri-cane of charges, countercharges, and accusations of a cover-up. And later, NCAA investigators would reveal academic irregularities involving ASU players who received credit for bogus correspondence courses, causing the football program to be put on probation and tarnishing the school's image.

The bottom line was that Kush's bosses didn't believe him when he denied that he had ever hit Rutledge. Despite his status as Arizona's leading sports figure, Kush was fired in October 1979. But Kush coached one more game after his dismissal was announced. And on Saturday night, the players carried Kush onto the field and went out and beat the Rose Bowl–bound Washington Huskies, 12–7. The players carried Kush off the field, too.

Kush's fall from grace left much of Arizona in shock. Kush later would be exonerated in court after Rutledge filed a civil suit against him. Kush would even receive a settlement from ASU. To this day, he denies striking the punter. But he never coached another college game. Conceivably, he still could have been at ASU if the Rutledge incident hadn't happened. But Kush didn't think about that. He said that when you grew up the way he did, you didn't ponder "what if" questions very long. You learned to deal with reality.

After ASU, Kush had a one-year coaching stint in the Canadian Football League with the Hamilton Tiger-Cats. Then he coached for four seasons with the Baltimore/Indianapolis Colts, but his teams struggled with an 11–28–1 record. He finished his coaching career with the Arizona Outlaws of the United States Football League, which faded into oblivion after he had been with the team one year. Coaching in the pro ranks wasn't the same for Kush. The blind loyalty he had received at ASU was missing. The best example of that came while he was with the Colts and a player became upset because Kush had chewed him out during practice for not running hard. Later, the player poured a soft drink over the coach's head in the chow hall. Kush ignored him and cut the guy right after he finished his meal.

By 1986, Kush was out of coaching. For a time he was a public relations man for a Phoenix horse-racing track and did some television commentary. He was searching for something. Then, Thomas called from the Boys Ranch. He wanted to know if Kush would be interested in a job as the Ranch's executive administrator. Among his responsibilities, he would be the Ranch's face in the community and help spread the word about what the Ranch was doing. "When I hired him, it wasn't just to be a P.R. guy," Thomas said. "He shows up to work every day. He gives more talks than anybody I've ever seen. I've never met a better people person." Thomas also was smart enough to realize that there could be some benefits to having the football coaching great Frank Kush on the staff when it came time to convince counties throughout the nation that they should send their delinquent kids to Boys Ranch.

"All I know is that as soon as Frank came here, we started getting kids from California right and left," Winchester said. "Frank had a lot to do with selling the Ranch. It's like he's back out on the recruiting trail. Instead of selling ASU's program in the homes of recruits, he was selling the Ranch's program to various courts and judges."

As time passed, Thomas also made a startling discovery about Kush. "For all his gruffness, I really think he's too soft," Thomas said. "Get him off the football field and he's a marshmallow. He can't say no to people. The kids love him because he's so easy to con." People who got the chance to get close to Kush expressed similar sentiments. The truth is there were two sides to the man. There was the tyrant with a whistle around his neck that the public saw, but there was also a gentle soul who would do anything for his friends. When Winchester got out of college, he tried to buy a house but couldn't get approved for a loan. He turned to Kush, who told him to call his bank the next morning. When Winchester did, he found out that Kush had authorized a personal loan for $20,000 so Winchester could purchase the home. Players hated him on the field, Winchester explained. But off the field, he would do anything for them.

At some point, Thomas told Kush about his dream of fielding a full-fledged high school sports program with a football team as the centerpiece. Kush warned him not to expect to win many games. The old coach knew that you couldn't just slap a team together in the summer with inexperienced kids who didn't know one another and go out that fall and beat squads that had been playing together for years. As long as Thomas had realistic expectations, Kush said, then football would be fine at the Ranch. There was one catch, though. As the Ranch planned to field its first football team in 1994, Kush made it clear that he didn't want to coach. The main reason was the Rutledge incident. The Ranch had already been inundated with bad publicity. Kush figured that it would be only a matter of time before some kid accused him of striking him on the practice field. Kush already could see the newspaper headlines. So he agreed instead to help the coaches in some minor capacity. That self-imposed exile didn't last very long, though. He was still a football coach at heart. Soon Kush could be found out at the blocking sled, demonstrating the proper technique to knock that "jackass" who lined up across you on his butt.

"Frank is sixty-six and he's had a lot of medical problems in recent years, but you'd have to duct-tape him to the wall to keep him from being out there on the field," said Whitfield, the Ranch's athletic director. It was a good thing for the Ranch that Kush was around. Because that first team had been rushed along at the last minute and none of the coaches had run a squad before, all the ingredients were in place for a disastrous season. Kush helped salvage the team. "We weren't very good, but we weren't an embarrassment, either," Thomas said. "That's because of Kush. Frank just saved us. This year he's doing the same kinds of things that help us."

And, strangely, Kush bonded with players who were young enough to be his grandkids. Some boys clearly were scared to death of the little man, who wore his cap pulled down so low that his eyes could barely be seen peering out from underneath. Others would make it their mission to please the curmudgeon. That first season, the Ranch didn't kick an extra point all season because the Spartans didn't have anybody who could come close to reaching the crossbar. But one day, Milbrandt remembered, Kush auditioned kickers. He had a holder place the ball in position and then got down on his hands and knees. He was pointing to the exact place where the football was supposed to be kicked. He asked for a piece of chalk so he could mark the spot on the ball. "So then," Milbrandt said, "you had forty kids suddenly patting their football pants looking for a piece of chalk. They were that eager to please him."

After the season, Thomas decided that he needed to get some experienced high school coaches. He added Gray and Winchester. "When Richard got hired, Frank brought him into his office," Winchester said. "Frank threw a list of offensive plays at him and said, 'Here's our offense. You do whatever you want with the defense.' Richard must have been thinking, 'Hey, I thought I was the head coach?' But that's just Frank. He's a general. That's never going to change." If Gray had a problem with Frank being Frank, he never let on.

This season, Kush would be working primarily with the quarterbacks and receivers, but in reality he would be sort of a coach emeritus, a guy who coached the coaches, came up with game plans, and sat in the press box and offered suggestions to Gray on the sidelines via a headset. Kush freely admitted that he didn't have the patience to coach at the high school level. Every day he had to explain the same drills over and over because the kids' retention of the instructions usually could be measured by the second hand on a watch. He had to show receivers how to line up in their stance. How to hit the blocking sled. How to run the passing routes. He spent much of his day throwing his hat up in the air in frustration. Part of it was real. Part of it was a calculated act of reverse psychology. "I'll walk away and act like I don't give a damn," he said. "I'll ignore them and that will make the kids think, "Well, I'll show him.' Then they'll do it right. I wouldn't be out here helping if I didn't care."

In his last coaching jobs, Kush had been working with well-paid professionals at the highest level of football. Now he was back on the lowest rung of the ladder. Although he never verbalized it this way, perhaps he still saw football as an escape. He often talked about what football had taught him: determination, how to deal with adversity, the importance of refusing to quit. The kids on this field weren't going to get anywhere in life if they didn't learn those basics. To Kush, football was as good a way as any to deliver life's lessons.

"I'm here because maybe I can help some kids," he said. "The wins and losses are insignificant. Shaune, our quarterback, had never thrown a football in his life before last year. Now he can play for any high school around. That's what I get out of it. If I can help a kid develop some confidence and some self-esteem, then maybe he can bring that to real life. I don't care if we win a game."

It never struck Kush as the least bit ironic that he had once been accused of pursuing a win-and-at-any-costs philosophy and now was saying that he didn't care if his team even won. He had completely recalibrated his goals. But true to form, he never looked back. He didn't have time for irony. One day at practice, several kids were trying out for the role of punter. One poor kick after another floated feebly into the air maybe 20 yards downfield. Kush only shrugged his shoulders. "I think we're going to have some punting problems," Kush said, a wry smile creasing his face.

A few days later, Kush was standing on the dais at the new College Football Hall of Fame in South Bend, Indiana, listing all the people who had made it possible for him to be there. Two people he didn't forget to mention were Kaiser Bussick and Gump Polansky.

ADVERSITY STRIKES

There is nothing any football coach loves to do more than look at game film. Give a coach some tape, a projector, and a screen, and he's a happy man. A coach rarely tires of watching game film, searching for subtle clues to why each play worked or failed. He will study his own team. He will study his opponents. It's often in darkened rooms, not on the fields, that games are won and lost.

The Ranch coaches were no different from their brethren. Early Saturday morning, six days before the season opener, the coaches began wandering into the classroom. Several held large cups of coffee or soft drinks from local convenience stores. Bleary-eyed, they plopped down in chairs and waited for the show to begin. These days "game film" actually was videotape. Winchester popped a cassette into the VCR. Gray, being the boss, controlled the remote control. As he punched the buttons, the grainy images on the TV screen went forward and backward. They moved at fast-forward speed and in slow motion. The camera eye missed nothing. The coaches would watch one play several times before deciding that they had dissected it enough to move on to the next specimen.

The picture that flickered on the screen was of the Ranch's scrimmage against the Wickenburg Wranglers. The Ranch had lost to Wickenburg the previous season. But the night before, the Spartans had worked them over easily. Less than twelve hours later, Gray couldn't decide if that was good or bad. On the one hand, it was a boost to the players' confidence that they could beat somebody. On the other hand, Wickenburg was nothing like the teams the Ranch would play in the 3A East Region. Nonetheless, Gray was in an upbeat mood. His team was coming together.

McKissic had proved himself to be a smart quarterback. Twice he had corrected the coaches when they tried to call plays out of the wrong formation. He understood the offense better than they did. McKissic was someone the other kids respected. And Gray's suspicions about his team's quickness had been confirmed. His kids could flat-out run. He had never coached a high school squad this fast. Ray High, the Ranch's first opponent, had scouts at the scrimmage, and they supposedly had left mumbling the word "speed."

Finally, although there were plenty of handicaps to coaching at the Ranch, there was one advantage: You never knew what the next van from juvenile hall might bring. Two new arrivals had Gray practically salivating. One was fifteen-year-old Reggie Miles, who already stood six feet one, weighed 235 pounds, and had quick feet for a boy his size. The other was Amenweah Yuoh (YO), who checked in at six feet two and 200 pounds. It was only a matter of time, Gray said, before they would be lining up with Tamar Armstrong on the defensive line.

As the coaches methodically pored over the film, some of the players began peering through the classroom window, hoping to catch glimpses of themselves. Because they had played a game the night before, nothing was planned for them this morning. But they quickly became bored and left as Gray kept running the same couple of plays again and again. He was watching the Ranch's center, a boy named Cody Jeffries. Only fifteen, Jeffries weighed 250 pounds. When Gray had first looked at him, all he could see was a round, soft Native American boy. He had been pleasantly surprised. "I'm telling you, Jeffries is a man," marveled Ray Perkins as Cody repeatedly dominated a Wickenburg defender who had been all-state the previous year. Gray could only concur. Cody would be the anchor of the Ranch's offensive line.

But all the news wasn't good.

"So Elliott is going to start?" Perkins asked.

"I think so," Gray said, rubbing his chin as if deep in thought.

A decision had to be made. Gray really wanted Cabell to start over Tim Elliott at tailback. They both were good running backs, but Cabell was a big-play threat every time he touched the ball. Yet the reality was that despite Cabell's electrifying performance in the intrasquad scrimmage, Elliott had looked just a little better in the preseason practices. Elliott also had performed best among the backs against Wickenburg. Gray worried that in their effort to get Cabell to work harder, the coaches had lost him. Maybe they had been too tough on him. His self-confidence seemed shot to hell. Instead of fighting to be the No. 1 tailback, Cabell was acting as if he didn't care if he played at all. "Right now he's a little bit of a broken runner," Gray would say later. "He's been in Coach Moore's doghouse, and I prefer that those two work it out. Cabell should be the best, but he hasn't been to this point."

There was one more order of business: choosing team captains. The coaches decided against McKissic and Armstrong because they were going to be leaders with or without the title. They wanted boys who might grow from the experience. Eventually, they decided on Sparkman, Letua, Jeffries, placekicker Alex Andrade, fullback Lloyd Peters, and offensive lineman Shibaka Miles. (Shibaka said his dad had named him after an Egyptian pharaoh mentioned during the *Roots* miniseries on television.) "OK, let's see," Gray said. "We've got every race represented—black, Hispanic, Samoan, Indian—except a white kid. It's like a Disney movie; we need a white kid." After some more discussion, though, the coaches decided six captains would be enough.

As the session concluded, Moore went to Cabell to break the news that Elliott would be starting Friday night in the opener. "He might as well know now," Moore said. "You watch, I'm gonna have to baby-sit him all next week. He's gonna ask three different coaches what's wrong instead of talking to the one he needs to. But that's the way these kids work. They play staff off one another."

————

Everyone on campus—teachers, counselors, even Mr. Thomas—kept telling Cabell how he was going to lead the Spartans to the playoffs. He was going to make All-State. He was going to attend college on a football scholarship. They had his future all mapped out for him. But they didn't understand. Nobody understood. How could he explain it to them? Every time somebody told him how great he was, he wanted to shout out, "Yeah, well if I'm supposed to be so good, then how come the coaches won't even start me?"

Others may have thought he was going to be the Spartans' standout performer, but Cabell sure wasn't feeling like a star. Rather, he was feeling pretty lousy. Losing his starting position was bad enough. All the pressure to be a star was even worse. How could he be the star if he wasn't carrying the football? The way he saw it, he was doomed to failure long before the first kickoff of the season. Then everyone would be coming up to him wanting to know what was wrong and why he wasn't the same player he had been the previous season. He thought the coaches were more interested in him concentrating on defense where he was a starter in the secondary. Cabell figured that ultimately would be the position he would play in college, but that the only way to get noticed by schools in the first place was to be a tailback. He thought colleges would have doubts about taking a player from a place like the Ranch, where everybody had a criminal history. Cabell believed he had to play so well that colleges would be willing to take that risk on him. Besides, carrying the football was what he wanted to do. He finally had found something he was good at, and he didn't want to let go of it.

"But I'm not even mentioned when they talk about running back," Cabell said. "It's been like this ever since last spring. When we started practicing, they had me at ninth-string, below every other running back. Then I worked all the way up to second-string. But now this season is almost here and Tim Elliott is starting. People are expecting a lot of me after what I did last year. They want me to do even more this year. When I started this year, I said that I wasn't going to let nobody take my position. Nobody. And I've been striving to work hard. Still, they put me down low."

The coaches — especially Mr. Moore — were testing him Cabell figured. That was what staff did at the Ranch. They put kids in adverse situations to see how they would handle it. Would they blow up, or would they show some maturity and act like responsible young men? He had been at the Ranch long enough to know how the game was played. But Cabell felt he had done everything asked of him, and still he wasn't getting a fair chance.

The coaches saw it differently. They thought Cabell could work even harder. The other variable was that Elliott had talent, too. Gray was thrilled with the prospect of having a one-two combination of Cabell and Elliott: the speedster outside and the bull moose running between the tackles. Few other teams in the state — regardless of their size — would have that kind of backfield duo. But Cabell couldn't see the big picture. All he knew was that he had lost his position. So his mood vacillated wildly. Sometimes he had a tendency to brag on himself around the other kids, something that wore thin with his peers and the coaches. But if anything, Cabell talked big to hide his insecurity because there were other times when the gauge on his self-esteem tank read empty. The truth was that Cabell had been as shocked as anyone by his performance the previous season. He had surpassed the 1,000-yard barrier, a magical plateau for a running back. He had run back kickoffs and punts for touchdowns. He had played defense. He simply had done it all, becoming the team's unchallenged star.

"I worked hard last year, but I couldn't believe I did so well," he said. "I thought everyone would be quicker, stronger, and tougher than me. But I pushed myself, and it was unbelievable what I could do."

His accomplishments on the field had far outweighed anything he had ever done with his life. His hometown was Evansville, Indiana, but he didn't have a home in the traditional sense. His father, who had been a shadowy figure in his life, had served time on a couple of occasions, Cabell said. When he wasn't around, his mother was forced to work to make ends meet. Nonetheless, some of Cabell's earliest memories were happy ones. His mother had a good job, and he remembered having everything he wanted. But then it all began to fall apart. When he was five years old, Cabell said, his mother suffered a nervous breakdown and could no longer take care of him and his sister. He went to live with his grandmother for a time, but that proved unworkable because she couldn't deal with the young boy.

"So they took me to a foster home and told me that I would be there for a weekend," Cabell said. "I was there for six years."

When his foster father passed away, a man with whom he had formed a bond, Cabell began to rebel. He ended up being shipped from one home to another in rapid succession. Somehow he got the notion in his head that his various foster parents were keeping him and his mother separated for some undisclosed but certainly evil reason. So he ran away at every opportunity. He was never mistreated. In fact, Cabell spoke kindly of all his foster parents. It wasn't their fault that he acted the way he did. He just missed his mother. He was allowed to visit her on weekends but could never stay permanently.

Cabell felt like he was living in limbo. He had no sense of belonging. He had family, yet there certainly wasn't a family unit. In a gang, he found a substitute. It was called the Vice Lords and was loosely affiliated with the Bloods. "I was twelve or thirteen when I started getting out of hand," he explained. "That's when nobody could control me. They tried. But I was a hardhead and did what I wanted to do. All I thought about was myself. I was selfish. I thought my mother and my father didn't care about me. My dad, he used to tell me not to hang out with those boys who were getting into trouble. But I didn't care what he said. It got to the point where I didn't want to be in foster homes anymore. I thought I could start taking off and start making my own decisions. Then I started breaking into houses, stealing, selling drugs, smoking weed. You know, doing a lot of crime."

Cabell described Evansville as a small town where there was nothing much to do other than drive around and get high. The people he hung with — cousins and their friends — all wanted to act like the gang members they had heard about out in California. The end result, Cabell said, was that he followed the crowd down the wrong path into the full-fledged gang-banging scene. Part of that included becoming part of a flourishing small business in the drug trade. Cabell wasn't a big-time dealer. "I was just one of the little ones," he said. But Cabell said he made some money, usually $250 to $300 a week. On weekends, he would hang around the parking lots of the adult clubs, looking for customers. Because one of his friends had an uncle who worked at one club as a bouncer, Cabell was sometimes able to peddle his wares inside, too.

"Sometimes, I look back and think I was doing the right thing just because I was doing what I had to just to get through each day," he said. "You know what I mean? Then there's sometimes when I think that it just wasn't worth it. But when I was doing it, I didn't really think much about it. Now I see that I maybe could have gone another route — maybe delivering newspapers or doing odd jobs. Something legal. But I wasn't thinking about that when I was just hanging out with my friends."

Eventually, enough was enough. He was too much for any foster home to handle. He had been charged with burglary after, in his words, he broke into a house and stole $5,000 from an elderly man, and was accused of criminal mischief for breaking an aunt's window after she was in an argument with his mother. Further, the court was fully aware of his history of running away from foster placement. The juvenile judge presiding over Cabell's case told him about the Ranch and that he thought the facility might be a good place for him. But the more the judge talked, the more upset Cabell got. Arizona? Why would he want to go all the way out there? He remembered getting angry and acting up right there in the courtroom. Fine, the judge said, have it your way. Cabell was shipped off to another Indiana Boys home for eight months. The next time he appeared before the judge, Cabell said he was ready to give the place out in Arizona a try.

Cabell didn't really want to go to the Ranch, of course, but his choices were limited. When he did arrive in January of 1994, he was scared. He didn't like the regimentation. He didn't like the way staff got on him. He thought about running again, but he figured that there was no place to run to. Slowly, when he looked around at the surrounding desert, he saw some positives to being there. He came to feel that the staff was sincere about trying to help him. Residents ate, lived, played, and worked together. In some ways, they were like a big extended family. He had left Evansville behind him. "I'm, I dunno, different," he tried to explain. And when he was back in Indiana on home visits, Cabell would find some excuse not to join old friends downtown. When residents returned after home visits, they usually had to take a drug test. Cabell said with pride that staff wouldn't even test him anymore because they knew he wouldn't use when he was away.

Cabell had been due to leave the Ranch in May, but the judge had been so impressed with his progress that he proposed a deal: If Cabell stayed at the Ranch so he could complete his degree in December, his court would keep paying the bill. Cabell talked about the offer with his mother, who was still having a hard time. "My mom told me to do this for her and finish what I started," he said. "I want to change for her. I don't want to go to prison. I want another chance. I might not be like I was now, but it's all in my files. I made that reputation for myself. I don't want that reputation no more. Nothing could make me go back to being the person I was."

The judge had laid out another carrot for him: If he got that degree in December, his record as a juvenile offender would be destroyed. He would get a fresh start. What really struck Cabell was how the judge seemed to suggest that in his case the system had failed. The judge told Cabell that maybe he wouldn't have had to go to the Arizona Boys Ranch if he had somehow gotten more direction earlier in life. "I could have got sent to a kid prison," Cabell said. "But my P.O. had been telling them, 'This kid, he really isn't that bad.' They knew. I think they felt it was sort of their fault. The judge told me that he was real proud of me." When he graduated, Cabell had decided he would not return to Indiana. He was going to attend college in Arizona.

But Cabell's plan to get a football scholarship seemed to be crumbling before him. How could he catch the eye of college scouts if he wasn't running the ball? Instead of preparing for what should have been the most exciting couple of months of his young life, Cabell was dreading the coming weeks. He appeared ready to shrug his shoulders and give up the fight.

When told that he could always make the most of his chance once he got into the game and carried the ball, Cabell answered despondently, "If I get in."

THE REGULAR SEASON

My name is Todd Anthony Harris Jr. I'm sixteen. I'm from San Diego. I've been here going on ten months. On the football team, I'm a wide receiver and backup quarterback.

I've been in different programs, and they weren't as structured as this. Those programs didn't teach you what they teach you here. Here, they want you to deal with adversity. So when I first got here, I couldn't really handle it. But now I'm learning to handle it better. The other places were a joke really. It was all about doing your time, and then getting out. Here, it's about learning how to change so you can be a better person in life. I want to change because I've got a daughter who's a year and a half old. Her name is Asa.

When I first got here, I thought it was going to be like my other programs. After about two months, I realized that this was different. It was tough at first. I had never experienced anything like this before. It was a shock. I didn't want to deal with it. When I did something wrong, they wouldn't let me play sports, and that's what I like doing the most. I didn't like that at all. Then I started talking to people, and I began to realize that they're just trying to make you a better person in life and help you so you can find a job.

It's pretty mean back home. There's a lot of peer pressure. That's my problem. I can't handle peer pressure very well. There, I didn't really care what happened to my life. I was into gangs, crimes. I did drugs. It's sort of hard to stay away from it because it's there. You don't want to say no because then everybody else will beat on you and stuff. They'll fight you. That's why it's hard.

I was in the Crips. When you're in that gang, you don't care about nobody except your own friends. That's all you care about. At first, I didn't want to be in the gangs. But when I moved to San Diego, everybody used to beat up on me. I wanted to be known. I thought that if I hung out with them, I would be doing fine. So I got in. Then a couple of months later, I got caught for strong-arm robbery. So I went to a placement. Then after I got out, I got caught for grand theft auto and got sent here.

I don't really know much about my daughter. I wasn't there when she was born. I felt kind of sad. Yes, sir, I have pictures of her. She can talk. She said "Daddy" and stuff on the phone. But I don't think she knows who I am. I'm not with her mom anymore, but we have a good relationship. It's real hard being away from my little girl.

Every day I write her letters. Every day. Anytime I start thinking about all the stuff I used to do, I just start thinking about my daughter, sir. I concentrate on doing what I have to do to get out and see her. When I leave here, I'm going to find a job and spend most of my time with her. I'm not even going to tell my friends that I'm out when I leave here. I might like to go to college. If a chance comes along, I'd take it. But I'm not really that good at school.

Having a child changes your perspective. It should have changed it out there. But I was only thinking about myself. Just myself.

MUTINY AT THE RANCH

Ray High School is located in the mining town of Kearny, southeast of Phoenix. There used to be a town called Ray, but now it's in a strip mine. When the people were moved to Kearny, they evidently took the name of their school with them.

The Ranch's first game ever was against the Ray Bearcats the previous year. The Spartans played so badly that the game bordered on a slapstick comedy. It would have been funny if it hadn't been so painful to watch. The coaches had wanted to find a rock to hide under. On one punt the Spartans had too few players on the field. On a kickoff, they lined up on the wrong side of the field. Thomas had vivid memories of seeing an irate Kush throw his headset around the press box. Ray had a big running back who was built like a bowling ball, and he knocked over the Ranch defenders like pins. Every carry, he seemed to roll a strike. At some point during the game, the Spartans nicknamed the boy Fat 'N' Nasty. They proceeded to make him look like All-State material. The only thing that went right for the Spartans was that Cabell ran back a kickoff for a touchdown. The Ranch was losing 42–6 late in the fourth quarter when one of the fast-moving monsoon storms that erupt suddenly over the desert during the early evenings of August and September came rumbling through. The officials called the game because of the torrential rain and lightning. It was almost as if the good Lord had been watching, decided he had seen enough, and ordered up a cloudburst to spare the Ranch further pain and suffering.

The Spartans would be opening the season against Ray again this year, and, thanks in large part to the returning Fat 'N' Nasty, the team was supposed to be one of the best 2A teams in the state. Gray began pulling the motivational strings early in the week when little notes like

"Fat 'N' Nasty wants you!" began appearing in the locker room and even on the blocking-sled pads. By late in the week, there was nothing subtle about his ploys.

"You know what I hate worse than anything?" he asked the team after practice one afternoon. "It's when a coach comes up to you after his team has just kicked your butt and says, 'Coach, great game. Your kids played hard.' I hate that. That's probably what the Ray coach said after he whipped you guys last year. But this is a new year and Ray doesn't have anything that you don't have. I look at them on film and I see two arms, two legs, and two eyes on all the players."

"What about their balls, coach?" Shofner asked.

"Well, I think they've all got two, except for one boy who was in a bike accident," Gray added without missing a beat. "But other than that, I can't figure out why everyone thinks that Ray is going to beat our butts. We've got them right where we want them. They don't respect you because they basically toyed with you last year. They rubbed your noses in it a little bit. But that was last year. Where I come from, we say that paybacks are a bitch. This is a payback. And I've already got my postgame talk down. I think about it every night before I go to bed. I'll walk right up to the other coach and say, 'Coach, nice game. Your kids played hard.' "

Gray maintained his air of confidence around the kids. Now if he could only convince himself that he was right. Back in the coaches' office, after the players had left for the pantry, Gray began talking about the upcoming game and his cocky attitude evaporated into thin air. He began ticking off a laundry list of worries: The Spartans had never punted in a game. They'd never had a kickoff. They'd never held a practice under the lights. They'd never attempted an extra point. Heck, the Spartans didn't even know what PAT meant. They were untested and unknown. This was going to be the first time most of them ever played a real football game. If we fall behind early, he concluded, the floodgates might open. There was one other thing that Gray noted. There was no mercy rule. Theoretically, Ray could score 100 points on the Ranch, and the referees wouldn't halt the game.

Winchester also thought the result could be ugly. But having worked at the Ranch for years, he saw things differently. He knew how far these kids had come. "Most of them have been failures their entire lives," Winchester said. "They never stuck with anything. When things got tough, they quit. To me, when they take that field against

Ray, then they've already won."

———

Game day had arrived.

The players had been up with the sun — that had been by design, because the team had been taken off-Ranch for a breakfast to kick off the season. But the kids would have been up early anyway. Some had barely slept all night, as they pondered what would happen when the lights began to glow over the football field the next evening. There had been the obligatory pep rally at mid-afternoon. The only difference at the Ranch, of course, was that there were no cheerleaders. At 4:00 P.M., the team had a light dinner. The pantry was practically silent and little food was eaten. The atmosphere in the room was like that at a last supper. Even the coaches were lost in their thoughts. "You know, somebody asked me what offense we run, and I was going to tell them the run-and-shoot," Milbrandt joked, trying to break through the dark mood. "That would be the right offense for us to run, right?" After some momentary laughter, gloom once again descended on the room.

Part of the reason for the coaches' dour demeanor was that just that day three boys had been dropped from the team and shipped back down to the Civics program. The goal of the Ranch might have been inclusion rather than exclusion, but the reality was that kids were here to straighten out their lives, not to play football. The three hadn't been doing their program on the main campus, so it was decided that the trio would get more out of being in Oracle in Civics uniforms than being on the main campus in football uniforms. Among the boys was the Hispanic youth who had been first in line to get his equipment a couple of weeks earlier. He wouldn't have been much of a player for the team, but he seemed genuinely excited about being part of the squad. "They could be the best ballplayers out here, but the program comes first," Milbrandt said. "You have to keep telling yourself that this isn't about football."

Nevertheless, none of the coaches was happy that three kids had been dropped from the team on the eve of the first game after sticking it out through all the rugged preseason practices.

Back in the locker room, players began to get dressed. Because the Ranch did not have its own field, home games were played at different area high schools that they rented out for the evening. Tonight's game was to be held at Highland, a new high school in the nearby town of Gilbert. It was located only fifteen minutes away by bus, so the Spartans would get ready in their own small barn of a locker room. As the players put on their gear, they repeatedly looked at themselves in the two mirrors in the bathroom, like homecoming queens making sure their makeup was applied just right. The home uniforms consisted of green pants and green jerseys with white numbers on the front and back. The word "Spartans" was printed on the front. The helmets were green, too. Each had an "S" on the right side. The outfits were exact replicas of the ones the Michigan State Spartans used to wear. That school happened to be not only Kush's alma mater, but Thomas's as well. Meanwhile, the coaches set about the usual pregame rituals. They went over their game plan. They looked at last-minute film. They checked the radio equipment the coaches in the press box would use to communicate with the assistants on the sidelines. They performed any busywork to keep their minds occupied.

Finally, just before the squad boarded the bus, Gray gathered the team together in front of a chalkboard and revealed the master strategy for the night: The Spartans would run Ray into the ground, wear them down, then win the game in the fourth quarter. "We're the best-conditioned team in the state," Gray explained. "We've been practicing in the midday heat. They've got a lot of kids who play both offense and defense. Their tongues ought to be hanging by the fourth quarter. That's when we're going to win. Now, if you have a chance to put them away early, by all means do so. Please, go ahead and cross the goal line. You don't have to stop."

Gray left the players with one last thought to digest on the short bus trip. "This is not," he said, "a democracy. Whatever I say, you do. The coaches make the decisions. You follow our instructions tonight, and we'll do just fine." The players' inability to abide by Gray's last order would haunt the Ranch later that night.

———

The boys' eyes grew wide as they walked into the spacious Highland locker room. Compared with their humble, confining facilities, this was a palace. It still had a fresh-paint smell. The kids acted as if they were afraid to touch anything for fear of somehow desecrating the place. Gray told the players to find somewhere to sit and to save their energy. Only they couldn't. Boys began to pace back and forth like lions in a cage. But other than the sound of their cleats clicking on the gray cement floor, a deathly silence had fallen over the room. Stanley Moultry, a linebacker, turned to Shaun Williams, a defensive back. "You nervous?" Moultry whispered. Williams didn't answer. He just bobbed his head up and down. With their pads on, the Spartans appeared menacing. In coaching parlance, they looked good getting off the bus. "We might be big, but we don't have any experience," countered Lono Hill, the tight end. Along with many of his team-mates, he resembled the proverbial deer caught in the headlights the moment before the awful impact with an oncoming vehicle.

As the players took the field for pregame warm-ups, the sun was just beginning to set in the distance and the field lights were being turned on. The coaches were abuzz: Fat 'N' Nasty would not be playing. He didn't yet have the ten practices required by the AIA to play in a game. The Ranch had caught a lucky break. While the coaches were discussing how this would change their defensive strategy, a singsong cadence began to fill the air.

First came the voice of one man, which was answered by the sound of maybe 150 boys responding in unison. *Sound off! ONE, TWO! Sound off! THREE, FOUR! Sound off! ONE, TWO, THREE, FOUR. ONE, TWO . . . THREE, FOUR!* The Civic Conservation Corps had arrived. Just about all of the boys from the Oracle campus had been driven up in a convoy of Ford vans. The boys wore matching black boots, khaki pants, white shirts with collars, and green Civics caps. Scattered around them was a platoon of Civics staff, all wearing simi-lar clothing and the same serious expressions on their faces. The group worked its way around the track in perfect formation, three abreast, singing different songs in military-style marching cadence as they loudly announced their presence. When they made it to their places in the stands, where they were handed green-and-white pompoms, they started chanting as a group: "Fire it up, Spartans, fire it up!" The bleachers shook as they stomped their feet. Thomas, who had taken his customary Jerry Jones place on the sideline, looked up at the Civics corps and smiled. "It's like a damned Army-Navy game," he said. Between the kids and the Ranch staff and their families, there were several hundred spectators. The Spartans may have been the team with no field, but they still had a home-field advantage.

Back in the locker room, the team recited The Lord's Prayer. Gray reminded the squad that the game was real simple. Either hit people or get hit. It was a lot more fun being the hitter than being the one knocked on his ass. Nobody was going to get arrested for popping somebody out here. All anyone would do was cheer. This was called taking out aggression in a positive manner. Then the Spartans took the field. Considering where this team was just four weeks earlier, that alone was an accomplishment.

The evening started off well when Letua intercepted a pass deep in Bearcat territory to set up a two-yard scoring run by Elliott. Ray had marched right back down the field to tie the game, 7–7. That lasted roughly fourteen seconds, which was how long it took Cabell to scamper 93 yards with the ensuing kickoff. When he caught the ball, he took one step toward the middle of the field which committed three Ray defenders in that direction. Cabell then broke outside and sprinted past everyone else down the right sideline as the Spartans fans cheered him on. It was exactly what he had done against his own teammates in the intrasquad scrimmage two weeks earlier. Cabell, it seemed, was ready to be his team's star again.

Another extra point by Alex Andrade made it 14–7. But the Bearcats responded with a 35-yard touchdown pass to tie the game at 14 near the end of the second quarter. Gray should have been a happy man heading into the locker room. Those floodgates hadn't opened. The Spartans could compete with the Bearcats. He had just wanted to keep the game close until the fourth quarter, and a tie game was as close as it could get. What he saw on the Ranch defense, though, horrified him. Everyone was lining up in the wrong place. Ray wide receivers were open on every play, and it was only a matter of time before the Bearcat coaches figured that out. Each time Ray ran the ball outside, the Spartan linebackers and defensive backs were getting caught inside as the running backs ripped off huge chunks of yardage. Even worse, players were pointing fingers at one another in the defensive huddle as they tried to pass the blame for their breakdowns on everyone else. The Ranch's best chance at victory, Gray told his coaches, would be to keep rolling up the points on offense, because it didn't look as if they would be stopping the Bearcats on defense.

Just before the third-quarter kickoff, Gray went up and down the sideline, looking at each player, telling him, "This is our time, and this is our half." In fact, it looked that way early as the Ranch forced a fumble on the second play. Then McKissic hit Sparkman with a 39-yard touchdown pass that was a thing of sheer beauty. Shaune and Juan looked like they had been making passes like that on a neighborhood sandlot their entire lives. Andrade's extra point made it 21–14.

Then it all disintegrated before the Spartans' eyes.

Less than two minutes later, the Ray quarterback tossed another touchdown pass. The play had been set up by a 27-yard Bearcat run that highlighted the Ranch's inexperience. Several Spartan defenders thought they had a Bearcat running back stopped behind the line of scrimmage even though they hadn't brought him down to the ground. But no referee had blown a whistle. So when the back wiggled free and started running, the befuddled Spartans just watched him before a defensive back finally made the tackle downfield. Gray could only slam his cap on the ground in frustration. A few plays later, the game was tied again, this time at 21. It remained that way only briefly. A poor McKissic pass was intercepted and returned 32 yards for a touchdown. Now it was 28–21, Bearcats. Ray forced a Ranch punt, but before the Bearcats could get too comfortable, Letua struck again. This time he forced a fumble with a hit so vicious that the running back was knocked flat and the ball popped straight up in the air before hitting the ground, where Stanley Moultry landed on it. Given new life, the Ranch went back to work on the ground with an eight-play drive culminated by a seven-yard touchdown run by McKissic early in the fourth quarter. It was a 28–28 game. It was the final quarter. This was when the Ranch was supposed to find a way to win.

In truth, the Spartans were hanging on by their fingernails. The Spartans' eggshell-thin layer of confidence seemed cracked. And they were tiring. The Bearcats were becoming the aggressors, not the Spartans. The tide had turned as Ray continued to move the ball with ease. With 7:39 left, a Bearcat running back took a handoff left. Cabell immediately stepped up from his safety position and hit him in the numbers . . . and bounced off. The Ray player high-stepped into the end zone for a four-yard touchdown run.

The Ranch was down, 35–28. Desperate times call for desperate measures, and it doesn't get any more desperate than this. On its next possession, the Spartans lost one yard on three plays. They were now faced with 4th-and-11 from their own 30-yard line with less than five minutes remaining. The safe play was to punt the ball away, hope the defense stopped them, and then regain possession with enough time left to have one last crack at the end zone.

Or they could gamble everything on a fake punt.

That's exactly what the Spartans did. Instead of snapping the ball back to Todd Harris, who was the team's punter, the football was hiked to the up-back: Lloyd Peters. A quiet kid who was a solid five feet nine and 175 pounds, Peters bulled his way up the middle. There was nothing pretty about the way Peters ran. He just lowered his head and plowed straight ahead. He caught the Bearcats by surprise and broke through the line of scrimmage. If he had been just a little quicker, Peters might have gotten the 11 yards. Instead, he was brought down after gaining only ten. The Bearcats would take over possession at the Ranch 40. It had been a nice attempt, and it was a gutsy play. Unfortunately, it was not one the coaches had called. As the punt team jogged back to the sideline, Gray went ballistic. "Who called that?" he screamed. "Who called that fake punt?" Nobody knew, and there was no time to find out. Five plays later, the Ray quarterback, who would throw only one incompletion all night, fired his fourth touchdown pass of the game. The extra point failed, but Ray now had an insurmountable 41–28 lead with 2:28 left. Even the Civics kids in the stands, who had been shouting all game, grew quiet. McKissic would march the Spartans down the field in the closing minutes, capping off the drive with a one-yard scoring sneak with twenty-two seconds remaining. The two-point conversion by Cabell made it 41–36. But when the Bearcats recovered the onsides kick, the game was over.

When the final horn sounded, Elliott fell on his back, staring up at the night sky in utter disbelief. Cabell walked around in circles, looking as if he was unable to express his anger in any tangible way. Others shed tears. Ta'ase engulfed Sparkman, who was visibly distraught, in a bear hug, telling him that everything was going to be all right and that he could hold his head up high. For a moment the entire team wallowed in defeat. Then came the curt order from Shofner: "Line it up!" Instantly, the players formed a neat row to shake hands with the victors. It was only then that the Spartans saw that with their helmets off, the Ray players were much smaller and younger-looking than they were.

Gray stared at the scoreboard. *How did we give up 41 points?* They had made the Ray quarterback look like Troy Aikman. In the fourth quarter, they had run out of gas. And the bickering on the field. He was going to have to do something about that, too. The coaches from the press box, including Kush, had come down to the field. Kush was incensed about the fake punt. "You wouldn't see that in Pop Warner or any other level of football," he growled. "In all the years I've been involved in the game, I have never seen a player rescind a coach's play. Never." Gray told the players to get close in the end zone. Real close. Regardless of whether they won or lost, they were still a team, he said. You need courage to play this game, he went on. That means having the strength to pick yourself up after you've been knocked down.

"Now, before we get on the bus, I have just one question," Gray continued. "Who called the play on the fake punt?" Nobody owned up. It was only later, after talking to the main suspects, that Gray was able to piece together the most probable version of events. He decided that three players had been in on the mini-mutiny: Sparkman the snapper, Peters the up-back, and Harris the punter. Gray figured that they must have decided among themselves that they were going to be Friday-night heroes. "And you know what?" Gray said. "They almost got it. If they did, they probably would have been carried off the field." Then with a bit of dark humor, Gray added that at least the trio remembered how to run a fake punt. The rest of the team had such a bad case of stage fright that they had forgotten their lines — or, in this case, their plays.

Gray could live with just about anything but players who had their own agendas. The following Monday was Labor Day, and the Ranch would labor during a four-hour practice while Gray reinforced the chain of command.

What nobody right then could possibly know was that Ray would go on to have an undefeated season and win the state 2A championship. This would be the Bearcats' toughest game all season. All the Spartans knew was that they had let one slip away. A grim truth was beginning to sink in among the players as they boarded the bus: Football could be exactly like the mean streets — they could lose. It was so quiet on the bus ride back to the Ranch that you could hear the team's hopes drop.

REELING IN THE YEARS

If nothing else, Otana Sengvong was consistent. Whenever he told his strange and mysterious story, it would not vary much. There were times when he would purposely become vague on details, particularly about why he had been sent to the Ranch. But that didn't make him much different from most of the boys. Other times, he would struggle with his English. He was somewhat uncomfortable with the native language of his adopted country. But he would get his point across, and the basic elements of his tale were always the same.

By the start of the football season, he had been at the Ranch for just over twelve months. According to court documents provided to the Ranch, he was to turn sixteen later in September. But he could easily have been mistaken for about fourteen. He could often be seen walking by himself on campus with schoolbooks under his arm. He also was the Ranch's most promising kicker. His small, slim stature belied the fact that he had a strong right leg. But, according to Sengvong, his best sport wasn't football. It was baseball.

A native of Laos, he said he was born in a refugee camp in Thailand. "The war was over, and we had no place to live," he explained. "So the Army made us move to a refugee camp. I was in the camp for a long time. I can still remember working in the rice fields." While he was still a young boy, around the age of eight, the family decided to emigrate to America. Sengvong already had an aunt living in the U.S., so, along with his mother, father, and grandfather, he relocated temporarily to a camp in Taiwan. The way Sengvong explained it, this was part of the process of getting into the U.S. You couldn't just go directly to America. The family stayed in Taiwan for less than a year. But it was there, Sengvong claimed, that his life was changed forever. "They saw me play baseball," he said. "I was pretty good."

"They" were Taiwanese Little League coaches. Taiwan is the home of some of the world's best youth baseball. Watch the Little League World Series on television from Williamsport, Pennsylvania, in August, and chances are you'll see a Taiwanese team playing. Just about every year Taiwan is in the thick of the title hunt. The country had won sixteen championships since 1969. Often there are whispers of controversy, too. The Little League organization constantly has to deal with rumors that some of the foreign teams are stocked with kids beyond the twelve-year-old age limit. In 1992, the Philippines was stripped of its title for using players who were too old. Similar accusations had been leveled at Taiwan as well, although none had ever been substantiated.

Sengvong, who said he had begun playing T-ball at the age of six, claimed that he was good enough to be noticed by Taiwanese coaches. Even though his family left for America in 1978 and eventually settled in the San Diego area, those coaches didn't forget him, Sengvong said. "I think they come scout me," he said. "They knew about my pitching ability." So, Sengvong explained: "They come pick me up and bring me back to Taiwan. Then we have spring practice and fall season there. So I didn't spend much time with my family. We would travel to different countries to play teams. Then we'd get to Williamsport to play in the World Series."

Sengvong said he started playing for a team from Taiwan in 1980, and in 1981 played for that country in the Little League World Series. And how many years did he go to Williamsport after that?

"Well, every year, until 1987," Sengvong added, rather sheepishly. "I felt bad because we were playing little kids." Sengvong said he was fifteen by his last season. He claimed that he could throw an eighty-three-mile-an-hour fastball, which would be an incredible velocity on a Little League diamond. Sengvong maintained that another nine players — the entire core of the squad — were too old as well. As for how the team got away with such brazen deception, Sengvong wasn't sure. He said the coaches took care of everything. He explained it by saying that it was all "paper," which was his way of describing paper-work, and added that the calendar he had grown up with in Asia was different from the calendars in the West. Somehow, upon his arrival in America, he claimed to have lost eight years off his real age.

"I haven't grown for a long time," he said. "I got this size and then my body stayed the same. So maybe we were able to do it because we're not too big. And we all looked the same because we all have shaved heads because of respect for Buddha."

He did remember one time when Little League officials suspected that something wasn't right with the squad and began to make inquiries. "They come and ask me one question," he said. "They ask, 'How come we've seen you year after year?' Then the coach interrupted and said, 'That's because he was here when he was nine, ten, eleven, and twelve.' I don't really know why my coach did that. I guess he wanted to win."

Several times Sengvong expressed remorse for not playing by the rules. "Everything was so small," he recalled. "The field was very small. I broke records, including for home runs. Hitting a home run wasn't very hard. I felt bad. It wasn't a challenge because it was unfair. They were just kids playing against us. I would like to be able to tell them that I'm sorry. We should have let them play against kids their own size. This was like an NFL team against a high school team. I want to apologize. But they won't let me go all the way to Pennsylvania."

Finally, Sengvong said, he decided that he had had enough. He didn't return to the team. He wanted bigger competition because his goal was to play professional baseball in Japan someday. But he was quick to point out that things hadn't changed much for the Taiwanese Little Leaguers. He had requested that Ranch staff videotape this year's World Series title game. A team from Taiwan would defeat a Spring, Texas, squad, 17–3, in the championship game. Sengvong claimed that his sixteen-year-old cousin, who had a seventy-nine-mile-per-hour fastball, was a pitcher on the team.

Of course, if Sengvong had done what he had claimed, his current age would have been . . . "I'm almost twenty-four," he said one day on the practice field as he waited for his chance to kick extra points at the end of the workout. Sengvong's claims weren't exactly secret on the Ranch. Almost everyone had heard parts of his story, but nobody took him very seriously. For instance, another afternoon Sengvong was sitting on a bench in the locker room when linebacker coach Gallen Allen walked by. "Mr. Allen knows how old I am," he said. "Hey, Mr. Allen, can you tell how old I am?" Allen looked down at him, rubbed his chin, and pretended to be deep in thought, and then said, "You've got to be forty."

Sengvong wasn't alone in claiming to be older or younger than he was. Many kids at the Ranch did it. Winchester recalled that another Asian youth had sworn that he was in his early twenties. He was so convincing that the California county that had sent him there eventually cut him off. But the Ranch staff wasn't convinced and put him on scholarship so he could complete the program. It was only later, when the boy left the Ranch and was trying to enlist in the military, that it was learned he was only sixteen. Instead of being older than he claimed, he was actually younger.

But even if staff on the Ranch thought that Sengvong's tales were nothing more than flights of fancy or a way of blocking out a troubled or even a more mundane childhood, the situation was different now. The Ranch had a football program that had to answer to AIA rules. The bylaws were clear: No one older than nineteen could participate. The Ranch had a birth certificate that said Sengvong was almost sixteen. Yet the boy himself continued to say he was about to turn twenty-four. That left the Ranch in a bind, especially because Sengvong already had kicked for the JV squad in its season opener against Ray.

"These Asian kids come off the boat and you just never know how old they are," Thomas said while watching practice one day. "The thing I don't understand about him is, what are his motives? He doesn't want to get out of the program. He wants to graduate from here. Why would he want to manipulate us on this? He's not a dummy. He'll graduate in June. He wants to go to college, and he certainly seems bright enough. So I don't understand. Obviously, the court thinks he's a juvenile or he wouldn't be here in the first place. But everybody wants to be a juvenile rather than an adult because, let's be honest, the juvenile system is a joke. So the courts double-check and triple-check this age stuff because they don't want adults sneaking into the juvenile system. But sometimes it's just hard to tell."

But ultimately, it came down to one question for Thomas. "What if Sengvong wins a game for us and it does turn out he's twenty-four?" Then we'd be in real hot water. We don't cheat here. We can't afford to."

So the Ranch reported the situation to the AIA. Thomas was told that as long as Sengvong didn't play until there was further verification of his age, there would be no penalties against the program. But that didn't solve the question of the boy's true age. If he was twenty-four, he couldn't stay at the Ranch. Depending on the severity of his crimes, he could be sent to a far more hostile environment, like a prison. Sengvong was cryptic about how he had wound up in the juvenile court system. A pained expression would cross his face when he was asked what he had done. He would respond by saying that he was trying to forget his mistakes.

"I don't respect people who got me involved in that stuff," he said. "They lie, and I don't like that. They lied to me about what they were doing. My cousin got involved with some gang, and I didn't know. They did a lot of things. Then I started to catch on to what they were doing. I start gaining more and more knowledge. They steal and rob. But I've never seen anybody killed before, and I don't want to see that. I'm respectful of life. The FBI catch me and talk to me about my responsibility, because I was older than everyone else. They were too young, so I was driving a stolen car."

While that raised more questions than it answered, that was the extent of his explanation. Sengvong claimed that when he was apprehended, he was presented two choices: be sent back to Asia or go to the Ranch. "I don't want to go back there," he said. "I like it here." Thomas said that Sengvong had been a good placement. He was on his way to completing a high school education. He was a member of the school choir. He wasn't hurting anybody. Thomas had no intention of terminating his stay, unless a judge could come up with some documented proof that he was too old to be there.

The evidence never did materialize, but a couple of serious holes did appear in Sengvong's tale. The Little League headquarters is hooked up to a computer system, and a check was run on the name Sengvong and another Asian name that he said he had played under, as well as the name of the cousin he claimed had competed on that year's Taiwanese championship squad. Little League officials found no listing for any of them. And although Sengvong had said that he played in Williamsport from 1981 through 1987, Little League officials said teams from Taiwan did not even qualify as the Far East's representative in 1983, 1984 or 1985.

Nevertheless, Sengvong's days on the football team were over. He may have been the squad's most promising kicker, but staff felt this was the time to show him that actions have consequences. "He's gotten into so much trouble because of his mouth, fantasizing and making up stories," Winchester said. "We know that there's no way he can be as old as he claims. But he's brought this upon himself. He has to learn a lesson."

If any of the coaches were ever upset about losing Sengvong from the team, they kept it to themselves. Football was the secondary concern. Even Gray, who had thought Sengvong would eventually become his varsity kicker, never groused about the decision. But Gray, who had the least seniority of the Ranch coaches, could only shake his head and crack a bemused smile whenever he was asked about Sengvong. He still was discovering that coaching at the Ranch could present unique problems.

"I think his birth certificate is in some rice paddy somewhere," Gray said. "When a boat drops hundreds of them off, or when they come across the border from Mexico at night, they're not carrying birth certificates and baptism papers. If they do have documents, they're not very accurate. What do they say, 'I was born in the Year of the Cow or the Year of the Pig'? I don't know how the courts figure this stuff out.

"It's a zoo here," he added. "We've got 'em all walking through here. I've been in public education twenty-five years, and I've never seen anything like this. I don't know if he's telling the truth or if he's a pathological liar. But I know one thing: He's not very smart for saying these things. If he were smart, he'd keep quiet. He'll stay here where he's running around, where he's got three meals a day, where he lives in basically a dormitory. Instead, he's telling everybody that he's too old to be here. Does he want to be in a cell with a guy named Bubba and out walking around in a prison yard with a guard training a rifle scope on him?"

Actually, Sengvong had expressed his thanks for what the Ranch was doing for him many times. He talked about following a different path when he left. "I like the staff," he once said while he was still on the football squad. "They help me out with things that I don't understand. They're nice. I respect them. Sometimes there will be things that I don't understand. So they sit down and talk to me about it. I have to learn to grow up."

The rest of the fall, Sengvong would play on the Ranch's club soccer team. The team often would go through drills in the outfield of a baseball diamond that was located next to the football practice field. Sometimes, during water breaks, he could be seen watching football practice from a distance.

Sengvong seemed a lot quieter.

MIGHTY, MIGHTY BOYS RANCH

The Ranch already had dropped one of its two "must" games. When Gray looked at the schedule and saw all the East Region powerhouses the Spartans would play down the road, he figured they needed those first two nonleague games in the worst way. Then the Spartans lost to Ray. Their next opponent, the Globe Tigers, would be even tougher. Globe, another mining town east of Phoenix, was ranked fifth in the state among 3A schools. They were well-coached. Gray knew this because he had coached the Tigers' coach in college. When he had been an assistant at Northern Arizona, Gray had even recruited him to the school.

NAU had marked the high point in Gray's coaching career. A California native, Gray had been a pretty fair defensive lineman at ASU. But he had no illusions about playing professional football. So he got his bachelor's and master's degrees and eventually took a job as a head coach at a Phoenix-area high school. That led to another high school position, in which he was named Arizona Coach of the Year in 1981 by a Phoenix newspaper. From there, he had joined the NAU staff as an assistant. He was in Flagstaff five years before the head coach got fired. In some ancient cultures, when a king died, his wife (or wives) and servants were sacrificed and buried with him. That's the way it is in college sports. When a head coach goes, so does his staff. But Gray wasn't out of work long before he landed as the head coach of Gilbert High, a school in an Eastside Phoenix suburb. There, he turned out a series of .500-level teams against the state's best 5A competition. While that was pretty good, it wasn't good enough to satisfy the parents, booster group, and administration who had put Gray under the knife with a win-or-else ultimatum.

Finally, Gray said the hell with it. School officials were making it clear that he wasn't exactly welcome as their football coach any longer. So he resigned before he was asked to leave. In 1994, he took a job as an assistant at Mesa Community College, helping out with the defensive linemen. He was at a crossroads when he learned of the Boys Ranch opening. Now, months later, he would be competing against a former pupil. It's funny, Gray said, how things can work out.

"He's a Globe kid," Gray explained of the opposing coach. "That's what Globe brings — tradition. Their brothers played for Globe. Their fathers played for Globe. It means something. But nobody wants to say, 'My brother played for Boys Ranch, and I'm going to play there, too.' We don't have any pride to build on here." Gray liked the other coach immensely, but not enough to enjoy losing to him. "We drop this one," he added, "and you can stick a fork in us because we're done."

———

"Jesus Christ!"

"Look at the size of that mother!"

"That ain't nothing. Look at that other one."

"Damn!"

The Spartan players were watching the Tigers begin their pregame drills, and they were in awe. For a high school team, the Tigers were mammoth, maybe even pachyderm-like. One kid, according to the program, was six feet four and weighed 360 pounds. Another stood six feet nine and tipped the scales at 315. They looked even bigger in person. There were a bunch of other players who weighed more than 200 pounds, too. Perhaps there was something in the water.

Globe is only eighty miles from the Ranch, but getting there had been an adventure. Outside of Phoenix, U.S. 60 is a mostly two-lane ribbon that connects the Valley to mining communities like Superior, Miami, and Globe before heading northeast to the New Mexico border. The highway winds around the Superstition Mountains, where, according to legend, the Lost Dutchman's mine supposedly is hidden. From there, the road goes up mountains and down through gorges where rock formations jut out at crazy angles. Some seem to defy gravity as they loom perilously above the highway. Near the towns, copper-mining equipment such as giant cranes can be seen in the distance, looking much like dinosaur skeletons in museums.

The trip, which took the Spartans past such places as Pinto Creek and Devil's Canyon, went from the desert floor to an elevation of 4,000 feet. That explained why the Ranch's venerable bus, which had "Spartan Pride" painted on its sides, had to stop twice because of an overheated engine. At other times, the bus was going about fifteen miles per hour up steep inclines. When they finally reached Globe, they found a picturesque little town built on hills. Some streets were reminiscent of San Francisco the way they went practically straight up and down. The football field itself was a small, beautiful bowl carved out of a mountainside.

As the teams went through their pregame warm-ups, lightning lit up the sky in the distance, while a full moon occasionally peeped through the cloud cover. The weather added an almost magical quality to the night. But the players didn't seem to notice. All they could see was those big mothers. It's their size against our speed, Gray told the players. You don't have to be six seven or weigh 360 pounds to play this game. You can be mean, ornery, and nasty at any size.

But it certainly helped if you were mean, ornery, nasty, *and* big.

The Ranch was down 10–0 before the game was even six minutes old. The Spartans fumbled away the opening kickoff, and the Tigers converted that into a field goal. Then Elliott coughed up the ball on the Ranch's first play from scrimmage, and that would be turned into a touchdown. As lightning began to crackle overhead and the low drum roll of thunder steadily got louder, a soft rain began to fall. It was shaping up to be a long, dreary night for the Spartans.

The Ranch finally found the handle on the football on its next possession, and Cabell capped a quick six-play drive with a five-yard scoring dash up the middle. But Andrade missed the extra-point try, and Globe struck right back. On the first play of the second quarter, the Tigers increased their lead to 17–6 with yet another touchdown, this one coming on a two-yard quarterback sneak. It was developing into a rerun of the Ray game. The Ranch's defense was being blown off the ball by Globe's heavyweight offensive line. Receivers were left wide open. Defenders kept getting caught out of position. Then, when the Spartans were in the right place at the right time, they missed tackles. The thought was beginning to dawn on some sideline observers that maybe playing serious football at the Ranch wasn't such a great idea. Perhaps it was expecting too much.

But then the rain stopped and a deluge of another kind began.

Over the next fourteen minutes, a shark feeding frenzy erupted, and Globe was the food in the water. A light bulb had clicked on over the heads of the Spartans. Suddenly they realized that they could play this game after all. McKissic started throwing bombs. Harris started catching them, one for a 49-yard score and another for a 50-yard touchdown. Cabell and Elliott discovered holes in the Globe line. Elliott alone found the end zone three times. The defense forced turnovers as they began swarming to the ball. As the storm passed through Globe without dropping many more raindrops, the Ranch poured points. By the time the horn sounded for halftime, the Ranch had racked up an astounding 32 points in the second quarter to grab a 38–25 lead. With Kush helping to call plays from his vantage point high on the mountainside, the Ranch had used its speed to perfection by running around the bigger, lumbering Tigers. All in all, it was a dazzling display of high school football.

The trouble was that if the Ranch gave up 25 points in the first half, it probably could easily give up that many in the second half, too. So Gray shifted from his we-can-beat-these-guys motivational tactics to a we-still-can-lose-to-these-guys approach. "The flavor is in your mouth," Gray said at halftime. "Now you know what it tastes like. But that flavor can be taken away and replaced with a real sour taste. We've been working our asses off for something like this. Let's not lose it. Let's taste it when it's over."

And sure enough, the Spartans did their best to lose the game in the second half. It took Globe less than two minutes to score a touchdown and cut the Ranch edge to 38–32. The Ranch retaliated with another touchdown midway through the quarter when the Spartans drove the length of the field, and then Sparkman recovered an Elliott fumble in the end zone. McKissic's two-point conversion run gave the Spartans a 46–32 lead.

The rest of the night, the Ranch was like a tired prize fighter leaning on the ropes as he tried to hold on to the decision. The defense got pushed down the field when Globe embarked on a twelve-play drive that culminated with a short touchdown run by the Tiger quarterback. Globe missed the extra point, making the score 46–38 with over eleven minutes left in the game. Meanwhile, the Spartans were just starting to warm up when it came to making mistakes. Cabell would race 54 yards for a touchdown, only to see it called back on a holding penalty. Then the Ranch had a punt blocked. But what saved the Spartans, miraculously, was their defense. Twice in the closing minutes, it stopped Globe, forcing the Tigers to turn over the ball when they failed to convert on fourth-down plays.

The Tigers would still get one last shot. Faced with a fourth-and-1 at their own 41 with 1:20 remaining, the Ranch gambled. This time, Gray called the play. Instead of punting, he had McKissic sneak the ball. A first down would have sewed up the victory for the Ranch, but Shaune was stopped for no gain. So Globe was left with great field position. A touchdown and a two-point conversion would salvage a tie for the Tigers. But after an incompletion on first down, the Globe quarterback faded back to pass again. He thought he had an open receiver. Instead, the ball ended up in the hands of the Ranch's Shaun Williams. The interception sealed the Spartans' first victory.

The boys didn't seem to know what to do after the game was over. Winning was not a feeling they were accustomed to. When a coach yelled to line up to shake hands with the Globe players, they immediately fell into single-line formation like a platoon. It wasn't until a couple of minutes later, when the team took a knee in the end zone, that the reality of what had just happened began to sink in. "Guys," Ray Perkins announced loudly, "you just took down No. 5 in the state!" It was only then that the celebration began in earnest. When the cheering died down, Shofner started singing a song, with the players repeating his words.

"We are the Boys Ranch."
"WE ARE THE BOYS RANCH."
"Mighty, mighty Boys Ranch."
"MIGHTY, MIGHTY BOYS RANCH."
"Butt-kicking Boys Ranch."
"BUTT-KICKING BOYS RANCH."
"Globe-kicking Boys Ranch."
"GLOBE-KICKING BOYS RANCH."
"Who are we?"
"WHO ARE WE?"
"And we tell them."
"AND WE TELL THEM."
"We are the Boys Ranch."
"WE ARE THE BOYS RANCH."
"Mighty, mighty Boys Ranch."
"MIGHTY, MIGHTY BOYS RANCH."

Nobody wanted to leave the field. Players kept looking at the score-board, perhaps to make sure they hadn't imagined the outcome. Even Gray was caught up in the moment. "It's an amusement-park ride," he said. "We're a roller coaster. We can score from anywhere on the field, and we can get scored on from anywhere. Talk about shooting your-self in the foot. We don't have any toes left after tonight." But Gray also knew he should have expected this. The boys were still learning the game. They were learning other things, too. Most had never worked with others to achieve a common goal, unless it was to rob somebody or something. "They don't even know how to get excited," he added.

Then Gray paused.

"But they sure can line up with the best of them."

THE TIMES OF TROUBLES

Lorenzo Johnson fit in at the Ranch. Sparkman, who served as the Ranch's unofficial resident historian because he had been there so long, said everybody seemed to like him. But Lorenzo, Sparkman added, had some problems. In fact, he had been running away his entire life. He had fled his home in rural Mississippi, Johnson claimed, to escape an abusive stepfather. He had bolted from numerous foster homes and group home placements, too. And he had tried to run away from the Ranch after Mississippi authorities sent him to Arizona.

The last tragic phase of Johnson's young life began at a Ranch spike camp near Williams, Arizona. Open six months a year, the camp where boys would do conservation projects in a wilderness area was considered an honors program. But on June 22, 1994, Johnson ran from the camp for the second time while on a fence-building work crew. He was on the lam for two days when he was befriended by a family who found him hiding in a nearby camp ground. They drove Johnson back to the Ranch camp when he decided to return, and then staff transported him to the main campus. From there, he was to be sent back down to the Civics program in Oracle as punishment for going AWOL again. Late in the morning of June 27, three middle-aged men — Ranch staffers Charles Fleishman and Michael Graham and a prospective employee, John Goldsmith — got into Graham's Ford LTD with Johnson, who was now wearing a yellow shirt, for the ninety-minute journey to Oracle. It should have been just another trip. But about fifteen minutes into it, the boy indicated that he had to go to the bathroom. Graham turned down a deserted dirt road and pulled over. With Fleishman escorting him, the boy got out, hid behind a desert shrub for some privacy, defecated, and hitched his pants back up. Then Johnson did what he had always done: run.

He ducked under a barbed-wire fence and began zigzagging across the desert under the searing noonday sun. Fleishman immediately went after him. So did the other two — Graham by car and Goldsmith on foot — once they realized what was happening. A "chase" is probably too dramatic a word to describe the game of cat and mouse that ensued for the next few minutes. The adults more or less followed the boy, hoping he would come to his senses and quit fooling around. The pursuit didn't last long, either, because Johnson soon was stopped in his tracks by a sight that must have surprised him: a Central Arizona Project water canal stretched across the desert floor. As Johnson pondered his situation, Graham approached the boy and briefly thought of taking him down by himself. Instead, he decided to wait for the reinforcements. Goldsmith had arrived and Fleishman was closing in when Johnson began looking for an escape route. Graham and Goldsmith were closest to the boy but didn't make any movements toward him. They tried to talk him into surrendering without doing anything rash. Johnson threw a rock in Graham's direction, then tossed another stone in the water as if he were testing its depth. Goldsmith asked Johnson if he could swim. The boy said yes, but later nobody at the Ranch would remember him ever leaving the shallow end of the pool.

After a few moments of this standoff, Johnson made a break for it. He ran under a nearby bridge and tried to scurry along the steep embankment beneath it. Goldsmith was the only one to see Johnson hit the water. Goldsmith thought he may have stepped in the water intentionally, believing the placid canal waters not to be deep. But looks were deceiving. The water was actually fifteen feet deep and a frigid 64 degrees, which was a shock to the body considering the summertime temperatures in the Sonoran Desert could easily reach 115 degrees. The currents were remarkably swift and tricky. The angle of the embankment was a sharp 33 degrees, and the walls below the water line were slick with slimy algae. Metal ladders stationed 700 feet apart along the canal offered the only avenues of escape. What appeared to be a harmless aqueduct actually was a treacherous death trap.

During the ensuing rescue attempt, all three men would enter the water as it became obvious that the boy couldn't swim. Goldsmith never was able to get close enough to Johnson to assist him. In fact, he never could remember how he got out of the water. Graham did reach the boy, but by then Johnson was in a full panic and he began pushing Graham underwater as he thrashed about desperately. Graham lost all semblance of time, so he wasn't sure how long the two struggled. Finally, the boy disappeared beneath the surface. At that point Graham went from being a would-be rescuer to being in desperate need of help. He was exhausted and in danger of drowning himself. Fleishman, who had also jumped into the water, reached a ladder and held on to it as he stretched out a leg. Graham, who was floating past, grabbed it, and with Fleishman's aid eventually was able to pull himself out of the canal.

When the news reached the Ranch, everyone was stunned. Never in the Ranch's history had one of its boys died. The residents assembled at the main campus chapel, where Thomas announced what had happened and said that Johnson was presumed dead. Tears followed. Sparkman remembered wondering if something like this could happen to Lorenzo whether it could happen to someone else, like him. Some wondered if Johnson had somehow, miraculously, escaped. That would have been just like Lorenzo. Thomas half expected him to show up one morning saying he was sorry for running again. But that would never happen. His body was discovered a week later about fifteen miles downstream.

After an investigation, the Pinal County sheriff's department ruled that Johnson's death was a tragic accident.

More than a year later, both Fleishman and Graham said they couldn't shake the horrifying memory of watching the boy slip below the murky water, never to reappear.

———

Johnson's death shook the Ranch to its very foundation. But it was only one of a series of tremors to rattle the facility in rapid succession. In late April 1994, three boys from California "went over the wall," as some residents called it, although there was no actual wall to go over. They went AWOL from the Civics campus and were caught in a stolen car near the Mexican border. Once apprehended, they told their captors chilling stories. The trio said they were fleeing abuse at the Ranch, and begged not to be sent back. All said they had been roughed up by staff, and one claimed he had been struck with a broomstick.

The boys' allegations prompted the Department of Economic Security's Child Protective Services agency to launch its fourth major investigation of the Ranch. In all, thirty charges of abuse would be examined. In July 1994, CPS would substantiate thirteen of those charges, including accusations that a boy's feet had been scalded with hot water so severely that he required skin grafts, that a boy had been hit on the head with a shovel, and that a youth's nose had been broken from being slammed into a table.

In June of that year, the chief juvenile judge of California's Alameda County pulled the fifty-nine residents it had placed at the Ranch after also concluding that the Ranch was engaging in corporal punishment. All the boys were forced to return to California although half stated they wished to stay.

Then on Sunday, August 28, *The Arizona Republic* published a devastating front-page article about Lorenzo Johnson. The headline said it all. The story was titled: "Kid Without a Chance." A smaller headline read: "No way out of abuse at home, no way out of punishment for fleeing, no way out of water pulling him to death." Yet another headline accompanying the portion of the story that jumped to an inside page said: "Death of youth raises questions about his care." It was a lengthy piece, the linchpin to a series of stories about the Ranch that raised concerns about the facility's practices and methods. While the entire article was damning of the Ranch's treatment of Johnson, buried near the bottom of the story was this quote from the dead boy's mother: "I think they killed him, but why, I do not know."

The unmistakable insinuation was that the Ranch had been responsible for Johnson's death.

———

The Ranch, which prided itself on treating the baddest of bad young offenders, was now being judged bad itself. The state had even granted the facility only a six-month provisional operating license. In other words, it was on probation. Something had to be done or the doors might be boarded up by the state. That was why a member of the Ranch's board of directors contacted A. Melvin McDonald in June 1994. McDonald may have been uniquely qualified to conduct an inquiry into the Ranch, but at that time, he knew absolutely nothing about the place. He didn't even know where it was located.

The main reason the Ranch sought out McDonald was because he knew his way around an investigation. He had been with the Maricopa County attorney's office for four years before being elected a judge to the county's superior court bench. In 1981, President Ronald Reagan appointed him the U.S. attorney for the district of Arizona, making him the lead federal government prosecutor in the state. After four years on that job, he left to join a private law firm in Phoenix. The Ranch board of directors knew McDonald had been on all sides of the bench: as judge, prosecutor, and defense attorney. He had credibility. If his examination of the Ranch resulted in a favorable review, it would carry some weight.

But what if McDonald came away confirming the charges? That's what McDonald himself wanted to know. So before he agreed to take the job, he asked that a stipulation be written into their agreement: No matter what he found, and even if the Ranch fired him, he would have the right to publish his findings. "I warned them," McDonald said. "I told them that I will write it as I see it. If I find abuse, I'm going to report it. If there are defects in your system, I'm going to identify them. I said, 'Don't hire me if you think I'm going to do a whitewash of your program, because it's not going to happen. I feel strongly about reforming kids, but if you're beating kids up, I'm going to expose it. So don't hire me if that's what's out there, because I'm not going to be your front man.' "

The Ranch agreed to his terms, and in the following weeks, McDonald, drawing on his contacts as a federal attorney, assembled an investigative unit that included former FBI and Secret Service agents. Together, the team had three hundred years of combined police work experience. They set about interviewing boys, staff, parents, probation officers, judges, and defense attorneys. Some team members lived on the main campus and at the Civics campus in Oracle for a week to get inside looks. They could walk in and out of barracks and cottages. They could watch boys who were restrained to see how staff did it and to learn what incidents led to the physical contact. They could talk to whomever they wanted. After logging 1,700 hours on the clock, McDonald and his team had published a mammoth series of reports on Johnson's death, the removal of the boys from Alameda County, and the CPS abuse charges.

"I walked away really awestruck at the program they've got," McDonald said. "The team members, almost to the person, said, 'Gee, this is the answer for troubled kids.' It's a structured program that's very tough, yet also very caring. It's giving some kids some direction, some self-worth. That football program falls right into it as it promotes the idea of teamwork and working together."

One report after another fired broadsides at the host of Ranch critics. The first to fall under the guns of McDonald's team was *The Arizona Republic*. The report said the newspaper, in its "Kid Without a Chance" story, introduced the theory that Johnson was murdered when it had evidence that clearly showed that he wasn't. It said the reporters "exploited" a grieving mother by fueling her fears and doubts about how her son died. It went on to say that quotes were doctored and other information was twisted and distorted. It pointed out that the newspaper never even attempted to interview two of the three men at the center of the story — Fleishman and Goldsmith — before running the article. "They published a libelous story against staff at Arizona Boys Ranch who risked their lives to save a troubled kid," McDonald said. "They wrote a story suggesting that these guys were murderers when they were really heroes."

Another McDonald report would find no grounds to justify why Alameda County pulled its boys out of the Ranch, especially after twenty-nine kids pleaded to remain and Ranch officials offered to pay their way while they completed their program. An article in the *Tribune newspapers* would later note that at least sixteen of the boys that Alameda County removed ran away from their new placements within a month of leaving the Ranch.

But McDonald saved his most venomous attack for Child Protective Services. Of the thirteen charges of abuse alleged by CPS, the McDonald team believed that only one incident — the one involving the boy whose feet were scalded — constituted abuse. And as McDonald pointed out, the Ranch had fired the responsible staff member even before CPS investigated the incident. Every other abuse charge, McDonald maintained, was false. "It was absolutely crazy the things [these investigators] were doing," he said. "It was like they wanted to clean house on a house that already was clean." McDonald's report ridiculed the agency's investigators as inept, gullible, biased, and unprofessional. That included one CPS official who McDonald claimed was "hell-bent" on closing down the Ranch. CPS staff never realized, he said, that these kids were street-wise and knew how to beat the system. When they made an accusation of abuse, they made sure their friends would offer collaborative accounts to back them up.

When McDonald's team checked out their stories, it often turned out that the witnesses would have had to be able to see through walls or around corners to view the incident. In some cases, "witnesses" hadn't even been at the Ranch at the time the abuse supposedly took place.

"I had kids sitting with me in an office and they would look me in the eye and say, 'Sir, this is the first time in my life that I've ever felt safe. I don't have to worry about being intimidated because staff here will protect me,'" McDonald said. "I've had little kids pull up their shirts and show me the scars on their body where they've been shot. I remember one little kid who had been shot with a shotgun. I interviewed kids who have done drive-bys and murdered people. One kid I talked to was going to blow up a store, but they caught him first. He already had blown up cars. My point is that they've got some real tough kids there, and the only way to deal with them is to be disciplined. You can't let the kids run it. CPS felt that these poor little darlings were being intimidated out there. Well, they would never look at their jackets. They wouldn't know anything about the criminal history of these kids. They would go down and interview them and look at their angelic faces and have no idea that they were drive-by shooters. They would say, "Well, Mr. Jones pushed me or hit me," and CPS would make substantiations of abuse without having the foggiest idea of what was going on there."

The CPS investigators, McDonald said, didn't understand that they were never going to find a happy boy when they talked to a red shirt or a yellow shirt. They were either new to the program or being punished. Yet the likelihood that they would be malcontents or searching for ways to get out was never taken into consideration.

"You can go to college for four years, go to work at Arizona Boys Ranch, and then have a kid with a rap sheet that's longer than both your arms make an allegation that you abused him," he said. "Then CPS will come out and ask you questions like, 'So tell us why you battered little Johnny's head into the shower stall. You mean to say that you don't remember doing that?' We literally had tapes of that kind of interviewing. After five minutes of that, they substantiated charges of abuse. Then you've got no right to a hearing. You haven't been able to cross-examine anybody. But you've been adjudicated as an abuser because CPS says that you are. Period. You have no right to an appeal. You have no right to confront your accusers. It is the worst system I have ever seen. When you empower some bureaucrats who have no investigative experience and give them police powers, prosecutorial powers, judicial powers, and literally department of corrections powers, you're allowing them to scar people for life."

In December 1994, the state's Department of Economic Security issued a new operating license to the Ranch. It was off probation. But the state also stood by its original conclusion that there were 13 cases of substantiated abuse. Meanwhile, the *Republic* stood by the accuracy of its Lorenzo Johnson story and continued to criticize the program on its editorial page, frequently noting that the Ranch paid handsomely for the checkup that led to McDonald's clean bill of health. None of the three parties was budging from its version of the facts. For their part, CPS officials told reporters that the agency was merely being a watchdog for youth. And no matter what good aims the Ranch was trying to accomplish, the ends did not justify the means if Ranch staff were violating the law. The Ranch countered by saying those laws were hopelessly outdated and not designed for a world where twelve-year-olds kill one another without blinking an eye. CPS, it said, was interfering with the last chance these products of the mean streets had to change before it was too late.

Here, in a state known for its Old West roots, everyone involved was claiming his right to a white hat, while the other guy was wearing the black one. It figured that eventually these showdowns would be settled in a modern, more civilized manner than six-shooters blazing on a dusty street at high noon. The lawsuits began to fly.

First the Ranch sued the *Republic* for libel. Then it filed suit against the state in an attempt, Thomas said, to clear the Ranch's name and the names of staff who had been accused of abusing kids.

"I've never sued anybody in my life, and I hope I never have to again," Thomas added. "But they make you pay money to hire investigators to set the record straight. Then when you do it, they ignore it. With CPS, there's no due process. They can act like the Gestapo and have complete immunity afterward."

McDonald's reports would become the blueprints for both legal actions.

"I will tell you that if one of my own children was incorrigible and I could no longer manage him, I wouldn't hesitate to put him in the Arizona Boys Ranch, because if I couldn't raise him, they could," McDonald said. "I feel that strongly about their program. I am now a disciple."

Caught in the cross fire of the squabbling were the boys. Residents at the Ranch had gotten used to being asked about charges of abuse. Some, like Sparkman, thought that staff did step over the line on occasion. Sparkman chalked it up to staff's becoming angry about being "disrespected by some little kid." No adult, he said, would want to stand for that. None of the boys were crazy about the strict, military-style environment at Civics, even the ones who admitted that they were getting something out of the program. Many football players said they had been restrained at various times when they lost control, and that included being put on the ground until they calmed down. But no football player questioned ever said he had been struck by staff.

Cody Jeffries, the team's center, said it was a joke among some residents how the "CPS people" would come in, ask the boys questions, and believe everything they were told. The CPS people never figured out that the residents spinning horror tales were saying whatever they thought would get them out, he said.

One day, McKissic was sitting on a bench next to the outdoor basketball courts. He had been talking about how his football season was progressing when the conversation turned to the perception that staff beat boys at the Ranch. McKissic said he also had been interviewed by CPS staff. They asked him if he had ever seen a resident being restrained, and he told them yes. But that was only part of his answer.

"I told them that it's not like their goal to restrain you," he said. "They treat you like you act. If you act like a complete fool, that's how they're going to treat you. Staff might restrain you or put you on work crew. But they don't want to put their hands on you. They'll talk to you first. Then when a kid is trying to punch them, that's when it gets out of hand.

"Nobody gets abused here," he added softly.

M y name is Thurman Wilson. I'm eighteen. I'm from San Jose. I've been here nine months now.

I'm just here to get my high school diploma. When you're eighteen, you can go home. Hopefully, that will be in December for me. I played football in real high school. I like playing here because it makes time go by a lot faster.

It's stressful here — very stressful. Your family is far away. I've been in other placements before, and your parents are right there. You know that they're close by. But here, they're so far away. All you think about is going home, and yet you know that you can't go home. When I first got here, I had a problem with following directions. You know, all that yes, sir, no, sir stuff. But the hardest part of the program is when you get near the end. You know it's almost time to go home, and it's hard to focus on doing things here. I think this program goes on too long. When you're eighteen, like me, you don't need any little Boys Ranch anymore. I already know that if I go back out on the street and do something wrong, I'm not going to get another chance like this. I can weigh it out. I don't want to go to the pen. Not me. Some kids got the idea that it's cool, that it's their way to get a rep. A reputation. But I'd rather be on the outside.

I've been fighting since the fourth grade. I'm a good fighter. But I was normal. I knew right from wrong. I just went out in the wrong direction. I made some wrong choices. I've got a big family. Out of my whole family, I'm the only kid to get into trouble. My mom would always tell me, "You're heading in the wrong direction. Don't hang with those guys." But I thought I knew what I was doing. I figured I wasn't doing anything bad, that I could kick butt. But I didn't know the consequences for what I did. I didn't want to believe what she was saying. I thought that I was grown. I knew everything. I didn't want to worry about nothing. I thought I knew the ropes.

I got into the system for strong-arm robbery. I just robbed somebody on the street. I had a past history. I had been in the system for a long time. When you get in trouble, on and on, then eventually they send you someplace. So I finally got sent here. I didn't know what to expect. It's different. I thought it was a real ranch with barbed wire and stuff. But it's open. There's nowhere to run. They'll catch you, then you have to start over. After you've been here a while, you want to make sure that time counts for something. I've never got in real trouble here. I've made my mistakes, and I've corrected them.

I look back on how I used to get into fights and hurt people. I feel sorry for them because I messed up. I know how I would feel if I got beat up. I understand now. I used to go to stores and just steal little stuff. I used to get a kick out of it. I would do it just to see if I'd get caught. I never got caught stealing, but I've changed. I didn't know how the owner of that store felt. You know what I mean? It wasn't mine, so how did I know what he felt? I wanted to raise a ruckus. I don't like stealing anymore. I guess as you get older, you mature. My family thinks that I've matured a lot. When I was on my home visit and went to church, everybody there couldn't believe how I showed them respect. I was telling everyone "yes, sir" and "no, sir." On the streets, you don't hear kids talk like that.

My dad was in jail for fifteen years. So I didn't have a dad to tell me right from wrong. All I had was my mom. She did a good job. We had our values. But I thought I was a man. I started running around the streets, hanging out with the wrong crowd. That's what happens. I didn't hang out with gangs. I know gang guys. I've got a lot of friends in gangs. But I'm my own man. I don't need to be walking down the street with five other guys. I don't like to handle other people's business. I handle my own business.

My dad's out now. I've changed because of him. He told me what it was like. He just broke it down for me. He didn't beat around the bush like some parents. He was trying to save my life. He told me to straighten up. He told me the consequences. I thank my dad for that. If he hadn't told me that, I wouldn't be here right now. I'd probably done something stupid and really be locked up.

My mom, she's proud of me now. I've changed my attitude. I show respect now. Before, I wouldn't talk to you. If I saw you on the Outs, just walking on the street, I wouldn't talk to you. Un-uh. I don't know you. Why would I want to talk to you? That's the way I was. Now I've learned to act different.

DIDN'T HAVE THAT KIND OF HEART

Five JV players were standing on the practice field looking a little confused. They were wearing blue mesh shirts over their Ranch jerseys. Each shirt had crude numerals made of white masking tape on it that represented one of the Blue Ridge Yellowjackets' top players. All the Ranch's varsity players were on one knee, watching Gray go through his scouting report.

"This is No. 44," Gray said. "His name is Greg Salyers. He's in his senior year. He's five eight. He's a fine young man who is looking forward to the prom." Then Gray went over to another JV player wearing No. 7 and put his hand on his shoulder. "This is Adam Reeck. He's a good quarterback. He's a bright guy. He's the valedictorian of his class, and he's probably going to Oxford. He never makes a mistake. But this week we need to temporarily put him out of the game." Gray patiently went from JV player to JV player, giving a make-believe thumbnail sketch of his alter ego and then going through the player's very real tendencies that had shown up on game film.

What Gray didn't point out were weaknesses. That's because there were none. Blue Ridge was defending state 3A champion. It currently was the top-ranked team in the state. The Yellowjackets had won fifteen consecutive games. The last time that Blue Ridge had even been behind in a game was when it played the Ranch the previous season. The Spartans actually held a 12–0 lead late in the second quarter before falling apart and eventually losing 43–12. After the game, the Yellowjackets' star tailback, a kid who would rush for thirty-eight touchdowns and nearly 3,000 yards on the season, told the Ranch coaches that he hadn't been hit like that all year. Now that running back was playing for the University of Arizona, and that was why some of the coaches at the Ranch thought that Blue Ridge could be had this season.

"We can beat these guys," Shofner whispered as Gray continued to bring Blue Ridge to life for the Spartan players.

All week Gray had been checking the state weather page in the newspaper. The high temperature in the twin White Mountains resort communities of Lakeside and Pinetop, where Blue Ridge was located, was 72. In Phoenix, the thermometer was hitting a stifling 105. It would be a home game for the Ranch Friday night, and it would still be hot at kickoff. Gray, who was hunting for any possible edge, thought the heat might wear Blue Ridge down because a lot of their kids played both ways. Gray was under no illusions. The Ranch would need lots of luck to win; perhaps even the sort of good fortune required to hit the lottery.

"Wouldn't it be great if the team that was ranked No. 32 in the state went out and beat the No. 1–ranked team in the state?" Gray asked the players. "We can do that. I'm not lying to you. It would be a great thing for you, for this program and for the entire Boys Ranch to beat them. But it's going to take playing hard on every down. The main thing is keeping your minds open to the possibilities of what you're capable of doing."

Then he paused.

"Can we see ourselves beating Blue Ridge?"

"Yes, sir!" came the automatic response.

One person, however, wasn't buying it. Kush was keeping his opinions to himself. He knew this was one challenge beyond the team's grasp. He, too, had watched the film. He saw flaws in Blue Ridge that a normal high school team might be able to exploit. Only the Spartans weren't a normal team. Kush had come up with a game plan, but when he tried to implement even small changes in the Ranch's offense that week, he had completely lost the players. "You call a backfield formation a 'T' and they're baffled," he said. "I get so pissed off sometimes I have to walk away or I'll explode. The lack of comprehension is incredible. There's things we could do to score points against these guys. But we can't do them with these kids. Blue Ridge will beat them by 30 or 40 points. It's as simple as that."

———

It wasn't Gray's fault. Before the Spartans left for Gilbert High, where the game would be played, he gave the team yet another scouting report and chalk talk. In the Gilbert locker room, just before the players took the field, he gave his most impassioned speech thus far, telling them everyone in this room was a brother, that they had to depend on one another, how he had dreams at night that the Spartans were the No. 1 team in the state, and how they could record the biggest upset in Arizona history over the next two hours. By the time he finished speaking, the players were ready to hit somebody right then and there.

"Let's go, baby, it's time to rock the house!" Sparkman shouted as they left the locker room.

Then the Spartans went out and got rocked as decisively as a football team could be beaten. The final score was 31–0, but it didn't indicate just how thoroughly the Ranch had been manhandled. That was the way it looked: men against boys. The Ranch would gain just 88 yards in total offense. The Spartans would have only five first downs. McKissic completed one pass all night, for nine yards. The defense had been little more than a speed bump as Blue Ridge relentlessly marched down the field with all the flair of a methodical steamroller. Despite the Yellowjackets' dominance, the score had been only 6–0 when, with just thirty-five seconds left in the half, Blue Ridge faced a fourth-and-21 at the Ranch's 24-yard line. The Yellowjackets needed to reach the Ranch 3, and somehow a receiver pulled down a wobbly pass and raced to the 2. First down. Two plays later, the score was 12–0.

The Ranch was cooked. It didn't matter that 12 points shouldn't be anything for a team that had scored 82 points in its first two games. It didn't matter what the coaches were saying at halftime as they tried to regroup their troops. It just didn't matter. The players were whipped. You could see it in their eyes. The game was over. Gray told the team that the second half would be a test of how far they had come. The Ranch failed that exam — miserably. The Spartans just went to pieces. McKissic spent the final two quarters running backward as he was chased by Yellowjacket defenders. Meanwhile, Blue Ridge just drove the ball down the Ranch's throat. Rather than fight back, the Spartans had slipped back into an old habit: They had simply given up.

Later, at the Ranch, Gray would tell the players that they shouldn't look back but rather keep their focus on the future. "This game," he said, "is over. I'm not happy. The coaches aren't happy. You shouldn't be happy. But there's nothing we can do about this one now. We're going to have to go back to the drawing board, figure out what's broken, and fix it. But keep your heads up because our season is not finished just because of what happened tonight."

As the clock finally, and mercifully, reached 0:00, all Gray wanted to do was shake the Blue Ridge coach's hand and leave. Like a general surveying a battlefield after a defeat, he wanted to put as much distance between himself and this place as quickly as possible. Before the Spartans could escape the scene, though, the Blue Ridge coach sought out Tamar Armstrong. He told Tamar: No. 44, you played a heck of a game. You gave our quarterback hell, and at the end of the season, I'm going to nominate you for all-state. You got my vote, he added as he shook Armstrong's hand.

Right then, Armstrong, an eighteen-year-old senior, was more concerned about not crying in front of the opposing coach. At six two, 215 pounds and with hair that was already tinged with gray, Armstrong looked like a man. But just then he was struggling to fight back the urge to break down in tears. Losing always ripped at his insides. The way the Ranch had lost — being completely dominated — made that pain even worse. For Armstrong, football wasn't just a game. It was a way for him to measure how far he had traveled at the Ranch. It was here that he had embraced the idea of work. And nobody worked harder than he did. He just couldn't accept that all the effort could go for naught. It wasn't right. It wasn't fair. Those were the thoughts running through his mind as tears began to dribble down his cheeks.

––––––––

Drugs, Armstrong explained, had been his family's major downfall. Lord knows there were other problems. But drugs, specifically crack cocaine, had been the root of most of the evils that infected his life. Then he demonstrated what he meant. Armstrong's most noticeable physical feature, besides his imposing size and prematurely graying hair, was an ugly scar and discoloration on his left arm that ran from his wrist to his fingertips.

"My mother did that to me," he said.

One day, when Armstrong was about two years old, his mom had bathed and dressed him. She had places to go. People to see. She was in a hurry. She had to score. But little Tamar was delaying her. After she finished cleaning him up, he went outside and got into some mud. Tamar remembers that when he went back inside, his hands were dirty. Despite his young age, he also vividly recalled what happened next.

"When I come in, she saw how bad I looked and I guess she just decided to clean me off," he said. "But she turned the hot-water faucet on and stuck my hands in there. It caused first-, second- and third-degree burns from the wrist on down. You can imagine how bad it was as a child. It was so bad that the skin was dripping. It was bubbling up and falling off. I don't know what was going through her mind. I can't recall it. But that's just how it was. It was all from her desire for drugs. She wanted so much to get out there and get busy, and I had set her back by getting dirty. She had to have those drugs."

Armstrong held up his hand, spread his fingers, and turned it over a couple of times as he examined what his mother had done. Then he began to talk about the scars that were not visible. "I went through a lot of physical abuse with her," he said. "But the mental abuse was tougher, just seeing her in the state she was in. Her condition was awful because of her drug addiction."

Armstrong had grown up in inner-city San Diego. Some of his other earliest memories centered around other drug addicts, homeless people, and random acts of crime he had witnessed in his neighborhood. That kind of stuff was his whole environment, he said. Armstrong would prove to be the product of his environment.

He didn't know his father very well. He was never in the picture when it came to raising him. Armstrong said he was too busy making babies. After doing some quick math on his fingers, Armstrong figured out that his father had fourteen children, including himself, and that he basically took care of only one son. His parents had never married. He said his dad left his mom when she became pregnant with him. "My mom always hated him, so I grew up with the attitude that she gave me," he said. "She was always telling me, 'Your daddy is so rotten. He's a coward. He's a whore. He's this and he's that.' So I've never really been able to get close to him."

Armstrong stayed with his father on occasion, but mostly he lived with his mother. During those years he watched her battle an addiction to cocaine and heroin. As he got older, he would develop his own taste for the two things that eventually got him shipped off to the Ranch: drugs and guns. His mother unwittingly helped usher him into the world of the first. He discovered the second all by himself. Armstrong demonstrated at an early age that he had a good head on his shoulders. If he saw something, he remembered it. He watched his mother closely when she was selling drugs. Soon it was a case of like mother, like son.

"I saw how she did it and the money that she made," he said. "I watched the transactions. I figured there couldn't be anything wrong with it because I never saw her getting into any trouble with the law. It started with marijuana. I watched how she bagged it up. From then on, I considered myself a drug dealer. The streets were a part of me. And part of that was getting high, selling drugs, and carrying a gun. I did some following with my friends. Then I did my share of leading."

Most adults who came in contact with Armstrong throughout his life knew that he wasn't the stereotypical juvenile offender. He simply was a sharp kid, and over the years, he would excel in school. Yet there were times when Armstrong, in his own words, would go "crazy acting."

By the age of ten, he had run away from his mom, leaving behind a younger brother and sister, and moved in with his grandmother. Two years later, his mother was dead. An overdose had put her in the hospital. She spent a week on a dialysis machine before passing away. Technically, her cause of death was kidney failure. The reality was that his mother had killed herself, one day at a time, by smoking crack. Armstrong may have been a wild child before then, but after his mother's death, he really embraced the street life. That was also when he got involved with the law. Before, most of his problems had been confined to school fights and other small-time acts of violence. But it escalated into more serious crimes as he began to indulge himself in the temptations with which he came into contact every day. "I didn't have no concerns for nothing or nobody," he said. "Since my mom overdosed, I didn't care about anything, where I was going, what I was doing. I felt I could do whatever I wanted."

He would get high and then go looking for trouble. Once, he was strong-arm robbing a man and ended up giving him a vicious beating because the guy wouldn't give up what he had. Armstrong considered that the worst thing he had ever done because the person had done absolutely nothing to deserve the pummeling.

Armstrong was never in a gang, although he did hang out with people who were into the gang scene. But Armstrong had an infatuation with one of the standard accessories of gang life: guns. He liked the feel of a weapon in his hand. He liked shooting at targets. He liked shooting into the air. And once he shot a man. The way Armstrong recalled it, he didn't have any choice. The guy brought it on himself. Armstrong was still basically a kid, and one night this man, who stood about six-feet-something and looked to be in his twenties was hassling him. He was making him look bad on the street in front of people. Finally, Armstrong had enough.

"He had knocked my Raiders cap off, pushing me and all that," he explained. "He was calling me names and I just wasn't taking it. So I shot him three times with a .22 caliber."

After realizing what he had done, Armstrong took off. He started running and didn't stop until he couldn't run anymore. When he finally did slow down, he was in an unfamiliar part of town. He turned into an alley and ended up walking into a trap. He got jacked — mugged — by two gang members. They took his marijuana, his money, and his gun, and they left him with a black eye. It was there in the darkness that the night's events began truly to sink in.

"I saw what bullets can do to a person," he said. "It didn't just stop the man. It actually knocked him down. The power coming from my hand just put his big ol' butt down. I was shocked by that."

Armstrong never got caught for the shooting. His conscience was spared, too, since the man didn't die. He knew this because months later, he walked right past him on the street. It had been dark when he shot him, so the guy must not have gotten a good look at Armstrong. But Armstrong never forgot his face. He knew it was him. After that chance meeting, they never crossed paths again.

"I believe that things happen for a reason," Armstrong explained. "I learned that anybody has the power to kill someone, but the choice is whether or not you want to do it. Do you want to take somebody's life? I felt I didn't have that kind of heart. That's why I stayed away from the gang banging." But he didn't stay away from other crimes. He kept getting arrested and eventually was sent to a group placement facility in San Diego, where he spent over two years. He did well in school there and became an active member of the Seventh Day Adventist Church. He was even considered a role model for his peers. He was just weeks away from completing the program when he was busted for stealing a vehicle and carrying concealed weapons.

"My mom really got into crack cocaine heavy the last five years of her life, and I've had my times with it, too," he said. "That was really the source of my problem. When I was off the stuff, my grades in school were excellent. I had a 3.83 grade point average my junior year in high school. I was doing all right. But as soon as I went back to get high . . . just one weekend is all it took. I got high and violated probation after one straight year of doing good. That one weekend caused me to get sent here."

Armstrong arrived at the Ranch in August 1994. It wasn't at all what he had expected. He was anticipating much worse. When the van first pulled up to the main campus, he kept looking for fences. He couldn't find any guard towers, either. He had been behind bars in juvenile hall, and it took him about five minutes to realize that this place wasn't even closed up. He could just walk away if that was what he wanted to do. But Armstrong also decided that there was a reason he had been sent here. He was being offered a choice. Did he want to run and eventually end up in California Youth Authority, or did he want to stay and tough it out? The Ranch was no walk in the park. But when you came from his background, it was a step up. There was a nice place to sleep. Three meals a day. They even let him play some football.

Early on in his stay, Armstrong said he was active in the party scene. Only the parties at the Ranch were a little different than the ones on "the Outs". The residents called them pity parties, because everyone felt bad for himself. There were times when he felt like quitting, maybe AWOLing and taking his chances back in San Diego. But gradually, he had fewer of those low days. He began reflecting on his life and the mistakes he had made. There wasn't one single moment when he had decided to change his life, but Armstrong felt he was gradually moving in a different direction. He was tired of taking one step forward only to take two steps back. "It was a roller coaster," he said. "I had been going up and down before I finally asked myself, 'Where am I getting?' I realized that I was going nowhere at all. As soon as I achieved something, I'd drop right back down, making all that work that I had done mean nothing. So I guess I learned that it never stops, that you always have to keep working."

For Armstrong, football was the embodiment of work. Armstrong liked the game because he could see his progress on the scoreboard. If he put forth the effort and did what the coaches taught him, he could achieve success on the field. This wasn't just theory. This was something he could touch.

Armstrong had played on the Ranch's first team and had done all right, although he had never really been in shape. But since he was one of the handful of returning players, the coaches were depending on him. They had asked for volunteers to stand up front at the beginning of practice and help lead the team in warm ups. For the rest of the season, Armstrong took that responsibility seriously. There were some days when he didn't want to be up there, barking out the count as the players did jumping jacks, sit-ups, or leg stretches. But he did it. Like McKissic, he was a leader. Armstrong was more vocal, though. Whenever it got too quiet on the field during practice or games, it was Armstrong who would start yelling at players to wake up and show some emotion. He also was the one who would gather the team around for brief speeches on the sideline. That and his devout religious beliefs were the reasons for his nickname. The other boys called him Preacher.

"That's been my name for a long while," he said. "I feel like I've been through a lot. When you know you have experiences that could affect others, you want to tell the world. When a person asks me a question, I just can't say a few words. I'm not a man of few words. I'm long-winded."

If you asked Armstrong a question, he gave a thoughtful answer — a long, thoughtful answer. There was absolutely nothing frivolous about the way Armstrong carried himself. In his mind, everything he did at the Ranch had meaning and represented the changes he was trying to make. For instance, one day he explained that on the Outs, he had worn his hair in a big Afro style. The reason, he said, was that he was lazy; that hairstyle didn't require any work to keep it neat. If he were to leave the Ranch and grow his hair out again, that would be a sign that he hadn't really learned anything here and was reverting to old ways.

Like McKissic, Armstrong often could be seen off by himself. But what was different about Armstrong was that he looked as if he bore a heavy weight on his shoulders. At the ripe old age of eighteen, Armstrong sometimes looked world-weary. Self-doubt was evident on his face, as if he knew he wanted to take a different path in life but was constantly worried that he might not be up to the challenge.

"The main thing that's in your mind when you're here is, 'Do I go back to what I was, or do I change?'" he said the week after the Blue Ridge game. "It's kind of an either/or thing. Part of my determination is that I don't want to go back. I don't want that lifestyle. It killed my mother. It destroyed my family. All I knew was southeast San Diego. When I come here, I started to learn what was outside San Diego. I'm starting to realize that there's a lot out there for me. It's great out here, to tell you the truth. I want to have a piece of it. But I don't want to have to manipulate my way into getting it. That's what I grew up learning. It was always negative. So when you get what you want, you don't really feel good about it. It's not legally yours. I'm a very materialistic person. I like the nice things in life. I want to get them legally. I'm setting some goals, and I'm determined to achieve them." Armstrong paused a moment to think about what he had just said. "I'll tell you, it's easier said than done," he added. "I can say all this and it sounds good, but I'm still in the middle of it."

The fear of failure was never far away. Even as the football season progressed and it became clear that Armstrong indeed was one of the best football players in the state, there was the sense that he never quite believed it. Maybe that was why he worked so hard every day. He felt the need to prove himself over and over again. But for all the questions Armstrong would ponder endlessly, he was absolutely sure of one thing: Being sent to the Ranch had saved his life.

"Sometimes you wonder, 'Where would I be now if I was still back there?'" he said. "Well, I know. I'd be six feet under the ground, as they say on the streets, pushing up daisies. I'd basically be plant soil. I know that's where I was heading."

Then he headed off to the pantry for dinner.

TAKING IT PERSONAL

One day the week after the Blue Ridge debacle, Gray decided to have a short practice. It was only the middle of September, but with a 1–2 record, the season already hung in the balance. Friday night's game was against a school called Round Valley, whose team was probably similar to the Ranch's in overall ability. Lose that one and it would be virtually impossible to have a winning season. The Spartans would be reduced to a spoiler role in the East Region. So Gray called over his captains. The squad wasn't knocking off early to relax. He wanted a team meeting, and he expected the players to run it themselves. Gray had detected little rumblings that the squad might be ready to pack it in for the season, just as it had in the Blue Ridge game. He needed to make football important to these kids. He was looking for something to pull them together as a team and remove the cancerous attitudes that were eating away at the group.

"Are you going to let somebody ruin your last year of high school football?" Gray asked the captains. "This is the year that you're going to remember for the rest of your lives. There's always a next year for the coaches, but not for you. Are you going to let some bad attitudes screw up your last year so you don't make the play-offs? You need to find out what the problems are and deal with them. This is your team. Take control."

The Spartans sat down in the shade on cement near two outdoor basketball courts. Moore and Perkins were there to keep an eye on things, but it was the boys who would do most of the speaking. None of them was very articulate, and they all kept looking at the ground when they stood up. The words, though, came from the heart. Sparkman spoke first. He talked about how they could still have a good season, and he wanted to know why so many of his teammates were talking about quitting. Lono Hill got up and apologized for saying that he didn't want to play anymore. He wasn't used to all the conditioning, he said, but now he realized that he was getting something out of it. Obediah Breer admitted that he had thought about quitting because he wasn't starting but now understood that he just had to work harder if he wanted more playing time.

That was the way it went for several minutes. One boy after another got up and said he was sorry for his bad attitude and behavior. A football meeting had turned into a group therapy session as kids poured out their souls about why they were unhappy, and then asked for understanding and forgiveness.

Finally it was Cabell's turn. He was still the No. 2 tailback behind Elliott. He hadn't played poorly, but he hadn't duplicated his feats of the previous season, either. It was here that his long-simmering feud with Moore was brought out into the open. "The reason why I wanted to quit was because I've been fighting through adversity since last spring and all the staff is down on me," he said.

"Like who?" Moore asked curtly.

"Just staff," Cabell said.

"You been telling everybody on campus who you're mad at all this season," Moore countered.

"It's you, sir," Cabell blurted out. "You're always down on me. You had me behind every other running back last spring."

"The problem," Moore responded, "is that you can't deal with the fact that Elliott has outshined you. You're out telling your peers about how great you are. You're talking about yourself. You're not talking about the team. You haven't learned what a team is yet."

Sparkman, of all people, then tried to play the role of peacemaker. He told Cabell that he couldn't let staff get to him. "When they get down on you, they don't want you to pout, they want you to take it like a man. Heck, nobody gets more criticism than me around here," he added. "Mr. Moore don't mean nothing by it. He's trying to help you."

"Why are you taking it personal?" Moore asked Cabell.

"Because it *is* personal, sir," the boy answered. "You're harder on me than anybody else around here."

By then, Moore had become exasperated.

"You know what the problem is?" he said. "You've got more talent than anybody else. More is expected of you, and you haven't caught on to that yet. But you've got that attitude, and that's why you're here."

Several other players would stand and talk about how they had to stick together. Armstrong briefly preached his gospel of work. Friday night was not going to be easy, Tamar said. But if everyone worked hard and purged all their negative thoughts, it could set the tone for the rest of the season. Many heads were bobbing up and down as he spoke. When Armstrong was done, Perkins had the last word.

"We've got six games left," he said. "If we win four of them, then we go to the play-offs. Our whole season is still in front of us. Now let's hit the showers."

Later, as he headed to the pantry, Cabell said he had reached his own conclusion about the rest of the season. "I'm going to show some of these coaches because they don't have faith in me," he said.

———

As he pulled up a chair for dinner, Perkins said he thought the meeting had been cathartic for the team. He had faith in the boys. The trick was making the players have faith in themselves. The kids they had at the Ranch, he said, got down on themselves quickly. They were ready to throw in the towel at the first sign of hardship. The coaches had to make them realize that they could prevail if they just stuck with it.

"They're all survivors," he said. "They had to survive just to get here. What they did to get here was wrong, but they all had to do that to survive. If we can channel that energy in the right direction, they can be successful. We shouldn't be so quick to give up on them."

Before he began to eat, Perkins blessed his food. A deeply religious man, Perkins was an active member of the Fellowship of Christian Athletes. A tall, imposing defensive lineman during his own playing career, he began volunteering at the Ranch while rehabilitating from a knee injury he had suffered while playing with the Arizona Cardinals. After he retired, the volunteer work turned into a full-time job. There wasn't a gentler soul on the staff. He considered himself something of an actor because when he had to yell at kids it was so out of character. If a boy acted up, he wouldn't hesitate to put the youth in a control position or on the ground with a restraining move if it was required because he didn't want somebody — including the boy — to get hurt. But he was personally offended whenever he read newspaper stories about allegations that Ranch staff were hitting kids. He chalked it up to people not wanting to give the program a chance or simply being naive to the situations that could arise in dealing with a large population of juvenile offenders.

Perkins liked working with kids. That's why he was still here. He had been the interim head coach for the first season. It was a chaotic time. None of the kids had played before, and few of the coaches, including himself, had actually coached. But all things considered, 4–5 wasn't a bad season. Another man might have taken it as a slap in the face when he was told that the administration wanted to hire a more experienced head coach. Not Perkins. He never once expressed any regret at being a defensive line coach. "It doesn't make any difference to me," he said. "I'm a team player. The only important thing to me is that I get to be near the kids."

A few minutes later, a small Hispanic boy, perhaps eleven or twelve, approached Perkins and asked permission to speak. He was wearing a bright yellow T-shirt. He had just been brought back to the Ranch after being AWOL for almost a month. In a roundabout way, the boy said he was sorry for running. Perkins was also the recreation sports director at the Ranch and had gotten close to the boy through one of the sports programs he ran. Perkins asked him: Don't you know how serious that was? Your parents were worried. Believe it or not, we were worried, too. "But I'm not disappointed in you," he added. "I'm only disappointed in your actions. I'll still be here for you."

Perkins briefly was lost in thought as the boy returned to the table where the other yellow shirts were eating silently. Then he came back to football. "You watch," he said. "Friday night will mark the turning point of our season. I have faith," he added.

———

One of the great disappointments of the season was that the game against Round Valley was to be played in Phoenix. It wasn't that the Spartans wanted to make the 200–something-mile bus trip to the tiny towns of Springerville and Eager, near the New Mexico border. But it might have been worth the long ride. See, Round Valley possessed something that no other high school in the United States had: its very own dome. The building had opened in 1992. Just three years earlier the towns that fed into the Round Valley school district had gotten their first traffic light. Just six years before, the first fast-food restaurant had opened. So it was understandable that many thought it was strange that a rural community located hundreds of miles from any metropolitan area would have a dome. That included Tucson Electric Power Co. When voters passed a bond worth $25.5 million back in 1987, including $11.5 million to build the dome, they knew full well that about 90 percent of the school district's assessed valuation was a generating plant owned by the power company. So voters wouldn't be paying for the bulk of the bill — rate payers in the Tucson area would. But Tuscon Electric lost in court when it tried to halt the dome's construction, and now Round Valley was the envy of every high school in the state.

Round Valley took its football seriously. Somewhere at the school there was a case full of state trophies. The Elks had been a powerhouse in the 2A level for decades, and they also had done well in 3A since moving up a classification. Mark Gastineau, the former New York Jet defensive lineman who gained notoriety with his "sack dances" and flamboyant style, had played there. But in recent years, the program had fallen on hard times. So a new coach had been hired — Jim Wagstaff — whose long résumé included tours of duty as an NFL assistant with the Los Angeles Rams, Buffalo Bills, and San Diego Chargers. He had been talked out of retirement to coach the team. Everybody at the Ranch was expecting a dogfight. "We got to help each other tonight," Sparkman had told the team before the game.

But although the Spartan coaches fretted all week because Round Valley and the Ranch were supposedly evenly matched, it turned out that they had worried needlessly. Either the Spartans were a far superior squad or the message about having to pull together had really sunk in. The Ranch was in control from start to finish. McKissic, who rebounded nicely from his dreadful performance against Blue Ridge, threw a 60-yard touchdown pass to a leaping Sparkman less than three minutes into the game. A long kickoff return by Elliott set up a 37-yard touchdown run by McKissic. Soon after, Armstrong would bury the Elks quarterback as he was trying to throw. The weak pass ended up in the arms of Sparkman for an interception. Elliott took over from there. First he rambled for 36 yards. Another carry went for 12 yards. Finally, he capped a quick drive with an 11-yard burst into the end zone with five seconds left in the first quarter. It already was 20–8. The game was over.

"This," Shofner said on the sideline, "is what we're capable of."

The Spartans would tack on another touchdown early in the third quarter to seal a 28–8 victory. It was a solid, if unspectacular, win. The Ranch players seemed to let up after taking that big early lead, but Gray wasn't complaining. For the first time, the kids seemed to be working as a unit. There had been none of the usual infighting. Players were supporting each another. But one emotion did engulf Gray and the coaching staff: sheer relief. They now knew that the Spartans wouldn't be at the bottom of the East Region barrel. The Ranch might not make the play-offs, but they weren't going to be an embarrassment, either. The coaches also knew that word of the decisive victory would spread quickly in the White Mountains. The new kids had worked over one of the old powers. People up there probably would be shocked.

As the players were climbing back on the bus, one of them yelled, "Party back at the Ranch!" Dave DiDomenico, the secondary coach who also was a teacher on the main campus, just chuckled. "Uh, no," he said. "It will be a little louder than usual. There will be some pizza and then back to the cottages."

It would be just another night at the Ranch.

———

Kush had been at the game, this time in the stands, not in the press box with the headset on. Over the previous couple of weeks, he had become less active with the team. Finally, he had stopped coming to practice entirely. Part of it was his schedule. The Hall of Fame induction process literally was a year-long series of events that wouldn't conclude until a formal dinner was held in December in New York City. There had been the trip to South Bend. He was going to back to Windber, Pennsylvania, to be honored as that town's man of the year, and NFL Films was accompanying him because they were taping a show about his career. He also was helping prepare for an elaborate roast to be held in his honor at year's end that he hoped would raise money for the Ranch's planned athletic complex. Then there were his regular Ranch-related duties, which consisted primarily of speaking engagements.

Something else was affecting his involvement, too. The other coaches said that Kush wasn't looking well. Kush wouldn't say anything to anyone, but it was an open secret that he was struggling physically. "The reason I'm kind of fading out of the coaching part is that I'm having some abdominal problems," he admitted one day. A couple of years earlier, Kush had had colon surgery to repair scar tissue from a long-ago appendectomy. Kush had been suffering from acute pain ever since, and it was getting worse. Standing on the football field for several hours a day wasn't helping his condition. When he woke up in the morning, he felt tired. He recently had gone to the Mayo Clinic in nearby Scottsdale for yet another battery of tests. The good news was that they hadn't found any cancer. The bad news was that they couldn't identify the source of the problem. Kush realized he had to slow down.

"I still get too darn intense," he said. "I'm as fiery now as I ever was. There's no halfway for me. I like working with kids and watching them improve, but I'm still the same SOB. I'm still the bull in the china closet. I must have spent eight hours breaking down film on the Blue Ridge. To put all that time and effort into it is too difficult. I'm too old for it. But I haven't changed. I call those kids jackasses. But I'm still king of the jackasses."

MORE THAN JUNIOR'S COUSIN

At five feet six, 180 pounds, Derrick Letua was hardly one of the biggest players among the Spartans. But he was the human embodiment of the cliché that big things come in small packages, at least big tackles. He was, by far, the hardest hitter on the team. When he zeroed in a ballcarrier and lowered his shoulder, Letua would drive his pads into the opponent with remarkable force. Usually it was accompanied by that crisp popping sound that pads make during the execution of a textbook tackle, the kind that makes coaches smile. Sometimes opponents were left slumped on the ground in a heap like rag dolls.

There was a sense of strength about Letua. He looked like a tough guy. His face, though, was a blank slate that didn't show even the slightest hint of emotion. In some ways he was like a fire hydrant: squatty and immovable. Opponents probably didn't know he was there until he knocked into them. Even Letua couldn't explain where he got his power. But time after time he would hurtle himself into harm's way, and usually the other guy got the worst of the resulting collision. He thrived on the exhilaration that accompanied a thunderous hit.

"For me, football is like a rush," explained the seventeen-year-old Letua. "It's something legal you can do. I'm not getting in trouble for it. I don't have to look over my back and watch to see if somebody's going to get me for something. I can even get a pat on the back sometimes. I always try to give my full effort on all of my hits to make sure that I get my point across to people. When they first see me, they think that I'm small and they start laughing at me. They think that they're going to run me over. But when they get a little taste of me, they start to see that I'm not nearly what they think I am. They start thinking twice when they come running my way again."

Letua was the Ranch's middle linebacker, which is sort of like the quarterback on defense. It was the glamour position. He was the one who called the defensive signals. He was also the one who would tell the others to shut up if they started arguing in the huddle. He was the boss. Because he was Samoan, a linebacker, and from the city of Oceanside in southern California, the obvious comparisons were drawn around the Ranch between Letua and another Samoan middle linebacker who hailed from Oceanside: Junior Seau, the star of the San Diego Chargers, who had the reputation for being perhaps the NFL's most intimidating player. Some people liked to call Letua "Little Seau." He was not entirely fond of the nickname. He wanted to be known as Derrick Letua, not somebody else. "Everybody always asks me if he's my favorite player, and I tell them that I like Derrick Thomas of the Kansas City Chiefs better," he said. "Then they start giving me funny looks."

The reason for the strange looks was that Seau was Letua's second cousin. Other kids at the Ranch thought it had to be neat to be related to an NFL standout whom they had watched play in the Super Bowl earlier in the year. But Letua never understood the attraction. He was quick to point out that there was a pretty large age difference between him and Seau, and they were hardly what you would describe as close. Seau was busy doing whatever it was a star football player did, and Letua was doing his own thing.

"We're not tight or anything," Letua explained. "I don't know him real good. I used to see him once in a while. I never really used to say anything to him. We're not even that close as cousins. We're related, but he's a distant cousin on my mom's side. But he would know who I was. We used to go to the same church. To me, he's just like everybody else."

The truth was that Seau and Letua had traveled far different paths. In addition to being a heck of a football player, Seau was known as one of the game's humanitarians. He had been named the NFL's Man of the Year for the 1994 season, in recognition of his good works in the community. He had created the Junior Seau Foundation, a multipurpose organization designed to help children as well as anti–juvenile delinquency programs. Once, when a gang member was shot to death in a shopping mall in Chula Vista, California, which is just south of

San Diego, Seau showed up unannounced and told the hundreds of people who had gathered there that being in gangs merely guaranteed that members would come to a bad end.

At the same time that Seau was preaching his anti-gang message, his younger brother, Tony, was active in that very same scene. On January 29, 1993, according to newspaper accounts of the time, Tony, wielding a baseball bat, smashed an apartment window while another youth fired a gun into the building. The one round wounded a man inside. No other shots were fired because apparently the gun jammed. Tony pleaded guilty to his role in the gang-related attack and later was given a ten-year sentence to be served in the California Youth Authority. "Luckily for Tony, he's alive," Seau told *Sport* magazine. "He gets a second chance. He didn't get shot. He didn't die. Now the choice is his: a life his family has for him or a lifestyle the gangsters have for him. To me, the choice is easy." Seau added that his brother "got caught up in the wrong crowd."

Maybe Letua didn't know Junior well. But he did know Tony. "I used to hang around with Tony more," Letua said.

Oceanside was well represented at the Ranch, and most of the kids from there told similar stories about where they had grown up. Usually, they kept coming back to the same word to describe their city: rough. "If you go in my neighborhood and don't know anybody, it's going to be tough for you because there's always people trying to rob people there," Letua said. "There's a lot more killings out there now. Oceanside is a small area, but there's a lot of gang members there, so it would be easy for somebody to try and look you down and get you if they wanted."

What made Letua somewhat different from the average Ranch resident was that his mother and father were doing their best to keep him in line. They were supportive, and they had tried to discipline him. But Letua said that they weren't always around to watch him. So despite their best efforts, they didn't get anywhere with their son, who was growing increasingly out of control. He began hanging out with relatives, and it was with those people that he started to get into real trouble.

"When I was on the Outs, I was into crazy stuff," he said. "I had a lot of relatives who were into gangs. At first I didn't pay any attention to them. But my mom had transferred me to another school district to try and keep me out of trouble. I started getting into trouble at that school, so she had to transfer me back to my old school district in

Oceanside. Then I started getting caught up with my old friends. Then everything started happening. It just seemed like fun at that time."

Letua began to rebel against his parents, to sneak out at night, or to just run away. One thing led to another and before long he was active in a Samoan gang called the Deep Valley Bloods, the same outfit to which fellow Ranch linebacker Ailepata Suiaunoa belonged. It was also about the time that Letua started messing around with drugs.

"I tried to keep everything real low so they wouldn't know about the things I was doing," he said of his parents. "I know they knew that I used to drink, but I don't think they even know that I was getting into drugs like crystal meth and marijuana. When I started crystal meth, it just grabbed ahold of me and wouldn't let go. I started getting worse after that. I once went two months without doing it, but when I hit it again, I started doing it constantly, even at school. That's when I started doing a lot more crime."

There was one incident that weighed the most heavily on Letua's mind, and it was because he really hurt his parents. The police took him to the station for questioning. What made it worse was that his younger brother was tagging along when Letua got taken in. His brother was around several times when Derrick found trouble, but this time it was as serious as it could get. The cops brought Letua and his brother in because they had fit the description of two kids who had done a drive-by shooting that night. "We went to the station and gave fingerprints," Letua recalled. "They tried to check for gunpowder on our hands. They were doing all kinds of stuff to us. I felt real bad because my little brother was with me. I didn't want him to go through the things that I already was going through when he still had a chance to make it. I mean, he's doing good now, but I'm mad at myself now that he was with me during all that." Letua said they weren't involved in the shooting, and as it turned out, no charges were ever filed against them.

While he ran the streets, Letua also demonstrated that he had some athletic talent. One of the few kids who had played organized football before arriving at the Ranch, Letua said that as a sophomore he had made the Oceanside High varsity squad. Apparently he had shown some ability, because his coaches took a particular interest in him. Letua said that with the strong gang influence in Oceanside, he had the feeling that most of the teachers at his high school were scared and did the bare minimum to help students. At least his football coaches tried to provide him with some guidance. "But they really didn't know what I was doing when I was away from football practice," he added. "I never really talked to them about my problems. But when I first got into trouble, they would write letters for me to the courts, telling them to give me probation so they wouldn't put me away."

Letua played half the 1993 season before he got kicked out of Oceanside High, in part because of poor grades and in part because he almost got into a fight with the school's wrestling coach. By the beginning of 1994, all the "little things" that Letua was into had begun piling up. He landed in juvenile hall for what he described as a pair of strong-arm robberies. From the hall, he was sent to a placement facility, where instead of working on his problems, he went from bad to worse.

"I got into real trouble at the other place," he said. "I was getting into gang fights. I was talking back to staff. One time they said I swung at staff, but I still deny that to this day. I ended up getting sent back to the juvenile hall after I was charged with assault with a deadly weapon in a gang fight." The weapon? "A pencil," he said, an embarrassed grin breaking across his face. Letua had broken it off in another kid's back during a brawl.

Letua was running out of options. Slapped with the tag "incorrigible," he had reached the point where the system could decide that he wasn't salvageable. He was sitting in juvenile hall and had a two-year sentence pending at CYA. At that point, Letua's lawyer told him that he could ask the court for another hearing and tell the judge that he was willing to consider being enrolled in another facility in order to avoid going to the Youth Authority. Either the lawyer was persuasive or Letua expressed a genuine desire to change, because the court agreed to allow Letua into another program — if any would have him.

Like other kids in the system, Letua had heard about the Glen Mills program, with its emphasis on athletics, and was excited when a man from the Pennsylvania school came to juvenile hall to interview him. "When we were through, the guy gave me a little smile and said, 'I'll be seeing you in court,'" Letua remembered. "I thought I was going there. But a couple of days later, another man came from Arizona Boys Ranch, and that's when I figured that Glen Mills didn't want me." The Ranch did take him, however. Letua arrived in January 1995.

Letua chose the Ranch not because he wanted to alter his lifestyle but because he wanted to play football again. He figured it had to be better than just sitting around somewhere behind bars. After nine months, his opinion of the Ranch hadn't changed much. He didn't like it. He especially didn't care for the military environment of Civics. But he also knew what awaited him if he failed here.

Early one evening, after football practice and dinner, Letua was standing outside the two army-style barracks that housed the Civics boys at the main campus during the football season. The rest of the Civics residents were being put through marching drills under the watchful eyes of staff while Letua talked about the program. He wasn't exactly sure if the Ranch was making him a better person, but he added that it was impossible not to change a little after you'd been here for a while. "It's just a matter of whether or not you want to make it or let this program get you frustrated," he said. "I get frustrated all the time. But I don't let it get to the point where I get myself in so much trouble that I get terminated. There are some parts of my life that have changed. But I think I'm still the same person. I still act goofy at times. It's just a problem when I take it too far. I think twice about what I do."

There was one thing he loved about the Ranch, though: football. The game was his means of expression, a way to excel. When practices first started, his goal was just to make the team because he saw there were a lot of kids who wanted to play linebacker who were much bigger than he was. But he had an inner drive that most of the other boys lacked. It ticked him off to no end that some of his teammates didn't share his pure hatred for losing. He took each loss as a personal failure. There also was nothing he disliked more than when things went against the defense and the Spartans began to turn on each other. Players would start cussing at one another, and Letua would end up having to shout the defensive signals over their bickering or scream at them that nobody talks in his huddle. Sometimes that backfired and they started yelling at him instead. Letua was certain that the lack of an all-for-one-and-one-for-all mentality cost them the game against Ray. "I guess I have to remind myself that we can't win them all," he said.

Often Letua found himself thinking about the past. He remembered the previous placement he was in and how the staff had tried to help him there but that he wouldn't accept it. He thought about all the times in his life when he could have chosen a different path, the things he would do over if given the opportunity. But then Letua would shrug his shoulders.

"You can't go back in time, so I just have to do the best with what I've got," he said. "I guess my mind is opening up to more things. I used to just have one side of the story to things. I always tried to save myself. It was always me. I never thought about nobody else. Now I've started thinking about my family more and the things that I've put them through."

His mother was proud of what he was doing in Arizona, but she kept suggesting that he join the military when he got out of the Ranch. Letua, however, thought that the tan uniform of Civics was as close to the service as he wanted to get. His father, he said, didn't care what he did, as long as it was something positive.

"There are some people back in Oceanside that I know who have died," Letua said. "I wonder how they died. Sometimes I think that it could have been me. Sometimes I wonder if I should be glad that I'm here or if I should keep on complaining. I have real mixed feelings about being in my situation. I think about being alive and the opportunities that I have, like going to college or something. The chances I had of making it in life if I was still out there was probably a very small percentage."

Letua was also spending more time contemplating the future. It was the first time that he had ever done that. The more he thought about it, the more he worried about what that future held for him. He wasn't sure what he wanted to do after graduating, but like all the boys at the Ranch, he knew exactly what could happen if he walked right back into his old lifestyle.

"I could be dead," Letua said.

He was scheduled to leave the Ranch in either May or August of 1996. "If it's August, I have a funny feeling that they're going to keep me around for the next football season," Letua added.

He didn't say if that was good or bad. And with that, Letua fell into formation with the rest of the Civics residents. He locked it in and began marching as darkness slowly descended on the Ranch.

SMOTHERED
WITH KINDNESS

If one could bottle the essence of everything that high school football is supposed to be, then this night's experience would be tight inside.

No town and no team could have been more intertwined than Snowflake and its Lobos. Football wasn't just a game to people here; it was a way of life. A conservative Mormon community, Snowflake is smack dab in the middle of nowhere, 200 miles northeast of metropolitan Phoenix. The town has no stop lights. The three largest structures noticeable from the main highway are the old Mormon church, the new Mormon church, and the football stands. And as kickoff approached, those bleachers were packed with several thousand spectators. The lights over the field twinkled in the clear night sky like a beacon. There had been a parade earlier through the center of town as the school celebrated its homecoming. But now the streets were deserted. It was hard to believe there was anybody in Snowflake who wasn't at the football field. If there was, they could have been listening on one of the two radio stations that broadcasted the game live throughout the White Mountains region.

"This community really supports the football team," Snowflake athletic director Paul Reynolds explained. "Generations of the same family have played on the team — granddads, fathers, sons. These kids are always trying to live up to the stories of what their grandfathers did, and you know how some of those stories can get exaggerated with each telling. So the kids end up living up to tales of greatness that never really happened in the first place."

Although the same family names would keep appearing on the roster year after year, each generation created its own legends. Snowflake entered the game ranked No. 2 in the state, behind only Blue Ridge. Such a lofty perch was expected. The Lobos had won three consecutive state titles before Blue Ridge snapped Lobos' string the previous season. Snowflake had captured seven crowns in the previous thirteen years. The locals had come to expect state championships as their birthright, yet somehow they were not obnoxious about it.

Snowflake was a town that seemed to spring to life from a Norman Rockwell painting. Its name was not derived from the obvious meteorological source, although it did snow here. Rather, strangely enough, the two founding fathers were named, Snow and Flake. On this night there was a chill in the air that left the boys from the Ranch shivering. While a temperature in the high 40s might not seem cold, it had been over 100 degrees in Phoenix when the team climbed on the bus that morning. There would be no snow, however, and that disappointed Reynolds. He wasn't hoping for bad weather so as to slow down the Spartans. Instead, Reynolds knew that many of the Ranch kids were from southern California and probably had never seen snow before. He wanted them to have the experience of seeing the white stuff fall from the heavens. Reynolds's explanation was so sincere that it was impossible not to believe him.

Earlier in the week, Gray had told the players that it was a different world in Snowflake. They wouldn't see any graffiti or low riders or drug dealers selling their goods on street corners. He said it would be like walking onto the set of *Leave It to Beaver,* and he was right. When they had arrived earlier in the afternoon, the Spartans had gotten out of their bus in a nearby park to stretch their legs. Several Lobos players had come over just to say hello. They had no hesitation about fraternizing with the supposed enemy. The Snowflake players were so friendly that, unsolicited, they began offering scouting reports on their team. A player even mentioned that one of the Lobos running backs was upset that he hadn't been elected homecoming king. When that very boy wandered over a few minutes later, Milbrandt couldn't resist making a little dig. He casually mentioned to him that it was too bad he hadn't been voted king. The boy just stared at him wide-eyed, as if to say, "How the heck did you know that?"

At the field, the Snowflake coach showered Gray with praise about how good the Spartans looked on film and how his team would have its hands full. The Lobo cheerleaders had even made signs for the Ranch that hung on their side of the stands that read "Good Luck" and "Go Spartans." They smother you with kindness, Gray said, while they're kicking your butt. The reality was that homecoming games traditionally were scheduled against inferior opponents so the visitors didn't ruin the festivities. Maybe the good people of Snowflake were merely being charitable to ease the sting of the slap they were about to give these newcomers to the East Region.

Football has been called the moral equivalent of war, and truth is supposedly a war's first casualty. So although it was unclear how it got started, the Ranch coaches held on to a rumor that Snowflake hadn't lost a homecoming game in fifty years the way a man thrown overboard clings to a raft. When questioned about that impressive streak, several Snowflake residents later said it just wasn't true. It had been a long time since the Lobos had been defeated on homecoming, but it sure wasn't half a century. Nevertheless, the Ranch coaches weren't going to let facts get in the way of a good motivational tool. They had their story, and they were sticking to it. Fifty years. They kept repeating it like a mantra. *Fifty years.* Gray wielded the words like a stick. What happened over the last fifty years didn't make a damn bit of difference tonight, he told his players. "This is 1995. This is their team versus our team. We're here tonight because they thought we'd just be another homecoming pushover. But let's make them wish they'd never invited us to their party."

There are code words in sports. "Athletic" is one. "Speed" is another. Opposing coaches often used those words to describe the Spartans. They're so athletic. They've got so much speed. What they really were saying, in these politically correct times, was that the Ranch had a lot of black kids. Many of the teams on the Ranch's schedule were uniformly white, with the possible exception of some teams with a few Hispanic boys. And the reality was that the Spartans usually were faster than the other teams. But Snowflake's No. 22, a tall, lanky boy with a pale complexion, broke all the stereotypes. For the next couple of hours, the Spartans would be eating his dust. The first time he touched the ball, he darted 13 yards for a touchdown. The next time the Lobos had possession, he sprinted outside and went 73 yards for a score as he easily pulled away from the Ranch defenders to give Snowflake a quick 13–0 lead. Lance Michel, the Ranch's lead trainer, shook his head in awe. "That boy's got a gear that most people just don't have," he said.

It looked as if the rout was on. The Snowflake fans in the bleachers hooted and hollered as they smelled blood. Then, within a five-minute span, the Ranch stunned the overflow crowd by rampaging for three touchdowns of its own. McKissic had rambled 80 yards on an option play as he wove his way through defenders like a skier on a slalom course. Cabell ran back a kickoff 75 yards for the second touchdown. Then fullback Lloyd Peters tacked on a 17-yard scoring run that gave the Ranch a 21–19 lead heading into halftime. The margin could have been greater, but a fourth Spartan drive had stalled deep in Lobo territory. So the good people of Snowflake didn't have much to cheer about as homecoming floats circled the track during the intermission. Evidently No. 22, who had already rushed for 161 yards, had been voted king. He was putting a regal cape over his shoulder pads and exchanging his helmet for a crown. But at that moment the expression on his face was one of genuine concern.

Neither team had been able to stop the other. It had been a track meet as both offenses raced up and down the field. It was like a pick-up basketball game in which as little defense is played as possible. Every Lobo play seemed to be a sweep to the outside, and each time there were no Spartans there waiting to bring down the runner; usually No. 22. The Spartans' inexperience showed as the defensive backs constantly were caught out of position. So instead of making a tackle, Ranch players ended up chasing the fast white kid, and that was a losing proposition. Yet Snowflake was no better on defense than the Ranch. The only time the Spartans had been slowed was when they stopped themselves either through penalties or turnovers.

If they could somehow revive the shell-shocked secondary and get the players where they were supposed to be on the field, the Spartans could score a big upset. The small locker room was as tense as a hospital emergency room. The coaches played the role of trauma doctors as they frantically tried to come up with solutions to halt the defensive bleeding. Hurriedly sketching *X*s and *O*s on the chalkboard, they tried to cram a refresher course of Football 101 into the defensive players heads. They alternately chewed players out for completely forgetting their assignments and then tried to restore their confidence with soothing words. Disregard the mistakes of the first half, Gray told them before they left the locker room. Just worry about the next play. Right before the second-half kickoff, Armstrong gathered the team together on the sidelines. "Let's show them who the Spartans are!" he yelled.

Then it all began to fall apart.

Snowflake scored touchdowns on its first four possessions of the half. The Lobos were like an avalanche, and they buried the Spartan defense. The Ranch still couldn't stop No. 22, who was on his way to rushing for an astounding 283 yards on this night. But then other Lobos started getting into the act as the Snowflake coaching staff realized that the Ranch's halftime adjustments to stop their speedy running back had created other holes. The Lobo quarterback threw two touchdown passes. Then, with 7:44 left in the game, the quarterback raced 56 yards on a draw play up the middle to give Snowflake a commanding 43–28 lead. The second half had belonged to the home team. The lone bright spot for the Ranch was a four-yard touchdown run by Cabell in the third quarter. Now the Lobo fans were breathing easier. With a 15-point lead, the game looked as if it was comfortably in hand.

That sense of security lasted about forty ticks of the clock. On the second play of the Spartans' next possession, Cabell took a handoff outside, turned the corner, and raced 51 yards down the sideline. He entered the end zone untouched. Peters's two-point conversion run cut the Ranch deficit to seven points at 43–36. With seven minutes remaining, it was a game again. But it wouldn't matter how many times the Spartans scored if they couldn't stop the Lobos at least once. They seemed utterly incapable of accomplishing that task. The Spartans had tried an onside kick, but that failed. So taking the ball over at midfield, the Lobos once again made quick work of the Spartan defense. It took six plays for the Lobos to reach the Ranch 3-yard line. With four minutes left, the Spartans were in need of a miracle.

One was provided.

The Snowflake quarterback took the snap and went to hand off the ball to a running back. Only it was a bad exchange and the ball was bobbled. Mike Miller, a Ranch linebacker who had been blitzing on the play, pulled the football out of the air and started running in the other direction. Half the Snowflake team, after momentarily being stunned by the sudden development that something was going wrong, quickly took up the pursuit. But only one Lobo was close enough to have a chance to catch Miller as he approached the Snowflake 40-yard line.

At fifteen, Miller was still a boy, but he was a fast-growing boy who was beginning to look very much like a man. He stood six feet tall and weighed 200 pounds. In many ways, he was like a big puppy. He had large hands and feet and little definition in his chest. There was sometimes an awkwardness about him that suggested that his still developing body was a size too big for him. He was quiet around adults and wouldn't speak unless spoken to first. He had attended the same Indiana school that Cabell did and shared a similar story of falling in with a wrong crowd. Whitfield, the athletic director, said that although he acted downright shy at the Ranch, Miller had been considered such a wild product of the streets at his previous placement that he had been kept in solitary confinement for a month. "And he's not even that tough," Whitfield added. At this moment there was something else of particular importance that Miller wasn't: fast.

Near the 50-yard line, the lone Lobo close to Miller dived at his feet, just barely managing to trip him up, and preventing what would have been a certain score.

That touchdown-saving play seemed to inspire the Lobo defense. The Spartans weren't able to capitalize on this turn of events. Elliott was stopped for a loss on first down, and then McKissic threw three incomplete passes, giving the ball back to Snowflake. Now it really was over. The Lobos ran down the clock, although they almost managed to fumble the ball away one more time. In the last minute, the Snowflake quarterback threw yet another touchdown pass to make the final score a deceiving 49–36. Afterward, the only criticism Gray would voice to the players was that they still hadn't learned to work together. There had been too much bickering and finger pointing on defense as things steadily got worse during the second half. If they could win together, they could lose together, too. Their goal had to be to make state and get another crack at these guys in the play-offs. But that wouldn't happen, he concluded, if the infighting didn't stop.

Later, as the players silently showered and got dressed, Gray squatted down outside the locker-room door. With his forearms resting on his knees as he stared out at the darkened field, he was the picture of dejection. "Everybody knows our weaknesses now," he said quietly. "We got problems. Serious problems." With a 2–3 record, his team's season was teetering on the brink.

As the gear was loaded onto the bus for the four-hour drive back to Phoenix and people from Snowflake — being the good hosts that they were — bid the Spartans goodbye, Reynolds offered a parting remark. "We were lucky to catch them now," he said in a hushed tone. "You watch, they won't lose again this season." Relief seemed to be etched on his face. But it still was unclear if Reynolds truly meant what he said or if he was merely being polite.

My name is Brian Coleman. I'm sixteen. I'm from San Bernardino, California. I've been here about a year.

I don't really like it here. I just do what I have to do to get through. I can work on my education here a little. It's brought me closer to my mom, too. Those are the things I like about it. I'm graduating in May. I'll get my high school diploma and graduate from the program. The Ranch gives you some opportunities. I know Mr. Winchester says he'll help me get a job in Long Beach, which is near where I live. Maybe I can get something in welding. Right now, I'm trying to get a car from the Ranch so I'll have my own transportation. I'm going to try to go to junior college when I get back home, maybe take a couple of night classes. That would be just something to get me started. I'm going to be living with my mom for a while and maybe help her out a bit. Then when things get better and maybe if I meet a girl, then maybe I can move out in a couple of years.

They say you build relationships here, but I don't really understand that. I can talk to people better than I could before. I sort of feel different. I feel better about myself and what I can do. This gave me a chance to get off drugs and that stuff. It got me away from the friends. I know what I'm capable of doing now.

I didn't live with my mom. I was always out on my own. I could have lived with her, but I didn't get along with my older brother or my father. So I didn't stay at home. I was away from home for four years. I would stay with girls, and then when I met some other people, I would stay with them. I was about thirteen when I started messing up and leaving home.

I jumped into a gang. If people talked about it, I'd back it up. If somebody tried to disrespect someone else in the gang, I'd back us up. Then I'd have friends who'd back me up if something happened. Our gang was CFA — Chucamonga's Finest Artists. It started out about four years ago as a tagging crew. Then, after one year, it stopped being a tagging crew and ended up being a gang where everyone was carrying guns and stuff like that. Then we had rivalries with gangs that we didn't get along with. We'd go steal cars and sell them for money and buy stuff. I got caught for receiving stolen property. Some girls that I was with told on me. I had a car, too. So I also had a GTA [grand theft auto] charge.

When I was living on my own, I was stealing stuff to get money, like cameras. Sometimes I would buy drugs and turn around and sell them. I used to sell speed mostly. That's how I made most of my money so I could buy clothes and food and give some money to the people I was staying with.

When I think back on it, I know that I'd be mad if somebody were to *carjack my mom and steal her stuff. Still, I don't feel no remorse about what I did. I'm not saying that I'm going to go out and do the same things. I still want to drink beer when I get home, but I'm not going to get deep into it like I did before. You can't go back and get into it a little bit. But I guess I think I might go back and get involved again because it's hard to say no.*

I always got along with my mom. This tattoo [on his forearm] is her name: Bethelise. My brother and my dad have tattoos, too. It's just that I didn't like being around the house. My mom tried to keep me in line, but I wouldn't listen. I feel bad, too, because when I was doing what I was doing, I'd be thinking about her and I'd get sad. But I'd just keep on smoking something and then I'd forget about her after a couple of minutes. I felt sorry for my mom and my little sister. My mom would always spend time out looking for me, and she didn't spend enough time with my sister.

I only had two weeks of high school my freshman year. But in May, I'll have my diploma. I'm not sure how that happened, but I've been going to school a lot. I got a lot of credits in juvenile hall and at other placements I've been in. My mom put me in Charter Hospital, you know, a rehab place. Then I was in one placement, and I messed up after I got out and got sent to juvenile hall before the placement people came and picked me up again. Then I got out again and was arrested and got sent to a place in Napa, California. I got terminated from there. Now I'm here.

I think football is fun because I like being aggressive. I like playing against guys who are bigger than me, because in games I get low and I fire out at people. I'm only five seven, 165 pounds, but I still start at guard on the offensive line. The big guys don't scare me.

I like Mr. Winchester. He's basically the one staff member here that I can deal with good if something is going on. See, I'm in Civics, and I really can't talk to staff there because I know that they'll use it against me and maybe extend my program. But I listen to Mr. Winchester. He has a lot of stories, like about when he was younger. I don't know if they're true or not, but I like listening to them.

In Civics, we wear the tans and we can't change our facial expressions. We look all straight. So I can understand why people look at us and have a hard time believing that we're here. But there's a lot of gang stuff going on here. It's just that staff doesn't know about it. I know a lot of people who will talk gang stuff. But as soon as staff is around, things change so you don't get in trouble. But people get along here, although I don't know why. Maybe it's because here you don't have nothing to fight for. There's no territory or nothing.

Frank Kush talks to offensive linemen during a practice at Arizona Boys Ranch.

Members of the Ranch's Civic Conservation Corps march around the track before a Spartans game.

Tamar Armstrong (left) and Ranch CEO and president Bob Thomas.

TOP: *Corey Cabell (No. 46) and Tim Elliott (center) talk to Juan Sparkman at halftime during a regular-season game.*

RIGHT: *Tim Elliott in the Ranch locker room.*

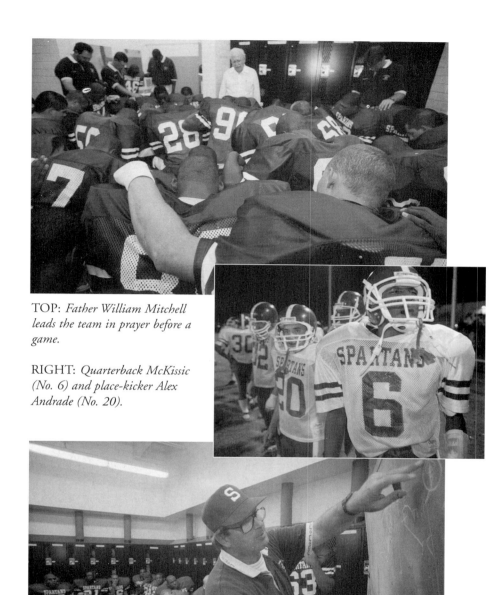

TOP: *Father William Mitchell leads the team in prayer before a game.*

RIGHT: *Quarterback McKissic (No. 6) and place-kicker Alex Andrade (No. 20).*

Spartans head coach Richard Gray sketches out a play.

TOP: *Members of the Civic Conservation Corps standing at attention.*

RIGHT: *Corey Cabell during the
National Anthem.*

Ranch fans during the Spartans homecoming game against Show Low.

Members of the Ranch's Civic Conservation Corps program at a regular-season game.

Ranch assistant coach Tunufa'i Ta'ase (center) instructs Tamar Armstrong (left) and Reggie Miles.

Spartan defenders converge on a Safford ballcarrier in the state semifinal game.

Spartans celebrate victory in state semifinals against Safford.

Ranch players hoist head coach Richard Gray on their shoulders after overtime victory against Safford in state semifinals.

Lloyd Peters and rest of Spartans shake hands with opposing players and cheerleaders after semifinal against Safford.

TOP: *Tim Elliott deep in thought before state championship game against Blue Ridge.*

LEFT: *Tim Elliott with the state runner-up trophy after the loss to Blue Ridge in the championship game.*

Juan Sparkman carries the ball in the state championship game against Blue Ridge.

Sometimes I do want to put all that behind me, but sometimes I don't. Sometimes I don't know if I can. I know there are some things that I want to do and some things that I don't. In the time I've been here, two of my closest friends growing up have been killed. Both of them was in gang stuff. One of 'em was just driving down the street in his truck. I've got an article from a newspaper about it. He was playing some oldies music and somebody just drove up beside him and shot him. It makes me think about how that could happen to me, too. What if somebody I was trying to jack had a gun? I think about things like that.

ABSENT
WITHOUT LEAVE

Life was looking up for Cabell. Although the Spartans had lost to Snowflake, Cabell had played his best game of the season. He had scored three touchdowns, including the long kickoff return. He had rushed for 86 yards on nine carries. Although no one had played particularly well on defense, he had played better than most. It was the kind of game that people on the Ranch were expecting from him every Friday night.

So even as Gray predictably railed against the team in Monday's practice, Cabell had a bounce in his step and a grin on his face. It was one of those days when the future's so bright that you gotta wear shades. He had had a good practice and, in a loud voice, encouraged his teammates with a loud voice to shake off the disappointing loss. The reason for Cabell's good mood was that he felt that he personally had turned a corner. His mind hadn't been into the first four games. He had been too worried about not being the featured tailback in the offense, too concerned about the coaches doubting his ability. But in the Snowflake game he proved that he could still be a big-play threat, and scoring touchdowns in bunches as he had done was exactly what got players noticed by college scouts. "I want to make all-state, and I want to make the play-offs," a bubbly Cabell said after practice. "Those are my goals."

With a plan fresh in his head, Cabell sought out Winchester before heading for dinner. Most players on the team liked Mr. Winchester, partly because the man was a born storyteller. He could hold the interest of kids with his tales, something that wasn't easy when your audience was the attention-impaired boys at the Ranch. Many of those stories dealt with his own youth. Winchester could relate to the kids because his upbringing had been a lot like theirs. Looking at them was like staring at himself at their age.

As a youth, Winchester had spent two and a half years locked up in California juvenile detention halls. By his count, he also lived in fourteen foster homes. His mother was an alcoholic, and he never mentioned his father. The family of seven kids lived on welfare, and that meant they had to go to the store on Saturday mornings to get boxes of bulk food items like powdered milk, bread, and cheese. He recalled getting into fights at school because his wardrobe consisted of clothes he received from charity organizations and other kids teased him that their moms had given those same garments to Goodwill the previous week. Once, while Winchester's family was living in a house at the bottom of a hill, heavy rains caused a mudslide. The force of the mud made the floor in the kids' bedroom buckle. The landlord tore up the floorboards and said he would be back the next day to replace them. "We lived that way for eight months," Winchester said, adding that they put down plywood themselves to cover the mess.

Sick of the charity clothes and food, Winchester and a brother turned to a life of petty crime. Winchester felt he was doing it just to survive. They would shoplift. They organized a bike-theft ring. Then once they committed an armed robbery during which his brother produced a gun and they stole $200 from a friend. That was how Winchester found himself in the juvenile justice system. But when the courts were done with Winchester, he couldn't return home because his mother was unable to care for him. Eventually, his mother would remarry and move to Texas. But he ran away and joined his brother, who by then was on a football scholarship at Oregon State. It was about this time that Winchester began to excel at the sport himself. He developed into a star offensive lineman and was recruited by major powers like Ohio State and USC. But he went to ASU, because on his recruiting visit Kush had called him worthless and said that he looked like a quitter so maybe he should go to one of those other fancy schools because he obviously couldn't hack playing for him. Winchester was so pissed off and determined to prove Kush wrong that on the spot he signed a letter of intent to play at ASU. He still remembered the Cheshire Cat grin Kush gave him when he saw his name on the dotted line. It was only then that Winchester realized he had been tricked. Nevertheless, he had a good career at ASU, as well as a brief fling in the CFL.

Sports had saved Winchester. It had given him the chance to get an education. He decided that as a way of giving something in return, he would become a teacher himself and help kids who were heading down the same road he had traveled. Eventually, he ended up working at the Ranch, although he certainly didn't need the job, since he and his wife also owned a thriving construction business. "But," Winchester said, "I wouldn't give this up for all the money in the world. If we can reach one kid in ten, then we've done something. I spent ten years in the public schools and felt like I was wasting my time. Not here."

When Cabell found Winchester, he poured out his heart to him. He told him that he was committed to playing football in college, specifically at Eastern Arizona, a junior college, and he wanted to know if Winchester would help him. Winchester said that Cabell definitely had the talent, so he would make a deal with him. If he kept working hard and showed the right attitude, he'd put his reputation on the line for him. He'd guarantee Cabell that he'd find a school for him.

"Coach," Cabell told him, "I'm going to show you that I can make it in college." Then he hugged Winchester. "Coach, you're a good man," Cabell added. Cabell walked out of the office.

And that night he went AWOL.

————

"There are people on this campus who are just sick," Winchester said the day after Cabell ran. "As for me, I'm just in shock."

Staff at the Ranch learn to expect the unexpected but this was just crazy. What the hell was Cabell thinking? One minute he was thoughtfully mapping out his future, and the next he was throwing it all away. Cabell and two other boys had run away from the Robson House, the transition home in Mesa, where they had been living. Slowly, Ranch staff were piecing together the story. Apparently, there had been some burglaries in the neighborhood where the Robson House was located, including the Monday night that the boys disappeared. In the course of the police investigation, area residents told the cops that boys from the Ranch had been seen out and about late some evenings. So while kids from the Ranch weren't suspects (and never would be), the police understandably wished to talk with them, if for no other reason than to find out if they had seen anything suspicious. When the cops arrived at the Robson House, the three boys were missing from their beds.

They still hadn't shown up, although staff had found a note from Cabell in which he apologized to everyone he was letting down at the Ranch. "That's a first since I've been here," Winchester said. "At least he was thinking of us." Four cars filled with Ranch staff had been out looking for them since early morning. At one point, the boys had been spotted walking down a street, so clearly they weren't working very hard to hide their whereabouts. When staff closed in, however, the kids bolted. They jumped over a fence and vanished into somebody's backyard as they lost their pursuers.

Meanwhile, Ranch staff tried to answer the obvious question: why? Boys had to reach a certain level of responsibility to live at Robson. Cabell had plenty going for him, and not just on the football field. It was clear from talking to the authorities that the police didn't believe he and his friends had committed the robberies. That left another possible explanation: girls. Other residents at the Ranch suggested that the boys were sneaking out to meet some members of the opposite sex. Shofner theorized that they had been out fooling around and that when they returned to the neighborhood they saw the cops and all the lights on in Robson House. Rather than walk in and face the music, they ran. It wasn't as if they had a plan, Shofner added. They didn't know anyone in Arizona. They had been spotted just strolling down the street in the middle of the day. They probably were holed up somewhere. It was just a matter of time before they got tired and hungry and called the Ranch to come pick them up.

There was simply no justification for running, Shofner said. The bottom line was that they didn't want to deal with the ramifications for their actions. Although they weren't going to be in trouble with the law, there was going to be a price paid, Ranch-style. They knew that they were going to be pulled from Robson House. After all, if they couldn't stay in their beds at night, there was a problem. They would have to come back to the main campus, live at the reorientation cottage, wear yellow shirts, and handle the hardships that came with that. But instead of accepting the consequences, they bolted. Street instincts had overcome common sense.

"You think you have a feeling for what these kids are like, but you never know," Shofner said. "That's what we're dealing with here. Corey is a good kid. He's never been a bad kid. We've got some bad kids out here who have done some really bad things in their lives, but Corey isn't one of them. Corey is a follower. He'd follow anybody. If he'd follow us, he'd be successful. Instead he's following some fools. He didn't think about everything he's got going for him. But we're the only family this kid has got. That's why he'll be back here."

The Ranch had to find the boys quickly. The law said that once they were missing for seven days, they were officially terminated from the program. Then, depending on what the original charges were that got them sent to the Ranch, they could become fugitives, not just runaways. Shofner had another thought: "You know who's taking this the hardest?" he asked. "Bob Thomas. He's probably out there looking right now." That was exactly what Thomas was doing, because of his close relationship with Cabell. But he couldn't locate the boys, either.

That night on the late-evening news, a breaking story involved three youths who had hopped a fence to cut through somebody's backyard in the nearby city of Chandler. A homeowner, mistakenly believing that the boys were prowlers, had shot one to death. Both Milbrandt and Winchester had seen the news report, and each one felt the same sinking feeling in the pit of his stomach. "I thought, 'Oh my God, it's one of ours,'" Milbrandt said.

As it turned out, it wasn't. Cabell and his friends were still on the run.

———

Cabell's breakaway run was the reason everyone at the Ranch was walking around with dumbstruck looks on their faces on Tuesday. But throughout the nation people were in a similar state of disbelief. In a Los Angeles courtroom, the verdict had been read in the O.J. Simpson murder case. Polls would show that most blacks felt that the not-guilty verdict was just, while a majority of whites believed that in spite of what the jury ruled, Simpson was guilty of killing his ex-wife and her friend. The verdict was the hot topic of conversation among the Ranch players as it was in the rest of the country. Probably not surprisingly, most of the boys had been pulling for O.J. Many said he had been framed by Mark Fuhrman of the L.A. police department.

Obediah Breer, who had come to the Ranch as an avowed white supremacist, was asked what he thought about the verdict. "I was happy for him because I thought he was innocent," Breer said.

———

The Cabell saga came to a conclusion on Wednesday.

He called from a convenience store that morning to say he wanted to come home. When Ranch staff showed up, however, he was gone. He had called from the west side of Phoenix — miles from Queen Creek — in a rough, decaying neighborhood. Since they were already there, the staff decided to check out the house of a former Ranch resident. It was such a bad area, the police had to be called to come knock on the door, in case things got out of hand.

Sure enough, the boys were there. One of the two kids with Cabell resisted when the police officers tried to bring him out of the house, and the cops ended up pepper-spraying him and taking him to a detention center. He would be terminated from the program immediately. The second boy, who was on scholarship at the Ranch and thus not legally bound to stay, also would be sent home. As for Cabell, he was brought back to the main campus. Their plan, Winchester said, had been to head to San Diego because one of the boys had connections there. Never mind that other than the city of Yuma, there was precious little besides 350 miles of desolate desert and mountains between Phoenix and San Diego. "But these kids are survivors," Winchester said. "They walk. They hitchhike. They find a way. They might have made it in another three or four days."

Cabell was coming back to the Ranch, but whether he was going back to the football team was an open question. He had been suspended indefinitely. He would miss that Friday's game at Payson. After that, nobody knew what would happen to him. Punishment at the Ranch was dealt out on a case-by-case basis. Cabell would get his yellow shirt and live with everything that accompanied it. He would be allowed to practice with the team, but playing was something else. Ultimately, Thomas would make that decision. For now, Gray was left trying to figure out how to replace one of his best players.

By Wednesday afternoon after practice, the word was spreading among the players that Cabell had been found and was being returned to the Ranch. Corey Luster, who, like Cabell, was from Evansville, and a former member of the Vice Lords gang, approached Milbrandt. Luster and Cabell had been flown out together from Indiana and had agreed that they'd give the Ranch a chance, but if they didn't like it, they'd run together. After five minutes at the airport, Luster said, they were thinking of AWOLing. Nevertheless, they had stuck it out. Luster was not one of the Ranch's fair-haired boys like Cabell. Instead, he had had more than his share of run-ins with staff. He had been addressed and restrained. Once Luster was talking in the locker room about a particular staff member in the Civics program, noting that they had been through some tough times together. Another Civics staffer overheard the comment and rolled his eyes. "Haven't we all, Mr. Luster?" he asked. Luster could only smile sheepishly. But as the clock wound down toward his graduation in December, Luster had grown and matured considerably. He couldn't understand why Cabell had run.

"See, I ain't never done that," Luster said to Milbrandt. "That's a long way from home for him. He don't have no family out here. So, have you heard from my friend yet?"

"He's been, well, apprehended," Milbrandt said.

"Can I talk to him when he gets back?" Luster wondered.

"Why?" Milbrandt asked.

"Because when I was getting in trouble, he told me not to run," Luster explained. "But now he went and ran."

"Hopefully, he can learn from this," Milbrandt concluded. "That's the important thing."

Luster walked away, shaking his head. Just like everyone else, he didn't understand.

———

It was another Friday, another game day, but not for Cabell. At 7:30 in the morning, he was with the other Re-Os, digging out a drainage pipe that was in need of repair. One of the staff members who were supervising the work crew was Gallen Allen. One of the basic tenets at the Ranch is that staff always work alongside the residents. There is no overseer-laborer relationship. If the job requires digging, the staffer picks up a shovel and sweats right alongside the kids. The Ranch philosophy is that working together is the perfect way to start cracking those walls that boys carefully erect to keep everyone out. Kids tended to let down their guard when they got tired. On this morning, Allen was shoveling earth right next to Cabell.

"I told Cabell, 'I'll ask you one question, and only one question: Why did you go AWOL?'" Allen said later. "He couldn't answer me. He had everything. But he ran because of some little girl. But I told him that I wouldn't bark at him, because he was going to have to deal with his peers, his teammates, the staff—all wanting to know why he ran. But I already know. It's the same thing that a lot of these kids can't deal with. It's freedom they can't handle."

Luckily for Cabell, Allen wasn't in a barking mood, because when he wanted, he could growl like a mean junkyard dog. Allen looked like he should have been playing linebacker in the NFL, which he had done briefly. Allen was constructed like a rock. His gruff demeanor suggested that he was impervious to everything around him. Even in the hottest days of the summer workouts, when the temperature soared past 110, Allen would stalk around the practice field wearing a sweatshirt. It would be soaked through with perspiration. He would carry a bandanna in his hand and constantly would wipe the sweat off his face. But he never would complain about the heat. Allen had one of those booming voices that traveled great distances on the football field. All of the linebackers dreaded being in a situation where they were caught in his steely gaze after they had done something wrong. Allen had a simple philosophy about life. When he played football, he gave everything he had. Now he had transferred that single-minded focus to the kids.

A junior college All-American at Nassau Community College in New York, Allen had come to the Southwest to play for the University of Arizona. The reason why he picked that school, he said, was because it was one of the few that didn't offer him something under the table that broke NCAA rules. For instance, he was making a recruiting visit at one Texas college when his host casually asked what kind of vehicle he preferred to drive. "Why do you want to know that?" Allen recalled asking. "He told me, 'Well, you know. Things could be worked out.'" Allen decided that they couldn't. While he played two seasons at Arizona, he didn't equal his success of junior college. Nevertheless, he had done well enough to sign as a free agent with the NFL's Seattle Seahawks in 1987. But Allen was already an injured man when he arrived in the Pacific Northwest. He had been beaten up in the college game. He had broken bones in one hand. He had rib and back injuries that had been so bad at Arizona that sometimes he temporarily was unable to walk. He had a torn hip-flexor muscle. But he did his best to keep quiet about all that because damaged goods didn't last long in the NFL. Hurt pro football players become ex-football players quickly. The people who stuck around the league simply had learned to play with the pain and keep their mouths shut. But one day, late in the season, Allen saw that Seahawks coach Chuck Knox was staring at him. For the whole practice, Knox had been watching him closely on the field. After practice, Knox called Allen over and asked him if he had any physical problems. Allen told him no. But a series of agility drills quickly confirmed that there was something wrong with the rookie. "Go see the team doctors," Allen was told.

Just about every part of Allen's body was X-rayed. Later, he was called into a hospital room, where all those X rays were illuminated on three walls. A small group of doctors huddled together and talked somberly as they examined them. The longer they compared their opinions and discussed possible treatments, the more nervous Allen grew. Finally, the lead physician approached him. "How the hell are you still playing football?" he asked. None of the injuries was particularly serious, they said, . . . if he just planned on living a normal life. But if he continued playing football, he would probably require at least three major surgeries. Even with that, there would be no guarantees that he would be any better.

"Well, it's been nice," I said. "I'd rather be able to run with my son," Allen recalled. "These kids ask me why it was an easy decision to leave football. I tell them that football wasn't my whole life. It was just a fluke for me. Football was the last sport that I took up as a kid, and I just happened to keep getting better and better. Football was fun. But I wasn't one of those guys who was going to play forever and destroy my body."

A couple of years later Allen found his true passion: the Ranch. He had been there six years now. Like many of the staff, Allen maintained that he would retire there. The metamorphosis boys underwent never ceased to amaze him. Allen looked around the gym at Payson, where the Spartans were putting on their gear and uniforms for game No. 6. His voice was soft now.

"Where these kids come from, they're heading to an early grave," he said. "They have no respect for society, their parents, nothing. We've got about eighteen months to do the job that nobody else could. They come in here at their lowest point. Maybe a kid takes a swing at you and you have to restrain him, and he's screaming, 'F——you, F——you, F——you!' Then, over a period of time, they deal with you on a daily basis. You never give them an inch. Slowly they understand the program and realize that they're changing and that they're changing on their own."

Allen said he didn't like to go to the Ranch's graduation ceremonies. It was too hard on him. Hard-core, gang-banging, tough-guy kids, who had arrived swearing that they'd never change, would walk up the aisle and receive their diplomas, maybe not perfect kids, but definitely different kids. "And after all the headaches, it really hurts to watch them leave," Allen said.

Earlier in the week, he had experienced one of those migraines. Walter Holmes, a boy who had played on the team the previous year, was having a difficult practice. The team was going through a one-on-one hitting drill in which a running back bulls straight into a defensive player. Allen warned his defenders that they'd better do the exercise at full speed or somebody was going to get hurt. Holmes kept going at half speed, and Lloyd Peters kept punishing him. Finally, Holmes grabbed a ball and threw it down in frustration.

"So I told him, 'Walter, pick up that ball,'" Allen said.

Holmes grumbled and refused to pick it up.

Allen again told him to get the ball, and again Holmes grumbled.

"Walter, pick up the damn ball!"

Then Holmes began swearing at Allen. So Allen grabbed him by the jersey with two fingers and lightly pulled him over to the ball. As he tried to tug Holmes down, the boy started resisting and somehow ended up on the ground. At this point Holmes temporarily lost it. "Then," Allen explained, picking up the story, "Holmes says, 'Hey, nigger, I'm going to fuck you up! I'm going to fuck you up!' Now I'm starting to get mad. I say to him, 'Walter, after all we've been through over two years, and now you're calling me a nigger?' Then he hit me with his left hand. It literally felt like a feather hitting me. It took everything I had not to break out laughing. I escorted him off the field. Then I told him, 'Walter, all you had to do was pick up the ball. But you refused. Then you call me a nigger and then you hit me. How could you do that to me?'"

Allen said he could see Holmes thinking for a moment. A sad look formed on his face, his eyes started to well up with tears. Finally, his voice cracking, Holmes said, "Mr. Allen, I'm sorry."

"Then," Allen said, "we could start dealing with the problem. I told him, 'What's going to happen if you run up to a cop and say "Fuck you" to him? I'll tell you what's going to happen. He's going to protect himself. And it's going to be your butt. Do we understand ourselves?'"

Holmes responded with a sharp "Yes, sir."

"Then he hugged me and went out and had a great practice," Allen said.

Just another day at the Ranch.

"People think we have big staff to intimidate kids," he said. "But what they don't understand is that these kids can't be intimidated. Size doesn't matter to them. In these kids' minds, they think they're invincible. They have zero fear of their parents. They're not afraid of the system. When they finally get to the point where they are totally out of control, they end up at Arizona Boys Ranch. The state thinks we take kids out back and beat them. Go ask Walter if he's ever been beaten."

My name is Walter Holmes. I'm seventeen years old. I'm from Phoenix. I've been here two and a half years.

When I first got here in '93, it was real rough. I was an angry person. I always used to have to get restrained. As time went by, things relaxed. But staff used to be real intense. Even if you blinked, staff would get after you. You had to be disciplined in order to survive. It's loosened up a whole lot. For instance, they don't run us as much as they used to.

Being restrained is for when you get angry and you get out of control. Staff, they have to put you on the ground. Most people think that being restrained is when they hold you up to calm you down. But that's just a control position. Restrained is when your whole body is actually on the ground. Then they want you to calm down. When you're down there, you get more mad. But they keep talking to you until you do calm down. When you're down there, it's a painful position. So you gotta calm down. You have no choice.

I'm here for assaults. I also burnt a porch. It was no accident. I was never a gangster, but I was angry. I come from a rough background. I have a deaf mom. It's hard to communicate with her. I knew sign language, but it was still hard for us. The Ranch has helped me and my mom build a better relationship. My dad was a little factor growing up. He left when I was about ten. Actually, we left. We ran away.

I don't know how I changed. I just settled down. I'm not as rough as I used to be. I think they broke me in or rehabilitated me. This is supposed to be a rehabilitation program. I think they've rehabilitated me real good. I'm not playing much this year, but last year I used to start and play pretty good. That's when all my anger was inside me. Now I'm relaxed, and I think that's why I'm not doing as well as I used to. I used to be mad because I wanted respect from my peers. I don't need that anymore. I don't really care if they respect me or not. I don't get no playing time, I hardly get any practice time, but I'll do whatever I can to help the team.

Mr. Allen and I don't talk as much as we used to. When I first got here, I went to Butler Cottage. That's the reorientation cottage. We went on work crew and I kind of gave him a look. He grabbed me and calmed me down. Ever since then, we've been talking. He helped me get out of Butler.

Did you see what happened the other day? See, I'm not that good this year. I kept going through these drills, and I kept getting rocked by Lloyd Peters. I kept getting blasted. So I just threw a ball down and said, "I don't get no playing time for this!" Mr. Allen tried to make me pick up the ball and I wouldn't. He brought me over to talk to him and I kind of gave him *a little nudge on the cheek. But he told me that he wasn't going to take it personal. We made up pretty good.*

I know there's people who want to shut this place down. They're looking for little reasons to close it. But I don't think staff abuses us. I'd be lying if I said they've abused me. They're just trying to help us the best way possible. But you have to want to be helped. If you don't want help, that makes your stay longer. For me, it was probably a year and ten months before I realized that. I've been here for a pretty long time, and I decided that I can't be here forever. I'm practically eighteen and it's time for me to move on. That's when I started changing. I'm at the Robson House in Mesa. That's the transition home. We're like the cream of the crop. There's just two of us there right now. There were five of us there, but the other three messed up. Two of them went home, and Cabell is back here on the Ranch.

Now I'm doing good. I'm about to get a car. The Ranch is helping me get my license. I'm getting out in May. I'll be graduating from high school. I'm going to be the only one in my family who has graduated from high school, and I think that's good. I'm thinking long-range. I'm going to the Job Corps in Phoenix. They say that if everything goes well, I could be making $16 a hour soon as a painter. That's pretty good money for just getting out of here. If that doesn't work, I'll just go back home.

I think things are looking up for me. This place has taught me a lot. It taught me self-control. That's all they wanted from me because I used to go off just like that. I had always been like that. They've helped me when I wanted it.

But I'll tell you one thing: I'm tired of looking at this Ranch. It's time for me to leave.

None of the coaches ever expressed disappointment in Holmes as a football player. They raved, however, about how much he had grown up in the last year.

"Walter's come a long way, and he knows it," Shofner said one day. "He's going to leave here with a high school degree, and that's a hell of an accomplishment."

A SLOW, STEADY CLIMB

It turned out that the Ranch didn't need Cabell against Payson. The Longhorns, well on their way to a winless season, were hopelessly outmatched. The hardest part of the game for the Ranch coaches was keeping the players interested. There were few spectators. Payson's field was a dreary and gloomy place, and the game followed suit. Payson is a cowboy town. It claims to be the home of America's oldest rodeo. Zane Grey, the famous author of numerous westerns, including *Riders of the Purple Sage,* once had a cabin near here. But the old place burned down in a forest fire a few years earlier. Payson is the sort of town where black folks stand out. And an administrator from the school had warned the Ranch coaches before the game that in the heat of the moment, some of their boys might say something. "We've been told," Moore said to the team just before the Spartans took the field, "they've got some players who could call you niggers. If you don't act with class and if you don't stop yourselves from retaliating, you'll have to answer to me on Saturday. There will be consequences."

As it turned out, nothing racist was ever said on the field. The Ranch was up 22–0 at halftime, and the coaches still weren't happy because the lead should have been even bigger. When it was over, the Ranch had won easily, 41–0. McKissic was the star on offense, rushing for 129 yards and two touchdowns. He was coming into his own as a player. He rarely made mistakes and had an uncanny knack for capitalizing on the errors of opponents. He never said much, but when he did, everyone listened. Other players talked about how there was a sense of security when they were in the huddle and they knew that Shaune was in control. Defensively, Letua had a big game that included returning a fumble 46 yards for a touchdown.

When it was done, one of the student trainers shouted, "We bent them over and spanked them like babies!" Maybe, but all in all the game had a just-another-day-at-the-office quality to it. Gray remained frustrated because the team still wasn't playing up to its full potential. Players continued to line up out of position. They kept making dumb penalties. They played to the level of the competition. But a win was a win, and it improved the Spartans' record to 3–3 on the season. The play-offs still remained a possibility. It just seemed like five hours on a bus, there and back, had been a long ride for an ugly game like this.

———

Early the next week, practice had finished and Cabell, now wearing a yellow shirt, was showered and dressed. After the regular workout, he had done extra gassers. Some other physical activity probably would be awaiting him after dinner, too. He was eager to tell his side of the story about his AWOL experience. It was important, he said, that people understand where he was coming from. He described the night he ran as a momentary lapse of reason. From the second he and the other two kids left Robson House, Cabell knew he shouldn't have sneaked out. But they were going to meet some girls a few blocks away, and, Cabell said, he thought that was only natural. Being at the Ranch, they never got to see any girls. So once they were out, they lost track of time. Somebody got some beer, and the next thing they knew, they were straggling back at 4:00 A.M.

That's when they saw the lights on at Robson House. They had seen police in the neighborhood, and when they went around the back, they saw through a window that their beds had been turned up. Putting two and two together, they figured they were the subject of some sort of mini-manhunt. Cabell said he told the others that they had been caught and they should just go into the house and deal with the inevitable fallout. The other boys said forget it, and they ran. Cabell ran with them. He said he had regretted that decision, too, but he just got caught up in the moment. Once he had made his choice, Cabell felt he had to see it through. That was why he ran when Ranch staff saw them walking down the street the next day.

"Mr. Moore saw us and was chasing us," he said. "I mean, Mr. Moore and I don't really get along, so I definitely wasn't going to go back to him. I saw two more staff, but they didn't see me. I just got tired of watching my back, looking for cars with staff in them. Being out there for a couple of days really makes you suspicious. Every van looked like a Ranch van. I wasn't trying to go anywhere. I told the guy who wanted to go to San Diego that I wasn't going there with him. I called from a Circle K because I hadn't slept in three days. I called the Ranch and waited for a while, then I just left. I went back to the guy's house where we were staying. I was lying down on the couch, when the next thing I knew, Mr. Saunders Montague was there, and I just got into the van with him. I wasn't going anywhere. I was coming back."

Cabell added that he and the other two boys didn't have anything to do with the burglaries. The last thing he wanted to do was get into trouble so close to graduation. He wasn't that stupid, Cabell explained. If he got into any legal trouble, the judge wouldn't destroy his record, and, most important, his hope of getting a college football scholarship would go up in smoke. Yes, Cabell knew he had made a dumb mistake by running. He knew he had disappointed people like Mr. Thomas, and he accepted the punishment. But he didn't hurt anybody but himself, and at least he had seen the error of his ways and tried to turn himself in.

"At first I felt like giving up everything and just going home," he said. "But that's probably what they want me to do. So I'm going to continue with this yellow shirt. It's just a little setback for me now. I feel a lot of pressure from staff and peers around here because I'm the last guy that they would think would do something like this. I've been here twenty-one months, and I've never been in a yellow shirt. I've never AWOLed. I've never made a major mistake, and I'm graduating in December. I'm going to bounce back."

He added that he wasn't going to let anyone take college away from him. With that, he took out a letter. It arrived at the Ranch the day after he ran, so he hadn't opened it yet. It was from Northern Arizona University. Although it was misaddressed to Corey Campbell, it obviously was meant for Cabell. He ripped open the envelope and read the letter aloud:

Thank you for your interest in Northern Arizona University and our football program. In order to evaluate you further, we need your assistance. Enclosed is a questionnaire that we would like you to complete and return at your earliest convenience. We are always looking for the best student-athletes. NAU traditionally is one of the nation's finest programs. We look forward to the return of your questionnaire.

Steve Axman, head football coach

Cabell carefully folded the letter, placed it back in the envelope, and returned it to his pocket.

"I'm gonna make it," he said. "You watch, I'm gonna make it."

———

There had been a spirited debate on campus that week about what to do with Cabell. He had already been placed in the reorientation cottage as was customary punishment for boys who went AWOL. That in itself was hard enough, and he had already missed one game. Should he be suspended for more games? Cabell's treatment team was divided. Hell, everybody was divided, even the coaches. Winchester said that some coaches were in favor of not playing Cabell that Friday because he had let down the rest of the team. Some staff felt he shouldn't play for the rest of the season. But doing that might harm Cabell's future irreparably because he still had a real chance to get a football scholarship, and that could be worth its weight in gold to a kid who had no money.

Eventually Thomas had to make a ruling, since he had the last word on every major decision at the Ranch. He let it be known that he wanted Cabell to suit up on Friday night. Whether or not Cabell actually played would be up to the coaches. He would not interfere with the inner workings of the football team.

That passed the final call to Gray.

"They left it up to the wrong guy," he said late Thursday afternoon. "My treatment is football. If they've left it up to me, then I'm going to play him."

———

Friday night's game against Holbrook was the only other soft spot on the Ranch schedule. The Roadrunners were struggling through a down year, having won just one game at this point. The Spartans should have won handily, considering the Roadrunners would have to make the 200-mile–plus road trip down to the Valley.

The Ranch would come away with a 19–0 victory. The game was anything but easy, however. The tone was set by a rather unusual performance of the national anthem by a Ranch resident. Just moments before the boy began singing, Thomas whispered that the youth had recently tried to go AWOL by leaping out the back of a moving van. The boy, Thomas added, had made considerable progress since then. But his vocal cords may have been injured in the jump because he went on to give what may have been the absolute worst rendition of the anthem ever sung. He was off key from the start and went downhill from there. He forgot not only words but whole lines. He even stopped once. Everyone on the sidelines, from players to coaches to game officials, did everything possible to prevent themselves from bursting out laughing until after ". . . and the home of the brave" was finally croaked out. "That was the worst I've ever heard, and that includes Roseanne Barr's version," Thomas joked.

The artistic quality of the evening improved briefly on Elliott's first two carries. The first time he touched the ball, he raced 65 yards up the middle for a touchdown. The second time, he went through the same gaping hole for 34 yards for another score. Two rushes, 99 yards, two touchdowns. The Ranch was up, 13–0, early. But then the game bogged down. The offense couldn't move the ball after that as McKissic had a rare off night. The only other score would come early in the fourth quarter when Peters pushed his way into the end zone from four yards out.

When it was over, the Spartans had yet another ho-hum victory. The wins over both Payson and Holbrook had been rather pedestrian, but the defensive unit, which at the beginning of the season had done everything except wave a red cape in front of opponents and shout "Olé!" as they raced past, had settled down and recorded two consecutive shutouts. More important, for the first time all season, the Ranch was better than .500 with a 4–3 record overall and 3–2 in conference play. If they could somehow split their last two games against Winslow and Show Low, they probably would squeeze into the fourth and final state playoff berth.

Elliott had clearly been the star that night. He had rushed for 176 yards on eleven carries to go along with his two touchdowns. There was no question who the big gun in the Spartans' ground game was now. Cabell, on the other hand, had struggled in his first game back from suspension, being held to minus-5 yards on six carries with a fumble. On the season, he was only the Ranch's fourth-leading rusher behind Elliott, McKissic, and the fullback Peters.

At halftime, Gray had exploded. The Spartans might have been winning, but they sure weren't playing well. He told Milbrandt to take

McKissic out to the parking lot and work on his passing mechanics because he had obviously forgotten how to throw the damn ball. If he couldn't remember how to toss it correctly, then he could have a place on the sideline and watch Todd Harris do it. Gray had also thundered at the squad that some players were worrying too much about themselves and not enough about the team. A football team, Gray had said, is like a motor. It's got pistons, spark plugs, and so on. "Well, I've got pieces of a football team strewn all over this locker room," Gray had said, "but some of you guys don't want to work together so the freaking motor won't run."

Sparkman had taken the criticism personally. When the rest of the squad had filed out of the locker room to take the field for the second half, Cabell and Elliott pulled Sparkman aside and told him how much the team needed him. Don't give up on yourself, because we haven't given up on you, they both said. There's no statistic for such an assist in football, but one should have been recorded for Cabell that day. In the second half, a rejuvenated Sparkman sprinted 49 yards on a reverse to set up the final touchdown of the game.

By the game's end, Gray's anger had dissipated into the cool night sky. He had made some kind of peace with himself in the second half. The Spartans were the Spartans. He had to keep reminding himself that most of them hadn't played any football before this season, and it was inevitable that they would make dumb mistakes all year long. It probably was expecting too much of them to think they could play a perfect game for 48 minutes and blow any team off the field. In hindsight, that 19-point victory was looking a lot better.

"There are enough times to be sad in this business," Gray said. "I think we better just be happy when we win. If winning 19–0 doesn't make you happy, then you're trying to feed your ego. We've got to let these kids be happy and enjoy their success after as hard as we work them. The bottom line is we've got the win and we're going to Winslow with a chance to do something."

————

The next night, Arizona State was playing against Brigham Young on its home field at Sun Devil Stadium in nearby Tempe. At halftime, the 1975 Sun Devil squad, which had gone 12–0 and upset Nebraska in the Fiesta Bowl, was honored. First the players were introduced and walked out on the field. Among them was Winchester.

Then Kush's name was announced. The loudest roar of the night reverberated through the stadium as the old coach received a long standing ovation. Representatives from the College Football Hall of Fame were there to present him with a plaque. When the ceremony was over, several players from the '75 team carried Kush off the field.

It seemed like old times.

———

There were days when the idea really hit home that the Ranch wasn't a normal high school and the Spartans weren't a normal prep football team. There were about three such days the following week.

That Friday night, when the Spartans would travel up to Winslow, would mark the biggest game of the season thus far. The coaches had their game faces on and were pushing the players. Only the kids didn't want to be pushed. The defiance had begun quietly early in the week as the boys just seemed to float through the motions of practices. It wasn't so much that their heads were swelling now that they had a modest two-game winning streak. Rather, it was that they wanted to take a little break and maybe glide some. The predictable result was that a lot of coaches were getting into a lot of players' faces.

Even the usual postpractice round of "consequences" had a lolly-gagging quality about them. After the workouts, players who had broken Ranch rules would be put through a series of extra drills. Sometimes it would be gassers. Sometimes it would be a grueling exercise called up-downs, in which the player would run in place until a coach blew his whistle. The boy would then have to dive to the ground, bounce back up, and start running in place again. This would be repeated until the player was worked to exhaustion.

One afternoon Ta'ase had been drilling two kids hard. One of them had sworn at a female houseparent: "Why are you always treating me like a little kid, bitch?"

"Have we learned how to properly address a female yet?" Ta'ase asked him.

The only response was a cold stare.

The other boy had been caught smoking cigarettes. After he finished his drills, he was flat on his back trying to catch his breath when Perkins went over to him and started breathing in deep gulps.

172 ● THE LAST CHANCE RANCH

"It sure is nice to have good, clean lungs to take in that fresh air," Perkins needled.

The youth wasn't amused.

With the exception of Gray, the coaching staff had as their first mission work with the kids. Through experience, they knew that the boys' demeanor could vary wildly from day to day, if not hour to hour. One day a youth could be in a great mood. The next, he could act as if he were lost in space. The third day he could pitch a world-class temper tantrum and need to be restrained and counseled. Dealing with rapidly changing emotions was simply part of the job. Yet as football coaches, those men couldn't accept such of behavior. They couldn't prepare a team for a big game when the players were focused on the task at hand for maybe two practices out of the week.

Then there were some days, like Wednesday, when the players were in open rebellion. The coaches would later say that they could see it coming. The team had reached a critical mass and had then proceeded to explode. All the elements were there for a sloppy practice. The temperature soared into the high 90s as Arizona's endless summer refused to give way to milder weather. It was scheduled to be a long afternoon on the field, and it was near the end of the season.

From the very beginning of the workout, the players hadn't wanted to be there, and they made that perfectly clear to the coaches. First came the halfhearted attempts to do what the coaches were telling them. Then came the quick glances of raw anger as the staff proceeded to chew them out. Then came the long, hard stares that Winchester referred to as the "F—you look." Finally, the inevitable back-talking began. Gray had seen enough. He decided it was time to quell the insurrection.

"Line it up!" he shouted.

Practice was halted to run some gassers. But the players liked that idea even less than having a real practice. So instead of sprinting to the end zone as the coaches demanded, the players actually were slowing down before they reached the goal lines, just to defy the coaches. At that point Gray forgot all about his carefully prepared practice schedule and threw his clipboard to the ground. The hell with trying to get them better, he decided. Let's just work 'em. The team would spend the next forty-five minutes running laps around the field.

"Those attitudes," Milbrandt would explain later, "can spread like wildfire. It's like a virus."

Pretty soon there was full-fledged dissension, and the more tired the players became, the more defiant some grew. Within minutes, there were little pockets of coaches snapping at individual players. One player had to be isolated when he clenched his fists and looked as if he might hit somebody. Moore and DiDomenico were addressing Jovan Davis, a reserve running back who had been at the Ranch for only a couple of months, on the side of the field. Davis apparently had made a smart remark to DiDomenico, the secondary coach, and it had escalated from there.

"You want to get physical?" Moore challenged, his finger poking Davis's chest. "Do you? Well, I'm ready for you. Why don't you make a move? C'mon, go for it." Davis dropped his helmet. Then it was DiDomenico's turn to get between Moore and Davis. After a moment, DiDomenico grabbed one of Davis's arms and Moore took hold of the other and they escorted a struggling Davis off the field and behind a cottage. As loud words were exchanged, two other nonfootball staff members followed the threesome.

Meanwhile, Allen was quietly lecturing Sparkman near the field under a tree. When Gray decided the team had run enough and wanted to finish the "practice" with some special teams work, he shouted sarcastically over to Allen, "Hey, can I have my punt snapper back, or should I get somebody else?"

As Sparkman returned to the field, Allen looked disgusted as he took up a position in the end zone, leaning on a goal post. He watched the team practice kickoff and punt return plays. Even with dark sunglasses, Allen's eyes seemed to burn holes in some players.

"They don't have the self-discipline," he said, practically spitting out the words. "There's a reason why they're in a place like this. It's all mental. They don't want to work. Then impulse kicks in and the mouth starts going. They don't understand that we coaches know what we're doing. But then they don't understand much. We've got too much talent to be 4–3. No kid out there, when a coach is telling him something, should be lipping. But then they've done it to their parents, to the schools, to the system, to their P.O.s, to judges. So why the hell not do it to us? That's what we have to turn around."

A moment later, Sparkman twisted his left ankle while fielding a punt and went down in a heap. He threw his helmet about 20 yards and began swearing up a storm. As the trainers started working on his ankle, Gray called the rest of the team around. Rather than deliver a vicious tongue-lashing, which the team richly deserved, Gray took the opposite approach. He presented himself as a hurt coach who had been betrayed by players with no heart. Gray softly told them that he was as disappointed as he could be. This was the worst practice of the season, and it was coming right before a key game. Don't look for somebody else to blame. Look at yourselves in the mirror, he said. We've got some opportunities to do something good. But we're limited by how far you guys want to go. If you're feeling sorry for yourselves, then you don't understand what we're trying to do here. We're trying to get you guys ready for the play-offs. But you're showing me that it's not important to you. Now get out of here and get showered.

As Harris, the wide receiver and backup quarterback, was walking off the field, he offered his own assessment of the day. "We deserved this," he said. "We had it coming."

Sparkman was the last one to leave the field. He slowly limped off toward the locker room.

"This is typical Boys Ranch," Shofner said later. "You gotta grab their attention. You gotta refocus them. It's like that old mule. You gotta kick him once in a while. You've got to hit him with a two-by-four." Then he thought about that last line for a moment. "Figuratively, of course," he added.

Gray, strangely, didn't seem too upset. After the players had headed to the pantry for dinner, he tilted back in his office chair and said he figured the team was due for one of these practices. You see something like this at every public school, he said. It's late October. It's still hot. It's not fun anymore. Kids have a hard choice to make. They can politely lose those last couple of weeks and be through with the season, or they can start working even harder and make a strong run for state. Maybe this would wake them up. "If this were a public school, I'd be in the principal's office the next morning, explaining why I ran my team so hard the week of a big game with the play-offs on the line," Gray continued. A wry smile crossed his face. "But I bet I don't get any calls from parents this time," he added.

The next day, the players went through a sharp practice. Davis looked good and attentive throughout the workout. Sparkman, miraculously, had lost his limp.

My name is Jovan Davis. I'm sixteen years old. I'm from San Diego. I've been here like two months now.

Football here is different. I played for another high school team in San Diego, and it was nothing like this. This is fun. I didn't want to get cut from this team. They told me there was a team here, but they explained that I was here for my program, not just to play football. I was gone for a week. I had problems. I was acting silly and not going along with the program. They sent me down to Oracle for a readjustment. It gets your discipline back. I wasn't locking it in the way I should when I was in formation. I was trying to justify my mistakes, and they don't like that. When I came back up here, I started doing my program the way they wanted me to. I'll be going back down to Civics, but not until after the season is over.

What was I like on the Outs? I was a gang banger. I really didn't listen to no one. I basically tried to look out for myself. My mother passed, and that's when everything started worsening for me and I started doing worse crimes and getting in trouble. She passed about a year ago last August. She had cancer. But I didn't expect that she would pass that soon. When she passed, I started messing around. But in a way, my life wouldn't have changed if she hadn't passed because the courts sent me here and now this is an opportunity to get my life straight.

I was selling drugs, shooting at people, fighting, all kinds of stuff. I look back on it, and it all seems dumb. But when I was doing it, it seemed like fun. I was a Roland 40s Crip. But I'm trying to get my tattoos taken off. I've got one on my back. I'm going to talk to the nurse and see what they can do about getting rid of them. I don't see no use for them anymore.

Me and my friends were involved in a hit-and-run. We hit somebody, and we just got out of the car and ran. I didn't think the person was hurt that bad. But they said that he had to go to the hospital and was in critical condition. I haven't heard what happened after that. I don't know what happened to him. They charged me as an accessory and I resisted arrest.

I have three brothers and a stepfather. I didn't know my dad. He wasn't in the picture. I also have two daughters: Imani Navoj and Arissa Joann. Arissa is two. Imani is one. Imani's middle name is Jovan spelled backward. I'm still with their mom. It's hard to be away. When I first got to the [juvenile] hall, I didn't think that I was going to be away for more than a year. But when I come here, I found out that I'm going to be here for like *two years. That's when I start dwelling. That's what Mr. Moore will say to me, that I be dwelling on things.*

Mr. Moore, he'll call me a crybaby. If I get into a problem, I'll just sit there and think about it. He says that I dwell on it a lot, that I stay on one problem for too long. Dwelling is no good. But I just think a lot. I'll try to think about the problem I did and the solution, so I won't do it again.

Sometimes it doesn't do any good when Mr. Moore gets into my face. But a majority of the time he does it because it was my fault that I did something wrong. But sometimes he'll be teasing me. Like last time, he said, "You're just a big baby. Stop crying. I'll bring you a bib to practice next time." I just try to control myself and not get mad. Mr. Moore, he'll be telling me that he's trying to get me mad just to see how I react. Now that I understand that he's trying to help me by doing this, I've learned not to get mad anymore. I like Mr. Moore. We get along swell. I don't have a problem with him doing that stuff at all. That's because I know it's for my own good. When they sent me down to Oracle for that week, it was Mr. Moore who got me back up here. They were going to keep me down there because they said that I wasn't meeting expectations up here. Mr. Moore told them that there was no cause. So when I got back up here, Mr. Moore told me that he had done me a favor, so now it was my turn to do him a favor. He told me I can't quit.

I've heard that there's been accusations of stuff here. I haven't had any abuse up here. But down in Civics it's a different story. They want you to act like robots. If you don't lock it in the way they want you to, you'll get addressed. They're hands-on. I don't like that. If you talk back to them, they'll put their hands on you. They did that to me once. It wasn't like a beating or nothing, but it did hurt me. I seen a staff almost push a kid's face into his food. They're real tough down there. I think they go overboard. They try to scare it out of you. But when Mr. Moore does it, I know that he's doing it to make me better. I know that, even when he's shaking me. Sometimes I think he's the only one who understands me.

Football helps you with discipline. It helps you develop coping skills. For me, it helps you control your temper because if you get hit hard, you can't jump up and fight. You learn to be tough the right way. Being at the Ranch is good. It's teaching me how to control my attitude. How to speak to people appropriately. How to control my demeanor. How to control my life without getting into trouble. When I was on the Outs, I didn't care what I had to do. I thought I was a big, bad macho guy. I'm not that way any-

more. I don't want to act that way.

Thinking about my kids makes me want to do my program better so I can get out of here quicker, so I can be more of a man than I was before. I want to be a good father and be able to take care of my kids. I didn't really do that before when I was on the Outs.

We're changing here, at least most of us are. That's because we want to. And it feels good.

STANDING ON THE CORNER IN WINSLOW, ARIZONA

The town of Winslow is just under 200 miles to the north of Phoenix, along what was old Route 66, in the high plains country of northern Arizona. The elevation is about 5,000 feet, yet it's still as flat as a tabletop. There are no trees or natural barriers of any kind. The town is known for the steady, constant wind and the accompanying whistling noise. "There's nothing to do there," Gray said. "It's either go watch the high school football game or go listen to the wind blow through the gas station."

Winslow was also the town immortalized in verse by the rock group the Eagles in the mid-1970s song "Take It Easy."

Winslow is not what would be described as the scenic town they sang about. But the song gave Winslow a claim to fame. Along the main drag there's even a sign that reads: "You're standing on the corner in Winslow, Arizona. Take it easy." The sign is a popular tourist destination. Visitors stand beneath it and smile as snapshots are taken.

This is also a town where cultures meet and coexist. There is a large Native American population there, and a strange story that would make headlines throughout Arizona a couple of weeks after the Spartans played the Winslow team illustrates how those cultures sometimes clash. According to the news reports, a white girl brought her deceased mom's ashes to school for some kind of show-and-tell demonstration. Why she did this was not fully explained. Neither was an explanation forthcoming of how some of her dearly departed mother's ashes spilled in the classroom. But when the parents of the Hopi and Navajo children who attended the school learned what had happened, they wouldn't allow their kids in the building because there was a "spirit" present. The boycott involved about one hundred students when school officials realized that something had to be done. Eventually, Native American medicine men were allowed to perform a religious ceremony to "cleanse" the school. This solved one problem, but it created another. Now Christian groups were upset that they hadn't been allowed to conduct any of their services in the school. Subsequently, they asked for, and received, permission to hold a prayer vigil inside.

"I told the kids that Winslow isn't Snowflake," Gray said. "It's a lot different town."

If Winslow was renowned for anything else besides being in a popular song, it was for the town's football team. The Winslow Bulldogs were the fourth-winningest team in Arizona history. The school's Emil Nasser Stadium, which was named for a famous Winslow coach, had a reputation for being a snake pit. The wind always seemed to blow right through the field, and in late October the temperatures could plunge.

All season long, Gray had expressed mixed feelings about the Winslow game. He was dreading a contest in a tough environment probably in lousy weather, after a four-and-a-half-hour bus ride. Yet Gray also figured that this game would be a good test for the Spartans. This would be the Friday night when he found out if the state play-offs were a realistic goal, or just a pipe dream. The Ranch would have to play well to win because Winslow had a damn good football team. The year before, Winslow had lost to Blue Ridge in the state 3A finals. Virtually the entire team was back from that 11–2 squad. So it was no surprise that the voters in the state's Associated Press poll had tagged Winslow as their preseason No. 1 team.

The star of the squad was a six-foot-one, 210-pound running back who had rushed for nearly 2,000 yards as a sophomore the previous season. He was big, and he was quick. The Ranch coaches had heard that Division I schools were lining up to express an interest in his services. Gray said you never knew what to believe, but the rumor on the coaches' grapevine was that the University of Michigan had begun inquiring about this back, who wore No. 32 and had already run for more than 1,000 yards this season.

Yet something wasn't quite right with Winslow. Although the Bulldogs were still ranked among the state's top five teams, their regular season had not been the cakewalk that many had been expecting.

Winslow had lost a competitive game to Blue Ridge early. The Bull-dogs had then visited Snowflake and been drilled by 29 points the week after the Lobos had defeated the Ranch. So both teams entered this game with 3–2 conference records. The winner would have the inside track for the East Region's No. 3 play-off seed. The loser would have to scramble for the fourth, and final, play-off berth. Gray figured that the Spartans could win this one, but it would have to be one of those trips when everything went right.

"We need a measuring stick to find where we're at," Gray said.

What they needed was a measuring stick before they left the Ranch, since Spartan Pride, the team bus, ran out of gas about halfway to Winslow. Gray wondered if it was an omen. The bus looked good, mostly because of a nice paint job. Beneath the paint, however, was an old vehicle with a lot of miles under the hood. Ranch officials first leased, then purchased the 1978 bus for a total of about $54,000 and reconditioned the engine themselves. As previous breakdowns had proved, every road trip was an adventure. One of the Spartan Pride's many problems was that the gas gauge didn't work, so the drivers at the Ranch used a dipstick to measure the amount of gas in the tank. Because of a mix-up before the team left for Winslow, no one had checked to make sure the fuel tank was full.

The Ranch coaches and players ended up having to sit along a remote section of highway in northern Arizona for two hours while they waited for a tow truck to bring them gas. Help eventually arrived and the Spartans were on their way, but they wouldn't roll into Winslow until just after 6:00 P.M. Kickoff was scheduled for 7:00 P.M., although Winslow officials agreed to push back the game fifteen minutes. Still, there wasn't much time to get ready. As the players got off the bus, each resembled the Tin Man from *The Wizard of Oz:* stiff. Getting to Winslow had turned out to be an all-day trip. And now they had to play a football game.

After their belated arrival, small annoyances kept pushing the coaches toward a slow boil. The field was a mess. Right next to the sta-dium, the Winslow school district was building a $5.8 million gym — complete with a weight room, a wrestling room, a dance room, offices upstairs, and three full-size basketball courts downstairs, with a seating capacity of 2,500. But it was being constructed on the site of the old football practice field. The Bulldogs had been forced to work out on their game field, tearing up the turf. The locker-room quarters were small, too. Most of the Spartans ended up getting dressed in the lobby of the old gym. And with only two toilets, boys were lined up five or six deep after the long ride.

On the field during warm-ups, a couple of things were noticeable about the Bulldogs. What caught everyone's attention first was that they were huge for a high school team. Then there were their uniforms. With garnet jerseys, gold pants, and gold helmets, the players closely resembled the Florida State Seminoles. The Bulldogs looked talented. They also acted as if they knew they were good as they strutted around the field. As Gray watched the teams go through their pregame drills, a Winslow player kept staring at him. After this went on for a few moments, Gray finally turned to him and said, "Good luck tonight."

"We're going to kick your ass," the player responded.

"We'll be here," Gray shot back.

The Spartans wouldn't just be standing on the corner in Winslow, Arizona, on this night.

————

Back in the lobby of the gym, where the Spartans had gathered before kickoff, the Ranch coaches were nervous. Several moved among the players, slapping hands with each team member. Then Saunders Montague, one of the part-time assistant coaches and a program coordinator on the main campus, led the team in a prayer back in the locker room. Lord, he said, we want to have fun, be safe, and kick butt. Then it was Gray's turn. He noted how his players had been watching the Bulldogs especially closely during the pregame drills. Something about the Winslow team seemed to just plain piss off his squad. Hell, he was ticked, too. Everyone was in an ornery mood. He wanted to exploit that. He wanted his team to take out that anger on the field. So Gray talked about how hard the Spartans had worked. Gray said he never had a team work so hard. But still, they lacked something. He told them that it was emotion. It was all right to let themselves go on the field. That was what football was all about. "We're facing a team tonight that is big, tall, and strong," Gray continued. "And we're what they call the new kid on the block. But it doesn't matter if you're the new kid if you can kick the old kid's ass. We want to show them that the new kid is the toughest one on the block. We're always regimented. We're always in line. We're always in order. But tonight, we've got to let loose. You've got to let your feelings come through. I say we form a rivalry right now tonight with the Bulldogs. I want to kick their ass and let them know who the new kids on the block are. This team is favored. This team has been ranked No. 1. This team has got black shoes and gloves and every damn thing on their uniforms except Christmas tree lights. But everyone in this room is wearing the same uniform. The same shoes. The same socks. We're the same team. We don't have any stars here. Now let's go out there and show them who we are."

The stands were packed with noisy Bulldog fans. It seemed that the whole town was there. As the Winslow team ran onto the field, a large "W" made of wood, just beyond one of the end zones, was lit on fire. As the flames flickered into the night sky, the fans worked themselves into a frenzy. There was a nip in the air. But, surprisingly, there was almost no wind. Even more miraculous were the Spartans themselves. On the sideline, they were showing more excitement than they had all season. Finally, they were acting like every other high school team in America.

Somebody, Gray told his squad just before the opening kickoff, is going to make a big play. We're going to need a play tonight that turns this game around for us.

The Ranch got the ball first and quickly marched down the field, thanks to a new wrinkle that the coaches had added to the offense that week. When McKissic received the snap from the center, he would take a step backward, then turn his back momentarily to the line of scrimmage, so that the Bulldog defenders couldn't see the ball. Instead of just going directly to McKissic, the defense would hesitate to see if the quarterback was going to hand off the ball to one of the running backs or turn and scamper with it himself. McKissic made the most of the defenders' hesitation. He looked much like a blackjack dealer dishing out cards. On the sixth play of the drive, he dealt the ball to Cabell, who burst through the left side of the Bulldog defense and raced 31 yards for the first score of the night. Andrade's extra point try was wide left, leaving the Ranch with a 6–0 lead. Andrade was distraught as he returned to the sideline, and Gray pulled him aside. "I'm not taking you out," Gray told him. "You're my man. You're my kicker. Don't worry about it. Just get the next one."

On its first possession, Winslow drove to the Ranch 22 before

McKissic, who was now playing defensive back in the Ranch's revamped secondary, stripped the ball from the Bulldog fullback and then recovered it. The Spartans went right back to work, this time mounting an 11-play scoring drive. The march was capped by a brilliant 6-yard run by McKissic. It had appeared that he was trapped back at the 10-yard line as he ran around the left side, but somehow he found a seam, snaked past several defenders, and dived over the goal line. The two-point conversion was good as Elliott forced his way into the end zone. The score was now 14–0. The four-headed rushing monster of McKissic, Elliott, Cabell, and Peters had Winslow on its heels.

Then the Bulldogs began to demonstrate why they were the preseason No. 1 team in the state. They put together a fourteen-play drive, capped by No. 32's 2-yard scoring run. The Winslow tight end was wide open in the end zone for the two-point conversion as the Ranch's lead was cut to 14–8. But the Spartans struck right back. First McKissic found Harris for a nice 11-yard gain. More important, the short pass set up the next play. Harris streaked down the field, outrunning the defensive coverage, and McKissic hit him on the fly with a beautiful rainbow pass that went for a 39-yard touchdown. Andrade's extra point made it 21–8, with 3:32 to go in the first half.

On the next possession, for the first and only time all season, a Spartan was thrown out of the game. There had been a lot of trash talking on the field. Finally, it escalated to something physical. The way Sparkman would describe it later, he and a Winslow offensive lineman were "having a little disagreement." Sparkman said he took the lineman down with a low, but clean, block. The lineman thought differently, believing Sparkman had gone for his knees, and he grabbed for Sparkman's shoulder pads. "I took a swing," Sparkman said. All the officials saw was the punch, and Sparkman was immediately ejected. Gray was incensed, of course. If one of his players was getting tossed, he wanted to know why one of the Bulldogs wasn't going with him. Not only would Sparkman miss the rest of this game, but the AIA rule book said ejected players had to miss the next game as well. But Gray didn't have time to worry about that right then. "We know that we're in Winslow," Gray growled at the lead official, "but let's be fair."

Thus far, the Bulldogs' No. 32 had shown flashes of why he was such a highly regarded running back. He could, to use a cliché, stop on a dime and switch directions to elude defenders. What he didn't have was pure, blazing speed. Fast running backs were the kind that had hurt the Ranch all season. Every time this kid paused to cut back or juke a defender, it gave the Spartans a chance to converge on him. So as the game approached halftime, he had rushed for only 46 yards on ten carries with a fumble. Even so, he was still the most dangerous player on the field as he dropped back to take a punt by the Spartans.

Then came the play that Gray had been talking about before the opening kickoff, the play that would turn the game.

When No. 32 caught the punt, Andre Hughes, a backup running back, hit him first, forcing him to drop the ball. As No. 32 bent over to pick it up, Jovan Davis barreled down and popped him, helmet on helmet. Meanwhile, the Ranch's Obediah Breer had come up with the ball at the Winslow 33.

On the next play, McKissic went around the right end on an option play. He kept the ball and took off down the field. Near the end zone, three Winslow defenders appeared to have McKissic cornered. His best bet looked to be simply lowering his head and getting as close to the goal line as he could. Instead, McKissic inexplicably slowed down. Then, just before he was about to be tackled out of bounds near the 5-yard line, McKissic suddenly cut back inside toward the middle of the field and bolted into the end zone with no one laying a hand on him. The maneuver left all three defenders twisting and spinning like tops before they fell to the ground. It was the kind of move made on Saturday afternoons in college games — or maybe even on Sunday afternoons in the pros.

Andrade's kick failed, but as the Spartans went into the locker room, they held a 27–8 lead. The Winslow crowd was in a stunned silence as the Spartans left the field. Many fans also were staring down their sideline, worried looks on their faces, as an ambulance pulled up. It wouldn't be until the third quarter that the Ranch coaches and players would realize what happened to No. 32. Davis said later that he knew something was wrong right away when the boy had trouble getting to his feet after fumbling the punt. In fact, he never made it back to the Winslow sideline; he fell down unconscious about halfway there. When he regained his wits, he temporarily couldn't feel his legs. He would be transported to the nearby hospital. There, the boy would spend the night as the doctors made sure that he had nothing worse than a bad concussion. But his evening was done. A couple of weeks later, Gray would learn that No. 32 had decided after this game that maybe baseball was his best sport and had elected not to play the rest of the season.

Back in the locker room at halftime, one of the Spartan players shouted: "Smell the play-offs, baby! Smell the play-offs!" That was exactly what the coaches didn't want to hear with two quarters left to play. Allen had already been screaming at the players as they filed into the locker room: "Now the game starts! We ain't satisfied. We're just getting started." Moore quickly added: "Everybody shut your mouths. We haven't started playing yet."

The coaches cautioned players not to be drawn into any confrontations on the field. They had already lost Sparkman; they didn't want to lose anybody else. The coaches were concerned that if the game really turned into a rout in the second half, tempers would flare on the Winslow side and players from the Ranch would retaliate. "Don't engage in anything cheap that they may start," Winchester told his offensive linemen. "Don't get suckered into that. You're better than that. Show pride. Show class. Just play football." Then Gray warned the team that a half of zero is still zero. It was unclear if the players understood his math, but they got the point that the game was still twenty-four minutes from being over. They expected an even rougher two quarters of football coming up as Winslow tried to claw its way back into the game. Back on the sideline, Armstrong gathered the team around him, just to make sure the coaches' message had gotten through. "Never give up, Spartans," he shouted. "Never give up."

The second half, though, lacked the passion of the first half. The loss of their best player had sapped the Bulldogs. The sobering sight of a boy being taken away by ambulance had quieted the crowd considerably. Winslow did score on a long touchdown run late in the third quarter to make the score 27–15. But the Ranch salted the game away with a lengthy, time-consuming drive that culminated with Hughes scoring on a 5-yard touchdown run with 4:58 remaining. The final nail had been driven into the Bulldogs' coffin.

Just about the only second-half fireworks occurred on the Ranch sideline. When the Spartans' offense couldn't move the ball in the third quarter, it was clear to Winchester that his offensive linemen had shifted into cruise control. From his vantage point in the stands, he radioed down the word that Coleman, one of his guards, wasn't doing his job. Winchester told Ta'ase that either Coleman needed to wake up or he was going to be pulled from the game. When Ta'ase relayed that message in no uncertain terms, Coleman became defensive. Ta'ase tried to explain that the Eye in the Sky — Winchester — was singling him out, but Coleman wouldn't hear it. Before long, Ta'ase was addressing Coleman, and Milbrandt and Moore had to go over and intervene.

After the Ranch's final touchdown, in which the Spartans had run the ball down the field behind the improved play of the guys up front, Ta'ase pulled the players in the offensive line over to congratulate them. He grabbed Coleman's face mask. "So, how does it feel?" Ta'ase said, pointing to the scoreboard. "I told you you could do it." Then Coleman gave him a quick hug, which seemed to be his way of saying he was sorry. When the game was over and the Ranch had won 34–15, the players hoisted Gray on their shoulders. The whole time Gray was pointing at the ground and saying, "Put me down, put me down." But the players wouldn't do it. Other kids were hugging each other and dancing around the field. They started up a singsong chant that they had prepared just for this occasion:

Go for the play-offs, Spartans! Go for the play-offs, Spartans!

"I hope you know what you just did!" Allen growled. If the Spartans didn't fully realize their accomplishment, the Ranch's staff sure did. Thomas was walking around with a huge grin on his face. Whitfield, the athletic director, pushed up the bill of his black cowboy hat and let loose a huge sigh. "These kids have been beaten down so long they don't know what success is," he said. "But give them just a taste of success and that makes all the difference in the world."

The one negative to the night Sparkman's getting tossed. Not that they excused his behavior, but the coaching staff gave Sparkman the benefit of the doubt back in the locker room when they talked to the players about what was happening on the field in the first half. Some ugly things had been said, and sometimes it can be hard for teenagers to ignore what they're hearing. "They were calling us all kinds of racial names, nigger and stuff," Sparkman said. "They said they were going to beat our little asses. They were just arrogant about it. Then I think they got frustrated. Oh, man, they were cheap. They were being nasty."

But Sparkman had been the one to act on the ugliness. He had gotten caught, and now it would cost him next week's homecoming game against Show Low. The officials, he said, had treated him unfairly. It was just the latest in a long series of events that had made this season difficult for him. "I know I have a lot of talent, but I'm just not using it all," he said. "I just feel that I can do a lot better than what I'm doing. But then they don't need me." Cabell was nearby and heard Sparkman downgrading himself. "Yeah, we do need you," he said. "We need you bad."

Meanwhile, the celebration continued as the players showered and got dressed. But despite all the hooting and hollering, the Spartans were not yet assured a play-off berth. Only a victory over Show Low in the season finale would clinch that. Gray was the one person in the locker room who realized this. "Nothing's been settled yet," he said. But he didn't want to spoil the party atmosphere. So, with a soft drink in his hand, he went into an empty hallway and squatted down on his haunches. It was the exact same pose he had struck after the demoralizing loss against Snowflake. Only this time, he had a smile of contentment on his face. The Spartans finally were becoming a team.

A few minutes later, as the players filed onto the bus for the long trip back to the Ranch, the Winslow High students were entering their gym for a school dance. Music was beginning to blare, and lights were flashing. Lono Hill looked over at the scene. "Why can't we dance?" he asked. "We won. Not them." Then he turned toward the bus. Life wasn't fair.

The Spartans would get back to the Ranch at 2:45 A.M.

My name is Charles Williams. I'm seventeen, sir. I'm from Merced, California. That's in northern California. I've been here about two years.

There's a lot of things that I've done that I just kind of fell into because I was hanging out with a group. I know the difference between right and wrong, but there was a lot of peer pressure. I was stealing cars — lots of cars, maybe about fifty, sixty. I sold 'em for parts. All kinds of cars are needed to get parts. The price we got depended on the parts they needed. Sometimes we'd get $200, maybe $300. It doesn't take long to steal a car. I only needed about twenty seconds at the most. The best car I ever took was a Caprice Classic. I also took a Mercedes-Benz. But I eventually got caught in a stolen car in a different county. They transferred me back to my county. They gave me ninety days and told me the next time it happened, they'd get me in a placement. It didn't happen again, but I violated my probation by staying out too late.

It's quiet there in my hometown now. It's not the same as it was before. There used to be a lot of gang activity. That three-strikes-and-you're-out law has changed things. I feel bad about stealing all those cars. I know that I hurt people, even if there was insurance to cover the cars.

I've been learning a lot since I've been here. I didn't want to be here at first. I didn't like being away from home. I was supposed to go to Civics, and I didn't want to go. I was scared. I had heard all about Civics, so when they told me that I was being sent there, I thought, "Man, I'm not going." So I tried everything I could think of not to go, but nothing worked. I twisted my ankle playing basketball, so then I tried to use that. I put my ankle in hot water to make it swell up. Then I tried beating on it. I tried sitting in a wheelchair. But I guess I didn't hurt myself enough. I ended up going anyway.

When I first got there, I tried to just walk away. Me and this other kid planned it. We just took off. We waited for a certain time when everyone was busy. We got all the way to the town of Oracle, which was about six or seven miles away. We could have just kept going. But there was nowhere to go. It's just desert down there.

It turned out that I enjoy what I was scared of. In Civics, you've got to go through the struggle. You've got to overcome things. I don't think about leaving now. I know what I need to do. I've got some goals now, to go to college and play football. I want to get a degree and help people like me.

What do I like about it here, sir? I like the football team. I like what I'm becoming. Back home, I was messing up. Here, I'm striving for my *dream, and that's playing football. I'm going to graduate with a high school diploma. I've changed a lot here. I'm not even the same person that I was at the beginning of football season. I feel more patient, relaxed. I've learned that if you wait patiently, you'll get your turn. Before I got here, I had learned to put myself in a shell and put up a front for everyone. Now, I know who I am and I'm not afraid to show that to other people.*

I've got a mom and dad. But my family is pretty messed up. Me and my little brother used to get beat up, so when I was five years old, they took us away. I've been staying in foster homes and group homes ever since. I don't have much contact with my parents now. The only person I have contact with is my foster mom. She's the only parent I have. I keep in touch with her every week. I've got a foster brother who is playing football at the University of Pacific. I've got another foster brother who is playing in junior college, and he tells me not to give up on my dream.

I'm not really mad at my parents. There's nothing I can really do now to change anything. It wouldn't be right for me to hold a grudge against them like that for the rest of my life. I've got to let go sometime. The only thing I can do is be successful. I'm doing something good. I'm not out there running around the streets, gang banging, stealing cars, and all that.

What's gang banging mean to me, sir? It means hanging out with a group and causing trouble. Serious trouble.

I guess it's all about respect. That's what I like about football. You can go out on the field and earn respect. I guess everybody talks about our backgrounds and stuff. But then you can go on the field and let them know that you're not bad. You're not trying to hurt anybody. It's just the way of the game. They're trying to do the same thing that they're trying to do. That's win the game.

GOD'S COUNTRY

The trip from the Phoenix area to Oracle is about 130 miles. The route travels through the heart of the Sonoran Desert. Saguaro cacti guard the way, like silent sentinels.

The small town of Oracle is located north of Tucson. To get there, you must pass by the Biosphere 2 project, a $150 million glass-domed laboratory that rests on the desert floor. For two years from 1991 to 1993, seven people were sealed into this man made ecosystem as an environmental experiment to see if conditions on Biosphere 1 (Earth) could be mimicked successfully. Among the intended goals was to learn more about how people react in a closed system and to get some clues as to whether we could someday put a "world" like this on a spaceship and travel to distant planets. The mainstream scientific community criticized the project for being more of a publicity stunt than real research, and many thought the folks out in the desert (Biospherians they called themselves) might be no more than New Age loons.

On the other side of Oracle is a closed environment of a different kind. Here, the goal is less pie-in-the-sky. One hundred and sixty boys spend an average of eighteen months trying to turn their lives around. A couple of miles beyond the town, the paved road ends and a dirt road begins. For the next six miles, the path cuts through rugged desert terrain. Except for the occasional ranch, there is little sign of life, except for the roadrunners that sometimes dart in front of vehicles. Eventually, the road, if you can call it that, snakes its way up a small bluff. Over the hill is a desert oasis. Set deep in a canyon, a small piece of heaven is revealed.

Thomas often referred to this area as God's Country.

Off the side of the road is a public campground. On weekends, the place is packed with families trying to get away from civilization for a couple of days. But about 100 yards beyond that, if you look hard, is a tall wrought-iron fence. Those were the only bars found at Camp Mary Mullaney, home of the Ranch's Civic Conservation Corps campus. The camp, which was built along a small creek, is almost completely hidden and sheltered by a forest that included sycamore, apple, and peach trees. Among the buildings are a chapel, barracks, classrooms, and a pantry, as well as an outdoor basketball court, a ball field, and an amphitheater. There is never a rock out of place anywhere.

Small bridges and walkways crossed the babbling brook. That little stream once figured prominently in an abuse charge a boy leveled against Ta'ase, who at the time was on the Civics staff in Oracle. The boy accused Ta'ase of holding him under the water while he was being restrained. "There were four people there, but he named me because I was the biggest guy," Ta'ase said. "I made the papers on that one. But that never bothered me because I knew that I didn't do it. I was cleared. But now they call me Ta'ase the Baptist."

In previous existences, this place had been a ranch and then a Salvation Army camp. It had been the home of the Ranch's Civics program since 1991. At first, the residents of Oracle weren't crazy about having a placement facility for juvenile delinquents so close to their quiet town. Staff members even remember a headline in a local newspaper that read: "Kiddie Cons Come to Oracle." Over time, the camp and the town had come to coexist. In fact, residents did work projects for the local school and in turn Civics received permission to use the gym when it was available.

Inside the main gate, the camp was serene-looking, yet it also had the unmistakable feel of a military base. Ta'ase, who was now with the football team up at the main ranch, had warned that the intensity level rose as soon as you stepped on the grounds. He was right. There was a palpable feeling of tension in the air. The Ranch proudly described the place as having a paramilitary atmosphere. As much discipline and structure as there was at the main campus in Queen Creek, it was nothing compared with the environment on the Civics campus. Generally, this was where the older boys went, the ones between the ages of sixteen and eighteen. If, during an initial interview in juvenile hall, it was determined that a boy had a problem respecting authority or had trouble finding the drive to accomplish anything with his life, this was usually where he was sent.

The Civics program motivated kids fast. The football team was about evenly divided between main Ranch and Civics kids. Gray loved working with the kids from the Civics program. "I call it Full Metal Jacket," he said. "They're so good when they come back up here. They look you in the eye. It's all 'Yes, sir' and 'No, sir.' They're real coachable. There's so much difference between the two groups. Now we coaches are telling the Ranch that we've got some more kids on the team that we need to send down there. There's nothing like a little Full Metal Jacket to get them focused."

Kids, of course, hated being sent down to Civics. Charles Williams, who had faked his way into a wheelchair in an effort to stay out of the program, was a perfect example of the lengths to which creative boys would go to keep away from Oracle. "I don't like it down there," added Sparkman, who had "joined" the program after years of being at the main campus. "It's not me. I just don't like the structure and the military stuff."

Residents of the Civics program wore a uniform that consisted of tan pants and shirt, a belt with brass buckle, shined black boots, and a green baseball cap. They marched wherever they went. They would stand at attention and "lock it in"; standing tall, they stared straight ahead with their hands down at their sides, shoelaces tucked in, with no facial expressions. Everyone wore the exact same outfit to reinforce the idea that everyone was being treated as equals. No one could wear jewelry. Residents weren't allowed to have money or material items like radios. Anything that could be construed as setting boys apart was against the rules.

Civics residents learned to ask permission from staff to do everything. If a boy was at the pantry eating and had to blow his nose, he had to ask the staff member sitting at his table if he could go outside and use a tissue so as not to disturb the other people who were eating. When kids made the trip to Oracle to use the gym, the van would be completely silent until the driver announced that it was all right to begin talking among themselves, quietly and appropriately.

The theory at Civics was that idle time and idle minds led to trouble. The kids were up at dawn and to bed early. In between, there was rarely a moment when the boys were doing nothing. The average day would begin anywhere from 6:00 A.M. to 6:30 A.M., when the residents would be rousted from their barracks. There was no reveille call. There was no need for one since most of the staff had backgrounds in the military, and their body clocks seemed permanently programmed for the service way of life. Before breakfast, the boys would police the barracks area and have inspection. There would be school until mid-afternoon. Then there would be P.T. — physical training. It might be something as simple as calisthenics or sometimes games. Only the games were devised as treatment tools to help work on issues such as self-esteem and cooperation.

In the game of dodgeball, for instance, which most kids have played, the object is for players on one team to hit the players on the other team with volleyballs (thus the idea of trying to dodge the ball). When a player is hit, he's out. The twist that Civics put on the game was that when a boy was hit, instead of leaving the court, he would lie down on the floor. Another boy on his team could then drag him back to a designated area where he could "regain life" and start playing again. The idea was to teach the concept of teamwork.

But the heart of the program was the work crews. The name said it all: Civic Conservation Corps. The boys did community-service projects around the state, putting up fencing for ranchers and building desert trails. They would do all sorts of odd jobs for the U.S. Forest Service, as well as work in state and city parks. They were involved in everything from clearing out rocks to cutting down trees. Anything difficult and involving hard labor, they did. Before they came to the Ranch, their idea of work may have been selling crack in an alley. The work crews were designed to show them the pride that could be gained from completing a rugged project. The aim was to make them feel good about themselves. On the right shoulder of their shirt was a patch that summed up the aims of Civics. It read: "Work-Pride-Success."

"The program takes all these kids who have never been very successful at anything in life and tries to get them to fight through that brick wall," explained Henry Johnson, a shift supervisor at the Oracle campus.

There were three steps to the Civics program. The first stage was orientation, when the kids wore red shirts, just like at the main campus. Then there was Phase One, which was the most military in style and the structure was as tight as possible. Then there was the Main Phase, when residents worked on their education and work crews.

"We're not teaching them to be military," Johnson said. "We're teaching them to be human beings. The military part is to keep discipline and organization. The marching is so they can't do that street, pimp walk. We're a reality-based program. We teach them how to act in society. We know if you get mad at your boss, you can't punch him.

You can't go in the broom closet and snort cocaine. They say we do brainwashing here. Well, yes sir, we do. We brainwash them into being responsible young men who are respectful and positive in life. Is that bad brainwashing?"

Civics clearly had a reputation. This was the state's most controversial juvenile placement facility. Or as Thomas bluntly put it, "This is the favorite program of DES [Department of Economic Security]." Johnson said parents who came to visit their sons would sometimes ask to see the room where staff would beat the boys when they got out of line.

"It's sad that people have that image of us," he said. "Parents hear all these horror stories about us. When they come here, they're expecting the worst. They're looking for the eight-foot walls, the wire, the dogs, and the armed guards walking around. Then they see how peaceful it is. They're looking for that prison mentality. We don't need that here. Instead, the trust that we develop allows the boys to relax. This is where kids don't have to worry about the pressure of the gangs and the drive-bys. Kids always have trouble sleeping when they first get here. Then you look in their files and see that they were victims of violent crime, or they did something and they were worried about reprisals."

No gang activity of any kind was allowed at Civics. No affiliations, no signs, no colors, nothing. Johnson said it was hard at first, but eventually staff became trained in looking for even the most subtle of hand movements that were gang signs. Also, staff would go out of their way to make former Bloods and Crips rack mates in the barracks. That way, they could see up close that their alleged "enemy" was a boy just like them. "A lot of friendships form in here," Johnson explained. "But back on the streets, they would have killed each other."

It was a pretty simple world at Civics. As they did at the main campus, the staff created the atmosphere. They made the rules. The residents followed them to the letter. The difference was that absolutely no deviation from those rules was tolerated. Staff would be in the face of residents for any breach of their code. They wanted to show the kids that they had to screw up only once to end up back in jail for good. Another reason for the toughness, Ta'ase explained, was human nature. When somebody gets away with something small, next time he may try to get away with something bigger.

"You always have to be on the lookout for bad behavior," Ta'ase said. "You take every little, minute mistake and blow it out of proportion. Kids say, 'But, Mr. Ta'ase, it's not that big a deal.' But what I tell them is that it's like if you steal a quarter from your mom's purse. Well, maybe next time you steal fifty cents. And on and on. You need to nip these behaviors in the bud. They have to know that you'll always hold them accountable for everything."

Perhaps the most important reason for the extreme structure at Civics was that the boys here were truly the hard-core cases. Some kids who arrived, once they had been separated from their gang, quickly showed themselves to be nothing more than scared boys who somewhere along the way had had their self-esteem destroyed and had tried to find a sense of belonging by joining the street crowd. Then there were the other kids, who came through the front gate firmly believing that they were the masters of their own universe, no matter what the judge may have said. They surely weren't happy about the sudden turn their lives had taken to bring them here. Most were certain that they could somehow beat the system. Why not? They had everywhere else. Johnson said he couldn't remember all the times that a probation officer warned him that a kid was pure trouble and that he had AWOLed or been terminated from every other program in which he had been enrolled. When he arrived, he met staff who were absolutely sure they knew how to solve juvenile behavior problems. What you had were two trains on the same track heading for a collision.

"Nobody gets threatened here," Johnson said. "Everybody knows the boundaries. When they step out of line, that's when they get addressed. When that happens, they know it was because of their behavior. They brought it upon themselves. At least the consequences here ensure that everybody will wake up the next morning. The consequences out there include getting killed. So we tell people to make your mistakes here and learn from them because if you make a mistake out there, you might not wake up the next day."

Inevitably, there was conflict. When boys acted out physically and it looked as if they might harm someone, including themselves, they would be restrained by staff. It happened more in Civics than on the main campus. "They've been on the streets their entire lives, and they only know one way to act, and that's to fight," Johnson said. "You're also talking about a kid who's coming straight from Youth Authority. Being in detention is about defending himself, and he thinks he can continue that mentality of toughness here. In Youth Authority, he had no choice but to be tough."

There seemed to be no single concern state investigators had about the Civics program. But if it had to be summed up, it was that the staff were too hard on the kids. They were too quick to get physical. They pushed kids to the limits of their endurance, both physically and mentally. They created an environment based on intimidation. Most of the Civics staff had done stints in the service. Johnson himself had been in the Air Force. They looked tough. Many were big. Most were in shape. They had an aura about them that seemed to scream: "Don't mess with me." And they were a little cocky.

A Civics staff member recalled how a state investigator, who was looking into a charge of abuse, accused him of putting his hands on a kid. He looked the investigator straight in the eye and said: "Yes, sir, that's exactly what happened. Now you tell me what's wrong with that? While you're at it, explain to me how I've been kicked, punched, spat at, called every name you can think of, threatened and somehow I'm made out to be the bad guy?" Nothing would raise the blood pressure of a Civics staff member more than to ask him about charges that he "terrorized" residents. Even Johnson, a soft-spoken man with glasses, got angry talking about accusations that Civics was little more than a fear-based program that scared the hell out of kids.

"How can a small group of adults terrorize a couple hundred gang members?" Johnson asked. "We've got Crips, Bloods, you name it. So how can these types of kids be terrorized by such a small group of adults, even if we were a bunch of Bruce Lee clones? How do you control some of the most negative behaviors through intimidation? If we're fighting, punching, and all that stuff, the natural reaction is to do the same thing back. We don't want that. Why aren't they beating staff in their sleep? It's not happening. How can people believe these things are happening when there's no mass retaliation? That's why I think it's funny that people think we're doing so much to hurt these kids."

Staff at Civics knew that they were often dealing with deep-rooted emotional problems. Yet, although they would empathize with the boys, they wouldn't sympathize. Residents weren't allowed to use anything as an excuse. They weren't allowed to rationalize their situations or attempt to justify their actions.

"We don't join their pity party," explained Jim Platten, another shift supervisor with an army background. "Suppose a kid was molested as a child. He says, 'Sir, why did he have to do that to me?' That's when I say, 'I don't know why it happened. But we have to deal with today. You can't blame everything that happens in your life from now on because of that. You have to put it behind you.'"

Johnson chalked up most of the problems outsiders had with the Civics program to perception and a lack of understanding of what kind of kids staff were dealing with. He recalled one time when a resident had to be terminated from the program because he beat up another kid. Staff flew back with him to San Diego, and when they arrived at the airport, the authorities were there waiting. They shackled his wrists and ankles as a precaution. "He was shuffling through the airport when two elderly women saw him," Johnson continued. "One lady said to the other, 'It's so sad. What could he have done that was so bad?' What he had done to land him at the Ranch was victimize elderly women, among other things. I wanted to say, 'Ma'am, if you only knew.'"

Generally, it took an awful lot to be kicked out of the Civics program. The theory was that if the staff just kept working with a kid for another day or even another hour, the boy might begin to realize that there was a reason for the uniforms, the marching, the staff being hard-asses about everything. "We tell them that we won't give up on them, and they test us on that," Platten added. "One time, we had a kid we had to terminate, and he told me, 'Sir, you said you'd never give up on us.'" Platten never forgot that comment, because he later learned that when the boy got out of the California Youth Authority, he killed someone.

Like other supervisors at the Ranch, Platten had a particular little speech he would give when he greeted a vanload of new arrivals. It would differ slightly with each group, but the central theme remained the same: This is different from YA. This isn't the hall. You will respond with "Yes, sir" and "No, sir." You will show respect to all authority figures. We are all the same color here. There's no racism. There are no gangs.

Of course, it would go in one ear and out the other. Kids expected the Ranch to be exactly like other placements. They'd just do their time in this damn desert and then go back to their same way of life on the streets. Only over time would they discover that it wouldn't be that easy. Their first hint, though, would be when Platten asked them if they understood the rules.

"Yeah," they would usually respond. Sometimes they would just shrug their shoulders.

"That's 'Yes, sir!'" Platten would bark. Then he would start chewing them out for not standing at attention.

Welcome to Civics.

Platten had gotten particularly tight with Tim Elliott, at least before the boy went up to the main campus to play football. Elliott, he said, had arrived as tough as they come. If you wanted a poster boy for what a '90s gang banger on the streets of inner-city America looked like, then Elliott was your guy. "Tim right away tried to pull the gang crap," Platten said. "He's affiliated with the Bloods. I heard him say something about crab-killing. The Crips are called crabs by Bloods. Tim wasn't subtle about anything."

Platten was there to meet the van when Elliott first arrived at Oracle to begin his indoctrination. He distinctly remembered the first words Elliott ever spoke to him.

"Fuck you."

THE AL CAPONE OF THE BOYS RANCH

Tim Elliott had two options when he faced the court: (1) be given a lengthy sentence or (2) attend and complete the Arizona Boys Ranch program.

That should have been a no-brainer for anyone. On the one hand, he would be behind prison walls. He would start out in the California Youth Authority, but might be transferred to an adult state penitentiary later. The way Elliott remembered it, he was looking at about six years. Or he could spend a couple of years in the Ranch's program. Maybe the Ranch wasn't a stroll in the park, but it sure wasn't jail, either. Besides, he could do the math; two years was shorter than six.

Yet for Elliott, it was a hard decision. And not long after arriving, he figured he'd made the worst mistake in his young life. Down in Civics, he was being told what to do every moment of the day: when to get up, when to sleep, when to eat, when to work. This wasn't for him. He actually found himself longing for a cell, bars, and a fence with that razor wire on top. Somehow he had convinced himself that he would be at this godforsaken place for an eternity. Looking back, more than two years later, Elliott knew his twisted logic sounded ludicrous. But he said people would understand if they had been in the Civics program. Staff were all over him, and he was damn sure he'd died and gone to hell. He liked the life he had chosen for himself, and he didn't want to change.

"I'm a mix of black and Puerto Rican," Elliott explained. "I have a quick temper. When I first came here, I didn't like authority figures, because of my father. He always had something smart to say to me. If I was trying to do what I had to do, like go places on the weekend, then he was always running his mouth and we'd end up fighting. Then

I come here and people are telling me what to do. So that's when I'd say 'F—you.'"

Elliott figured he fought the system for about three months after arriving in September 1993. He almost got himself terminated from the program by lying about his age. Elliott thought he had convinced the staff that he was eighteen going on nineteen, making him too old for the Ranch. His true age was fifteen going on sixteen, which is what officials confirmed when they contacted Elliott's mother, who was trying to take an active role in the rehabilitation of her son. "I said, 'Mom, why'd you tell them? I'm trying to get out of here?'" he recalled. "And she told me, 'No, you gotta be honest with these people.'"

Elliott's mother had been dealing with the gang life for a long time. It ran in the family. Elliott had an older brother who was a Blood, and he kept telling Tim that when he grew up, he was going to be just like him. Sure enough, before long Tim was hanging with his brother. By age eleven, Elliott considered himself a Blood and a member in good standing of the gang-banging community. That meant defending his colors. If he saw somebody from a rival gang, he would fight. If he saw somebody he didn't know in his neighborhood, he would fight. Sometimes he would fight just to fight. Growing up in both Oceanside and San Diego, Elliott knew Peters, the Ranch's fullback. He knew that Peters was a Crip. That's all he had to know about him. At the Ranch they had become good friends. But if they had ever crossed paths on the Outs, Elliott said with absolutely no hesitancy that they would have squared off.

The way Elliott described that period in his life, there were no rules, except for the ones he and his friends made up as they went along. When somebody crossed them, they'd quickly even the score. They get you, you get them back. "You know how people say that it's exciting?" Elliott said one day after practice. "Well, it's not exciting. But the adrenaline is pumping. Plus you have peer pressure to do stuff. You've already got drugs in your system. It's easy to be manipulated to do something."

That was what had happened the time he got shot. Elliott didn't want to get into the details. He said it had something to do with gangs, and he'd leave it at that. But the result was that he was shot in the leg during a street skirmish. Elliott was thirteen at the time. "What do you do when you're shot?" he asked incredulously. "You walk. You run. You're in pain. You're in shock. You think you're going to die as soon as it hits you. You think you're going to die right then. Then the next thing you know, you're up and running. Later you wonder if you should keep on doing what you're doing. Then the next thing you know, you're right there running with your brothers again.

"But, hey, when you live the life, you gotta pay," Elliott added matter-of-factly. "A lot of people ask me, 'Well, how can it happen?' It's no mystery. That's what happens. When you live that life, you reap what you sow. You're either going to die or get locked up. That's the cycle. Party, money, girls, get locked up, die."

Eventually, it all caught up to Elliott with a vengeance as he reached the "locked-up" portion of the cycle. There were some particulars of "the whole little ordeal," as Elliott called it, that he wouldn't divulge. The gist of what happened was that Elliott's gang decided to do a drive-by on members of a gang with whom they were having a serious "rivalry." There were four of Elliott's gang in the car. Shots were fired, and a guy in the other gang was shot in the neck. They were lucky in that the boy survived, although it was touch and go for a time. They were unlucky in that they were caught. Elliott claimed that the authorities couldn't prove who had done what because nobody in his gang broke the code of silence. But Elliott was charged as a knowing accomplice because he was driving the vehicle. That's how he ended up at the Ranch.

Maybe Elliott did figure out after a couple of months that it served no purpose to buck the staff. But whether he did or not, he continued to have his share of troubles. And then he went AWOL during the Ranch's first football season.

The source of the problem was Elliott's son, Alan. Like any father, he loved his child. He noted that the boy had a mouth on him and wondered if his mother had been teaching him bad language. Then, the next minute, he talked about how the boy acted just like him. Alan, who had recently turned three, was with Elliott's former girlfriend. At the time he went AWOL, Elliott was still close with his son's mother, but she had reservations about letting Tim back into their lives. She vividly remembered how he used to act. Elliott kept telling her by phone that he was trying to make positive changes. But he said that she was skeptical and wanted to see those changes for herself and not just hear about them long-distance. Elliott said, "Fine, then, I'll show you."

The Ranch isn't a hotel, however. Residents don't just check out as they please. Home visits must be earned. Elliott wasn't allowed to have a visit right away. "They wouldn't let me see my son," Elliott said. "They said I couldn't get no visit, so I couldn't go home and at least talk to him. So I told the staff that I'd find my own way home. I just got mad and left. There has to be a lot of built-up anger to make some-one run."

When asked how a resident goes AWOL, Elliott smiled and point-ed west. "It's right there across the street," he said. "It's easy to leave. There's nothing to it. Just wait for a moment when nobody is looking and start running. It's only after runners have put some distance between themselves and the Ranch that the reality of their situation begins to sink in. For one, the Arizona desert is not easy to traverse, especially when someone is trying to stay off the beaten path. For another, the runner has no food, no water, and little money.

Nonetheless, Elliott and two other boys started walking. Elliott knew one person in the entire state of Arizona, a girl who lived in the town of Goodyear, which is on the far west side of Phoenix, maybe sixty miles from the Ranch as the crow flies. That's where they head-ed. They just kept on shuffling. They were dead tired. They were hot and thirsty. They talked among themselves several times about giving up and just calling the Ranch and asking someone to come get them. Eventually, they made it to Goodyear, and from there they got a ride back to San Diego. But even when he got home, Elliott was a wanted boy. If he was caught, he would be sent to the Youth Authority. He fig-ured that if he reverted to the gang life, it would only be a matter of time before the bullet he caught wasn't just in the leg.

"When I AWOLed, it was rough," he said. "I had no place to sleep. I was always on the run. Money was getting short. I was either going to rob somebody and end back up in CYA or come back here."

Elliott realized the one way he could help his son was by doing something with his life. As far as he could see, there was only one way to do that. So, after talking over the situation with his mother, Elliott decided to turn himself in. After that, he was transported back to Ari-zona.

"Doing the Re-O [reorientation] thing didn't really bother me," Elliott said. "I can do consequences. Anything they give me, I can do. I don't have a problem with that. It's just when they get to yelling in your face for nothing. That's what gets me mad. If I don't disrespect adults, then I don't want them to disrespect me, either."

There was one other reason why Elliott came back to the Ranch: He still wanted to play football. By the time he returned to the team, Cabell had established himself as the team's No. 1 tailback, the position that had belonged to Elliot before he went AWOL. It was Cabell's spot now, and Elliott spent the remainder of the season playing mainly on the defensive side of the ball. Elliott said he had no problem with that, either. Cabell had a good season, and Elliott felt he was needed on defense more. Besides, he accepted the fact that there would be repercussions for his actions.

Elliott and Cabell had a strange relationship. On the field, they seemed to get along fine. In fact, for two guys who clearly had some talent and were competing for the same position, they seemed to be remarkably friendly. They were different kinds of running backs. Cabell was a speedster. He had breakaway speed that a coach can't develop. A player either has it or doesn't. Elliott didn't have Cabell's quickness, but he had a tenacity that Cabell lacked. If the Spartans absolutely had to have one yard, they gave the ball to Elliott. He didn't so much find holes as create them. A compact five feet eight, 185 pounds, Elliott could run over people. He was the running back who went between the tackles, while Cabell would go around end. The trouble was there was only one football on the field. It would have been easy to understand if jealousies had developed between the two. Yet each one professed to be a friend of the other. Both pulled for the other. Neither pouted when the other was running the ball well.

Nevertheless, the two had a history. The only reason Elliott was even at the Ranch for this football season could be traced to an incident involving Cabell.

"We had our moments, but the reason why we had our moments is because Cabell runs his mouth," Elliott explained. "He ticked me off one day. Now I'm used to him because we've been around each other so long. We're tight again. People have blown it out of proportion. But in this environment, everything is blown out of proportion."

The trouble began back in May as several friends, including Elliott, were preparing to leave the Ranch for good. Cabell had decided to stay until December so he could get his high school degree and play another season of football. Cabell was acting a little tense, and some staff thought that he may have been feeling as if he were somehow being left behind. What started as simple teasing of Cabell by the others quickly escalated. Suddenly, Cabell and Elliott weren't so tight.

Elliott picked up the story from there.

"I got mad at Cabell, and I told a friend to take some money from him," he said. "He went in there, asked for his money, and socked him. Later, Mr. [Mike] Smith asked me what we know. I told him I don't know nothing. So he said he was going to call the sheriff. I told him to go ahead and call the sheriff because I wasn't going to talk. Well, people started talking about how it was my idea to jump Cabell. Well, I didn't jump Cabell. I tried to stick to the story and it didn't work. They told me that the story I was trying to stick to didn't work because everybody had already snitched on me. So I said, 'I'm done talking to you guys. Do what you gotta do.' "

Elliott was charged with aggravated assault for instigating the attack and fined $250, which came out of his bank account at the Ranch. (He had earned the money from summer jobs.) But that was a slap on the wrist compared with what happened next.

Deciding what to do with Elliott fell to Smith, one of the Ranch program coordinators. The day before spring graduation, Smith sat in on a meeting at which Elliott's probation officer was in attendance. They concluded that Elliott wasn't ready for the Outs yet. So the next day, at the same time the graduation ceremony was taking place on the main campus, Elliott was in a van heading back to the Civics camp in Oracle.

"He's like the Al Capone of the Boys Ranch," Smith said. "When that happened with Cabell, Elliott didn't touch him. Elliott sent people in after him."

Elliott was well aware that he was known as the Ranch's No. 1 gangster. He thought the reputation was ridiculous. Elliott said that later he and Cabell talked things out, and on several occasions Cabell said that he didn't have a problem with Elliott and that they had made their peace. At the time he was shipped back down to Civics, Elliott had been at the Ranch for more than eighteen months. He may have been moving in the right direction, but he had yet to see the light and make a complete break with the past. He clearly had made some good decisions that indicated he wanted to change, such as turning himself in after going AWOL. And some staff thought he was close to making a revelation.

Amazingly, about that same time Elliott came to the same conclusion. There was no one reason why his attitude was improving. He certainly didn't give any credit to Civics, which he detested. It could have been his mother, who kept telling him to work the program because he just might find that he was learning something valuable. It could have been seeing his brother change his life. He was no angel, Elliott said, but he was married, had a kid, and was out of the gang scene. His brother kept telling him that the gang lifestyle just wasn't worth it. Elliott figured that he had always followed in his brother's footsteps, so if he could get out, then why couldn't he change, too? Or maybe it was the news from the home front.

"I really can't explain it," he said. "But the [gang] life is getting old. I've had about fifteen friends die. I hear about it and it gets me mad. It makes me think about how I could go home and might die, or maybe I could go on to college. When you've been here as long as I've been here, there's times when you feel like you're just doing time. But I know that this is my last really good chance, so I'm trying to take full advantage of it. There's nothing else you can do."

Like everyone else in Civics, he acted like a clean-cut, all-American boy. He looked you directly in the eye. Everything was yes, sir and no, sir. Yet there was more to it than just physical appearance. The Elliott who was now playing for the Spartans was very much playing the role of a leader, and not of the gang variety, either. Gray gushed over his work ethic. While coaches often could be heard grousing about attitudes of various players, Elliott's name never came up. Elliott knew that the tales he told about himself were in stark contrast to the way he acted now. He said that six months earlier, he wouldn't have been telling his life story in such graphic detail to somebody he didn't know. Elliott said he truly had changed. He wanted people to know what he was before so they could better appreciate what he was becoming.

Elliott felt that some staff members believed he was just putting on a good show for a couple of months. He would not make any waves, get out in December, and then go back to his old ways. But Elliott said a person was either good or bad. You couldn't be both. The way he explained it was that you can't gang-bang and then try to be an upstanding citizen and then go back to gang banging. It doesn't work that way. There are some things you just can't fake.

Besides, football had opened up opportunities he hadn't envisioned for himself. By staying at the Ranch through December, he could play for another season. He used that as the inspiration to deal with more grueling months in Civics. Now that the season had progressed, it was clear that Elliott was a damn good player. Gray was already talking about how Elliott could easily play for an Arizona junior college. If he did well at that level, there was every reason to believe he might earn a scholarship to a four-year university.

"Being shot once was enough for me," Elliott said. "I wish I had gone down the other way. Really, I do. But unfortunately, I didn't."

When Elliott graduated, the court would seal his record. He would have no criminal history. He would be a free man. That would be his reward for sticking it out at the Ranch.

"When I get out of here, all that's in the past," he said.

My name is Lloyd Peters. I'm eighteen years old. I'm from San Diego. I've been here for a year and four months.

I had never thought I was going to change and get out of the gangs and stuff. But then after a while, it hit me that I should try something different. I'm tasting something different. I smell it now. The scent smells good. I'm sure going to taste it when I get out of here.

The change came over a long period of time. It was probably about a year ago that it started. But it was only about four months ago that I decided that maybe I should try something different. When I first got here, I looked around and thought to myself, "You don't want to be here." I wanted to go back to juvenile hall and do my time there. That's when my head was screwed up.

Before, I was selling drugs, gang banging, stuff like that. I guess it's tough to stay away from. I liked being out on the streets. It wasn't like I was living out on the streets. I would go home. And if I didn't go home, I'd stay at my baby's mom's house. I've got a little girl. Her name is Tina Monique. She's two. Her mom and me aren't really together right now.

I was kind of calm out there, but I could be wild at times. I was always on my feet, on my toes, ready to go out and make money. I was into money and women. Sometimes we would go downtown knowing that we was going to get into some trouble, like fight for something or get into some kind of argument. We'd go out looking for money. We basically were on a mission. We'd call it set-tripping. That's when we went out as a gang looking for trouble.

I was young when I got started. We moved to L.A. when I was eight years old, and I got around it there. I gained the attitude and the walk. Then we moved to San Diego. We lived in a place called Oceanside. I just started meeting some friends, and we formed our own little clique. Then we grew up and started claiming the neighborhood as our own.

I was in a gang called WSC. That's for West Side Crips. My nickname was Little Peanut. That's because I was a nut. I was crazy. I was just way out there. There's a Big Peanut. When you get jumped into the gang, you get named after somebody that you remind people of. I always used to want to fight all the time and do crazy things. Wild stuff. Real wild stuff. Once I went to somebody's house, looking for that person, and I was ready to shoot him. But he wasn't there. His mom was there. Some babies were there. I had a gun in my hand. We kicked in the door. He had just shot one of my homeboys, and we wanted to get him. And the mom was screaming, "Policia, policia!" It was just stupid. That's why I'm glad I'm out of it.

You could make a lot of money selling drugs. I used to get a quarter piece of crack, and I would pay about $150 for it. But I got connections where I would sometimes pay only $135. Then you could turn around and sell the dope for $700. And some nights I would sell it all. I'd be out there until 3 or 5 in the morning selling. And if I run out, sometimes some guys would come up to me and say, "You got some more?" I didn't have none, but I'd just snatch their money and run. I'd just act like I was getting change for their hundred and then I'd run.

I tasted that. It tasted good for a while. Then I had to spit some of it out. I'm never going to forget where I came from. Like, I used to have my hair long in braids. That's the style. I'm not going to change in terms of looking all squared up. I'm not going to change totally. But I'm going to stop all that gang banging and live an honest life. I'm going to have my money and have my women. Those are things that I like, and I'm sure a lot of men are like that.

A lot of people say they can't believe I used to do that stuff, but this isn't the first place I was in, although I hope it's the last. But I used to do so good. I would fake it. I would get As. But then something would happen and I would AWOL, or I would get out and start stealing cars or selling dope again. When I first started here, I was faking it. But now I realize that this stuff is serious. It just hit me. I'm glad I came here. I've got an opportunity to taste something else.

I don't think they abuse people here. I think some kids just want to get out of the Ranch. Hey, they restrain people here. But those kids take it overboard. If they realized that the Ranch was doing something good for them, then they wouldn't say that. A lot of the kids here, they need to be restrained, not that staff is going to punch you or nothing. Restraining you keeps you under control. But they keep running their mouth and getting all out of control. If they just shut their mouth and say, "Yes, sir" and "No, sir," that wouldn't happen. It's easy to stop. But it takes some maturity, too.

I graduate on December 22. I'm going to stay out here in Arizona. Mr. Winchester has lined up a job for me in construction, making like $9 an hour. If I went back there, I would probably just end up getting back into the same kind of trouble myself. All that stuff is in the past. My mom likes the way I act now. Before, my speech was kind of messed up. I'm getting good grades, and she likes that. She's happy, and I'm happy that she's happy.

Now I'm glad I didn't find that guy when I had the gun.

Winchester and Milbrandt were in the coaches' office after a midweek practice talking about the offense when Thomas walked in. He wanted to know how Peters had been performing on the field. The coaches said he had been doing fine, especially considering what had been going on with him. Peters had gotten a phone call from his mother, who had told him that she was basically destitute. She was living in a horrible area. She had no food. The electricity to her place had been turned off. "His mom is scared to death just to go out of the house," Thomas explained. "She's in a gang-infested neighborhood. It's awful. I guess they had a murder there a couple of days ago. We're going to put her up in a small hotel in San Diego for a couple of days until we can figure out what to do."

Thomas ended up bringing Peters's mom to Queen Creek and she stayed at one of the Ranch's visitor's cottages for several weeks until she could find a place of her own. The plan was for her son to live with her after he graduated.

"I just wanted to get her out of San Diego," Peters said later, after his mother had arrived in Arizona. "There's a lot of trouble going on back there. She was going to wait until my brother got out of YA back there, but things were getting too rough. The coaches knew that something was wrong with me. I wasn't acting the way I usually act. So I told them what was happening, and they got right on it. They brought her here. I didn't think they would do it so quick. I respect the people here for doing it."

NO KING AND QUEEN AT THIS HOMECOMING

It's a coach's nature to worry. Perhaps it's even part of his genetic makeup. The obstacle that is directly in front of him is always the "biggest challenge" of the season. Gray was no different. No sooner had the Ranch dispatched Winslow than Gray began to fret about the Show Low Cougars, who would be the Spartans' opponent in the final week of the regular season.

The stakes were high. Win, and the Spartans were in the play-offs as the 3A East Region's No. 3 seed. Lose, and there would be a three-team mini-play-off between the Ranch, Show Low, and Winslow to determine the final two postseason berths. The Spartans would have to make the four-hour drive back up to the neutral field of Snowflake on Halloween night the following Tuesday for the play-off. Making that trip was the last thing anybody at the Ranch wanted to do. Gray hardly expected Show Low to roll over, either. The Cougars had started off the season slow but had come on strong late in the year. They were 4–4 heading into the game. The Ranch and Show Low had been on parallel tracks all season, with the only difference being that the Cougars had lost to Winslow and the Ranch had beaten the Bulldogs. Like many other towns in the White Mountains, Show Low was a small, predominantly Mormon community with a long history of having good high school football teams.

There was a great Old West kind of story surrounding Show Low's unique name. The legend was that back in 1876, two feuding business partners — Mario Clark and Indian scout Croydon Cooley — decided to dissolve their land venture and settle their disagreement with a card game. The deck would be cut, and each man would draw a card. Whoever would "show low" got the ranch. Cooley drew the two of clubs and won. Thus the name: Show Low. The main road in town was named Deuce of Clubs.

Something else concerned Gray. The game was on the Ranch's homecoming weekend. The Spartans didn't handle distractions well, and the week would be nothing but one big distraction for the players.

So who attends homecoming at a placement facility for juvenile delinquents? A couple of graduates of the program were planning on coming back for a visit, but most of the guests were going to be family members, and probation officers and judges who had sent boys to the Ranch. All told, the Ranch was bringing in 150 parents for the weekend and putting them up in a motel. About 50 were being transported from San Diego by chartered bus. But it wouldn't be homecoming in the traditional sense. There would be no floats or parade. No girls meant no queen. There would be no king, either. And forget a dance. But as the week passed and Friday approached, signs began appearing around campus. "You Can't Beat the Green Machine." "Go Spartans." "Stomp the Cougars." "You Can't Hide Spartan Pride."

As the parents started arriving on campus Thursday, the coaches became even more nervous. They expected a river of emotions to be flowing Friday night, and they had no idea where those currents would take them. "Who knows where these kids' heads are going to be at," Moore said.

Most of the Ranch's residents had complicated relationships with their families. Some kids hadn't seen their folks in months. Although others were close to their parents, rebelling against them was a primary reason many were here in the first place. By the time a boy landed at the Ranch, the parents were often exhausted from trying to deal with their wild child and ready to give up on him. One of the goals of the Ranch's Parents as Partners support group was to rebuild the bridges between mother/father and son. That was why homecoming was a big deal. It was a chance for the boys to show their parents what they had been doing at the Ranch to change their lives. It also gave the parents an opportunity to show their sons how proud they were of those changes.

"The biggest thing we're worried about is the kids who don't have parents here," Gray said. "Some of these kids, it's real familiar for them. Their parents don't want them around, like during Thanksgiving and at Christmastime."

Some boys, like Sparkman, didn't even have a mom or a dad. Others had folks who just plain didn't care. Milbrandt said that the previous year, one resident's parents had their tickets in hand to come visit their son during homecoming weekend but then for whatever reason just didn't get on the plane. Some of these kids, he added, had been discarded and shunted aside most of their lives. Feelings of abandonment and rage could grow quickly when forgotten boys saw other kids having tearful reunions with their families. It was common at the Ranch for trouble to start over something as small as a phone call from home not being made as scheduled. Then another kid would tease the first boy, saying something like, "Your mom didn't call. Ha, ha, ha."

"It goes to the next level real quick from there," Winchester explained.

As an example of what they were dealing with in this game, Winchester said that Cody Jeffries, the team's quiet center, was upset because his younger brother, who was in another placement facility, couldn't come down for the weekend. At the last minute, the other group home said it didn't have anybody to drive the boy to the Ranch. Winchester was livid because if staff had known earlier, someone at the Ranch would have brought Jeffries' brother down. But at least Ranch officials weren't going to make one mistake they had made the previous season. That year, they had held meetings before the game was played between the kids and their parents and probation officers to discuss the residents' progress. And by the time they got on the field, some kids were in a daze because they weren't happy about what they had heard. This year, the meetings would be held later in the weekend.

When Friday finally did arrive, it was exactly the kind of hectic day around the Ranch that the coaches had feared. There was a breakfast for the parents, who then toured the Ranch. Later the families made banners for the game. There was even a pep rally. While the parents were taken to the stadium to decorate it and have a pregame meal, the players took a nap in the weight room. If the Spartans lost this game, Gray darn well wanted to make sure it wasn't because they were too exhausted after a day filled with activities. He had learned a lesson from the season-opening loss against Ray.

As the players rested, several coaches gathered in their small office. A tape of a previous Show Low game was running on the VCR, but nobody was watching it. Instead, Allen, Milbrandt, and Winchester were shooting the breeze about kids who had passed through the

Ranch over the years. Perhaps it was a way to block out the mounting pressure of the impending game. Milbrandt reached into his desk and pulled out a stack of snapshots. One of Milbrandt's jobs at the Ranch was to oversee the Citizen of the Month program. He would take a picture of each winner, just as a keepsake. He divided the photos and passed some around to the other two coaches, and each started thumbing through them.

Every so often, Allen would smile or shake his head. A couple of times he lifted up a photo to show it to the other coaches as he offered a comment.

"This one's locked up for some kind of shooting."

"This one's dead."

"This one is sharp as a tack, but he's dealing with that KKK stuff back there in his family. Man, it's amazing the stuff we send them back to."

"Remember that one?" Winchester asked, showing everyone a picture. "He was the biggest gang banger here. Now he's running anti-gang workshops. It's true. He's been doing programs, talking about how he's been there and how you can get out of it. Who would have thought he'd go straight?"

The thing you learn quickly, Milbrandt explained, is that it's impossible to predict what these guys will do after they leave. Some kids who you believe have finally seen the light and gotten their acts together will slip right back into old habits the minute they walk out on the streets. Maybe they were just destined to fail no matter what anybody did to help them. Other kids who seemed to have learned nothing during their stay at the Ranch and who were just all-around pains in the asses somehow turned out all right. It was all one big crapshoot.

Shofner walked into the office. He was carrying several copies of a letter, which he gave to the other coaches. It was from a guy who had been a resident of the Ranch a couple of years earlier. He had been a bright, articulate kid. He had also been far too smart for his own good, Shofner added. The kind who think they've got every angle figured out were the boys who always proved toughest to treat. They're intelligent enough to know that they should go straight, but they still think that they're bright enough to beat the system. This boy had eventually AWOLed from the Ranch. Nevertheless, staff thought he was either going to do really well down the road or really bad. There would be no middle ground with this one.

The letter had been sent from San Quentin.

Dear Mr. Shofner:

Hello there! How are you doing? I'm fine under the circumstances. I have not spoken to you or written to you since I left, or anybody from the Ranch for that matter. I did what I did and there is no going back, but I hope that you will accept my apology for all the problems I caused in my leaving. I know you were pretty disappointed in me for doing something so completely foolish even after I really started to get somewhere. I ask that you read this letter to anybody in hopes that they start believing that [going to prison] it can happen to them if they don't take their program and, more importantly, their lives more seriously — especially those foolish hard heads who are sure in their minds that the Arizona Boys Ranch can do nothing for them.

Let me tell you a little something about what the Ranch did for me. The Ranch built up in me self-esteem and self-awareness that I had never known by simply introducing me to some good hard work and by teaching me some basic morals and values like responsibility, discipline, honesty and trust. These simple but seemingly hard things can take a man a long way in the society today. These things make life a lot easier. I don't mean easy in that you will go out and your first job will be for $10 an hour or that you will find a nice place to stay cheaply. What I'm saying is that these things will help you struggle through the rat race today and eventually give you what you want tomorrow. The sad thing is that some of you listening to this are still going to end up in prison or worse because you don't believe that it can happen to you.

My stay at the Ranch wasn't all full of trouble. I achieved two of the most important things in my life during my stay at ABR. A few days before I turned 17, I graduated from high school. I was the first one in my family to do so in a long time. The other was that I started college. I'm the only person ever in my family to do that. Also, while I was attending college, I lived in Wilbur Cottage and had a very good job at the pantry, ordering and maintaining the inventory for all foodstuffs in ABR. So I pretty much had it made. Then it all ended in one very stupid move. I was faced with a little adversity and I turned tail and ran like a coward. I guess I had still figured I could run away from my problems. I was also coward enough to drag someone down with me by taking him with me when I ran. I only took him to use him to get what I wanted, and then I ditched him in Phoenix while I flew back to California and temporary freedom.

Well, enough about what I did. Now let me tell you what I am currently doing. I went to California Youth Authority and did a year and a half in Preston. I was paroled on April 4, 1995. On April 10, I was back in county jail with 10 new felony charges. I still had not figured it out. Let me rephrase that. I had it figured out, but I just chose not to use the qualities that ABR had taught me. Now I'm 19 and in California's oldest prison, San Quentin, where every day it is not a guarantee that you will live to see the next day. I'm under a guard with a rifle all day, every day. There is a big sign on the wall across my cell that says: NOTICE — NO WARNING SHOTS ARE FIRED IN THIS UNIT. If that's what it takes to snap you back into reality, then so be it. Just remember in the end it's nobody's fault but your own. Don't wait for that. Change now. It's not too late yet.

I guess I had better quit my preaching. To wrap this up, I have a poem I want to share with you all, staff and kids. Take it how you want to, but believe every last word, because it is true. Don't let this poem apply to you in your life. You don't have to, so why even go there?

The enclosed verse was a fairly well-known piece of jailhouse prose. Shofner had seen it before. It was called "Remember Me."

> *Prison's no place for an innocent child.*
> *There's no room for the meek, no room for the mild.*
> *The nights are so lonely I toss in my bed.*
> *The days are so weary, I face them with dread.*
> *Grant me one prayer as you did from the cross,*
> *For that thief who knew that his life was a loss.*
> *Please come to this prison where I sit alone.*
> *Surrounded by razor wire, guard towers and stone.*
> *Broken and penitent, forgotten and lost.*
> *On the trash heap of regret where my life was tossed.*
> *I've no other place left on this earth.*
> *Remember me, O Lord. Renew me my birth.*
> *Come to the prison, enter my cell.*
> *Save me, forgive me, in this man-made hell.*
> *And if in this life, no home here I see.*
> *In your kingdom of forgiveness Lord,*
> *Please, remember me.*

The letter ended with a goodbye to Shofner and a final note that the writer now had two strikes against him under California's new three-strikes-and-you're-out law. The next time he was caught for something, the sentence automatically would be 25 to life.

"We always knew he was going to be something," Shofner said, rubbing the back of his neck. "He was the total package. He could be whatever he wanted to be. It's just a shame. Whatever he did, it was serious. That's why he's at San Quentin."

It was too bad, Allen said, because this kid could have done anything with his life.

"When he was doing well, that's when he would run," Allen added. "Every time he'd run, we'd go out and bring him back. He was just bored. That's when he got into trouble. His family life was shot to hell. He literally was living in dumpsters before he got here. But anybody who ever trusted him, he screwed them over by stealing from them. He did whatever he had to do to survive. That's the story of a lot of these kids."

Allen folded up his copy of the letter.

"I keep these," he explained softly. "I've got a million of 'em. Well, not really. But I've got a lot of 'em."

There were good letters, too: from former residents who said they had straightened out their lives and had steady jobs and were raising families. But these were the ones that really stuck with staff. On an intellectual level, they knew they couldn't save everyone. They understood that kids who arrived here were already traveling down a road to ruin. If the Ranch turned out to be only a rest stop along that highway, at least the staff had given it their best shot. Maybe they would get through to the next kid. It wasn't their fault that somebody left the Ranch and immediately reached for a gun or a hit of crack. That kid made his own choices. At the Ranch, staff were big proponents of the concept of free will. Yet it was impossible to get close to a kid and learn everything about him and his family and not develop an attachment. A bond would form, even if it wasn't a tight relationship. The staff would have been less than human not to feel pain upon learning that one of their boys had failed — or worse.

"It's tough when you get that phone call that tells you one of your former kids got shot or just robbed a bank and now is serving life," Ta'ase once said. "Those are the bad times. We're not a cure-all here.

We just try to share our knowledge, and hopefully these kids will get a grasp on what we're saying."

At that moment Allen, a huge and powerful man, looked incredibly sad as he put the most recent letter in his pocket.

———

The Highland stadium was decked out with banners, just as any high school would be on homecoming. There were even cheerleaders: the daughter of a Ranch staff member who attended ASU and some of her college friends were wearing green-and-white cheerleading uniforms made especially for this night.

The Ranch had drawn large crowds all season because most of the staff showed up, and residents usually were brought in to watch the games. Friday night had become central to the Ranch's social schedule. Everyone had a role at the games, even if it was just waving green-and-white pompoms and yelling "Go Spartans!" Part of the reason for starting high school sports was to "normalize" the Ranch, make it more like any other school. In that respect, the football team had been a huge success. There was an electricity on the main campus every Friday that was missing other days. The game was something everyone looked forward to, something that was not part of the ordinary grind. This crowd was even bigger and more vocal because of the contingent of parents. Some families were watching the boys play football for the first time. You could almost reach out and touch the anticipation.

And some of the players looked scared to death.

Adding to the carnival-like atmosphere was a four-person television crew from California in town to do a story about the Ranch and the football team. The crew had followed the players around during pregame drills and had filmed in the locker room before the game. Kids are kids, and several Spartans were doing their best to mug for the camera. So, instead of trying to pump up the emotional volume, Gray decided to take the low-key approach before taking the field.

"We don't need a big pep talk to go out and play football," he said. "Show Low has to win the game. We can't let them. That's what makes sports fun. That's what makes it exciting. When we coaches met for the first time last spring, we said that we were going to do one thing." Then Gray unfolded the T-shirt he was holding. It was one of the shirts printed with the team's slogan: Whatever It Takes.

"That's what we're going to do tonight: whatever it takes," Gray added. "Let's go out and prove what you're made of. Let's go take care of some business."

It sounded good, but privately Gray had no idea what was going to happen in the next two hours. "There was so much apprehension in their bodies today," he had said earlier while watching the team stretch during warm-ups. "You could literally see it. The players were nervous wrecks. Now we'll see what the night holds."

Less than four minutes into the game, Gray was already finding out. The Ranch received the opening kickoff but was forced to punt after going nowhere on three plays. After taking the kick near midfield, Show Low marched smartly down the field on just four plays, scoring the game's first touchdown on a 15-yard run. The extra point made it 7–0. The Ranch would not be in for an easy night.

But the Spartans struck right back. Elliott made a 30-yard run, which helped move the Ranch deep into Show Low territory. Still, the Spartans were facing a fourth-and-8 at the Show Low 9 when McKissic, as he had done so often all season, took matters into his own hands. The Ranch called an option play, and he ran around the right side, faked the pitch to a running back, lowered his head, and pushed his way through what seemed like the whole Cougar defense and fell into the end zone. There was a bad snap on the extra point try, and little Andrade was quickly tackled when he made a feeble attempt to run with the ball. That left the score 7–6 midway through the first quarter.

After that, things slowed down for both teams. They spent virtually the next twenty-one minutes punting the ball back and forth and occasionally giving it up on downs. The Ranch side of the stadium fidgeted. The Civics kids made their customary thunderous noise. The visiting families were quiet as they watched the proceedings. They had expected to witness their sons' crowning achievement: making the state play-offs. Instead, the possibility was dawning on them that they might end up having to console their boys after a bitter defeat.

In the closing moments of the second quarter, the Ranch finally caught a break. After a short Show Low punt, the Spartans got the ball at the Cougar 41. The Ranch immediately ran a trick play. McKissic pitched the ball to Cabell, who then threw a halfback pass across the field back to McKissic that went for 20 yards to the Show Low 21. After an incomplete pass, McKissic scrambled for 6 yards, and an inadvertent face-mask penalty on Show Low tacked on 5 more yards. So, on the last play of the half, Andrade lined up for a 27-yard field-goal attempt. In its two-year football existence, the Ranch had never tried to kick a field goal. With Andrade, even extra points could often be an adventure. But Gray still sent the kicking team on the field and hoped for the best. The snap was good. Andrade's boot was high enough and long enough . . . and just barely slipped inside the left upright. The Ranch crowd, which had had precious little to cheer about all night, came alive. The horn sounded, and the Ranch lined up and jogged off the field clinging to a tenuous 9–7 lead.

The Ranch coaches were far from happy. Their worst fears were coming true. The players seemed unfocused. Playing in front of their folks seemed to have unnerved them. Maybe they were so desperate for parental approval that they were just trying too hard. But even worse, they had been turning on one another again when things went poorly on the field. It was as if the tension of the moment had gotten to them. But back in the locker room, it was deathly quiet. As most of the coaching staff huddled outside the locker room to discuss halftime adjustments, Ta'ase prowled around inside. Anger poured off him like sweat. "Don't be hanging your freaking heads," Ta'ase shouted. "We're winning. We should be winning by more. Don't give me that freaking negative attitude. Think positive." But the players kept staring at the locker room floor. This had been a team the week before. Now it seemed to be every boy for himself. Nobody wanted to look at anybody else.

Despite what's shown in the movies, the best locker room talks are not the "Win One for the Gipper" speeches. The best way to fire up athletes is not by telling them to win for somebody else, but by reminding them why they need to win for themselves. Win, and all their hard work has been worthwhile. Lose, and they're left wondering if maybe, somehow, they just don't have what it takes. All the effort that the collective group has committed to the cause will have been wasted in defeat. This was the point Gray sought to emphasize as he called for the team to gather close. Like a veteran roadside preacher working in his tent, Gray started slowly and gradually picked up steam as he went on, building pace and volume with each sentence. The flock of faithful hung on his every word.

All their lives, he told them, they had been battling stuff like this. "You ever notice how it's not as fun when things turn negative? It's probably the same way at home, and the same way at the Ranch. It's not as fun when you've got a negative attitude. I come in here and look around at our faces and I see a lot of little things that don't need to be in our minds right now. Are we in this together?"

"Yes, sir!" came the automatic, almost robotic, response.

Don't just say "Yes, sir," Gray growled back. I want to know if you really mean it. Are we just eleven guys playing on the field and everybody else just standing around on the sideline not caring? I hope not. I hope that we can learn to stand together. I'm not going anywhere. Win or lose, I'm going to stand right next to you. I'm not going to turn my head to blame anybody, and I don't expect anyone else to do it, either. But what I see right now is a team that's not working together. I see people thinking about "I." Not the team. Not the goal of the team. Not the good of the program. But "I." We're out there arguing. If you don't feel like you're part of the green, then take your shirts off right now. Guys, it's not the game that's important. It's what's in the game. This is a team effort. What, can we only do it one time at Winslow? Is that the only time we can be brothers? Good things will happen to us if we stick together. But right now, we're all standing alone. This is football. It's a team sport. There's no "I" or "me." Now let's go play like a team.

When Show Low's first drive of the third quarter went nowhere, the Cougars had to punt. Only there was a high snap, and Armstrong corralled the punter before he could kick it away back at the 13-yard line. Two plays later, Cabell was sweeping in from the 9-yard line for the Ranch's second touchdown. On the two-point conversion try, Peters forced his way up the middle and into the end zone to give the Ranch a 17–7 lead.

On the sideline, Thomas was doing Jerry Jones proud. After the touchdown, the film crew from California did an impromptu interview with him. Caught up in the moment, he talked excitedly about what kids can do if they are just given the chance. Then he went on to say that he knew the Spartans would come alive in the second half after they got the jitters out of their systems. Now, he concluded, viewers were going to see the real Spartans.

But it was Show Low's turn to demonstrate its resiliency. The Cougars went down the field on twelve plays. It was like a long, slow cattle drive. Round 'em up. Move 'em out. It was capped by a 4-yard touchdown run with 3:17 left in the quarter. The two-point conversion attempt failed, but the Ranch lead had been cut to 17–13.

That was the way the score stayed until the middle of the fourth quarter. The Ranch's high-power offense had been bottled up most of the game. The defense had spent a long night on the field and was starting to wear down. Show Low began moving the ball again. Like every other team that had played the Ranch this season, the Cougars were having some success with the short passing game. One throw-and-catch went for 23 yards, moving the ball into Spartan territory. It was beginning to look as if the Ranch might be in serious trouble, not to mention heading back up to Snowflake on Halloween night for a play-off. The worst-case scenario was on the verge of playing itself out. Then, faced with a third-and-4 situation at the Ranch 37 with 5:25 left, the Show Low quarterback faded back to pass. He thought he saw a receiver open, and maybe he was free for a moment. But by the time the ball got there, McKissic had stepped in front of it and intercepted the throw at the 26-yard line.

Given the opportunity to throw a knockout punch, the Ranch tossed a haymaker. With Cabell and Elliott taking turns, the Spartans started ripping off chunks of yardage. Seven. Fifteen. Ten. Those were the body blows. Then Elliott went for the chin. He took a handoff from McKissic, headed off tackle, and raced 45 yards down the right side of the field. He didn't stop until he reached the end zone. There, he dropped to one knee and said a quick prayer of thanks. Behind him, Show Low players fell to the ground in despair because they knew that their season was over. The final score was 23–13.

A wild celebration began as the final seconds ticked off. The players began dancing and jumping around. Even the coaches let loose. "We're in there, we're in there!" a player shouted. "We're going to state!"

They were. Three months earlier, many of them didn't know if a football was pumped up with air or stuffed. Now they had finished the regular season with a 6–3 record and a third-place showing in the toughest small-school league in Arizona. They had not lost in a month. With every game, they were improving. Each week the coaches were expanding the playbook as the Spartans' grasp of football improved. The coaches had known from the start that they had some God-given talent on this team, but thoughts of actually making the play-offs were entertained only in their daydreams. Yet here they were, going to state. The festival-like scene continued after the teams shook hands. Boys hugged one another. Parents and family members came down from the stands. Gray got another ride on the players' shoulders. Some players even posed for pictures with their probation officers.

"I knew that to get here would be a long trip," Gray said once the players had put him down. "I didn't know if we were capable. What you can't measure is what's in their hearts. These kids are growing. You hope that they're learning some lessons. You try to make them believe that what's on the scoreboard isn't the important thing."

Then Gray turned around and looked at the score himself.

"That sure is a beautiful thing to look at, though," he added.

The TV crew from California was still filming when Gray pulled the team from friends and family for a few moments and brought the players together in the end zone. He told them how proud he was of how they had come together as a team again in the second half, of how they should be proud of what they had done this season. They had opened some eyes around the state, he said.

"When we first started, you were thirty-second out of thirty-two teams," Thomas added. "But now you've learned how to win. People at Boys Ranch know what effort is and what you get when you give 100 percent. We accomplished something tonight as a football team. But you did something else. You proved to the world that you can do any doggone thing you want to."

That night, Armstrong didn't get any sleep. He just kept replaying Gray's halftime pep talk in his head over and over again. He remembered how Gray had told them not to let all their hard work slip away from them now when they were so close to reaching their goal. Armstrong had refused to let his season end that way.

———

The following Monday, Milbrandt took Armstrong to a local resort for a lunchtime meeting of the East Mesa Rotary Club. The group sponsored the Ranch's Citizen of the Month award. Winners received a plaque and a $50 savings bond. Armstrong was that month's recipient. A snapshot of him would join the rest of the Polaroids tucked away in Milbrandt's desk. Dressed in slacks, a blue shirt, and a stylish tie, Armstrong looked like the model for upstanding American youth. His gray hair, which Armstrong said ran in his family, made him appear a little distinguished as well. When Armstrong stood up to receive his award, he told the Rotarians that he was hoping to attend a local community college after he graduated in December. "I plan on majoring in general business and playing a little football," he said.

Later that night, after dinner, Armstrong was walking past the practice field from the pantry toward his cottage. As the sun set on the Ranch, he talked about his personal goals in greater detail. He didn't know what he wanted to do, but he knew exactly what he didn't want.

"I don't want to go back to where I've been," he said. "I don't want to be anywhere near that place. I want no part of the lifestyle that I once lived. That's why I have high expectations for myself. My long-range goal is to start a family, and do it the right way. I want to show my kids the childhood that I never had. I had to learn everything myself. That meant a lot of times I had to learn the hard way."

For weeks Armstrong had been filling out college financial-aid forms, and he had been stunned to learn that there was scholarship money available for someone like him, who was a ward of the court and, for all intents and purposes, had no parents. The government actually was going to give him the cash to attend college. Imagine that. Every school he had sent the aid information to had responded favorably. They all wanted him. College wasn't just a dream anymore. It was only weeks away now. But which school? That was when he received his second shock. Colleges were beginning to seek him out because of what he was doing on the field. Like Cabell, he had received a letter from NAU. Eastern Arizona was interested in him, too. He was beginning to realize that football might be a boarding pass that he could use to transport himself somewhere else.

"I've surprised myself," he said. "I really have. It all comes down to work. I've found that to get what you really want, to have the best, it takes hard work. I've been told that a lot, but stubbornness made me learn it the hard way, by coming here. Football has brought a big change in my attitude. It has made me learn that you really have to work for a cause. It's just like in life. Sometimes you don't want to work hard. You want to take the easy way out. You can't really do that in football."

Gray believed that Armstrong was one of the best high school players in Arizona. He was having a great season, making three or four tackles a game behind the line of scrimmage and chasing players down all over the field. Gray added that Armstrong was everything a coach wanted in a defensive lineman, and it would be a crime if he wasn't picked for the all-state team. Gray also thought that Armstrong could go on and play at one of Arizona's junior colleges. But he was a little worried about Armstrong, too. Gray noted that he was always so serious about everything. He was always worrying, and he never laughed or smiled. Gray just wished Armstrong would enjoy football a little more. After all, it was supposed to be a game.

Most boys at the Ranch maintained that they had no desire to return to their old ways but would admit that their previous lifestyle had been good for some kicks while it lasted. Ask Armstrong if his pre-Ranch days were fun, and he would tell you that you were asking the wrong question. Armstrong had a difficult time with the concept of fun.

"When you're here, of course you say what you did before was dumb," he said. "But when you're out there, you love what you're doing, like getting high. All you want to do is eat, drink, and be merry. The only way to be merry is without going through the struggles. I learned from Frederick Douglass that without struggle, there is no progress. To me, that means if you're not struggling to do something with your life, then you're not progressing. With my generation, the only way you can have fun is with a drink, or a smoke, or a snort. A shoot of this, a shot of that. I've learned that's not the way to go. Maybe a lot of it was fun. But I try to separate fun from whether it was responsible or good for you. It was fun, but it wasn't the best for me."

Sermonettes like this one made most adults wonder what the hell Armstrong was doing in the juvenile court system. Armstrong obviously was a deep thinker. In fact, he was sick of being told he had so much potential.

"I've heard that from preschool on up," he explained. "They look at me and say, 'That boy has potential, but . . .' I'm tired of hearing that word, 'but.' I want to know what comes after potential. I have a little arrogance. My English teacher taught me that a little arrogance is OK because it shows a sense of pride. But there are times when my self-esteem drops so low. I look around and think to myself, 'What's to be proud of? I'm still at Boys Ranch.' If I do anything wrong here, there's a net to catch me. It's like circus-act people. It's all nice what they're doing up there when there's a net below to catch them. But you take that net away, then that is the most amazing thing. It's breathtaking.

That's how I want to look at myself. If I can do all this good stuff out there where there's no net, then I can step back and say to myself, 'Now I'm somebody.'"

My name is Amenweah Yuoh. I'm seventeen, sir. I'm from San Jose. I've been here a couple of months.

I like the sports program here. On the Outs, I wouldn't be in school. But the sports here, it makes you want to go to school. I played football at Oak Grove High School. It's on the south side of San Jose. When I got to high school, I played basketball. Then the basketball coach told me that I should play football. So I went out for the team my sophomore year and started at tight end and outside linebacker for the JV. Then I started getting into the system, so I couldn't play any more sports.

When I got interviewed, I heard there was a sports program here. They asked me if I want to come here, and I said yes. The court took it from there. I was in juvenile hall at the time. It's a detention center where you go while the courts decide what they want to do with you.

My problem was that I started hanging around with the wrong crowd. I started drinking, doing drugs, chasing girls, selling drugs, stuff like that. And before I knew it, I was here. If you don't have any self-discipline, it's not real hard to get involved. It was real easy to get me involved in that stuff, and it went from there. My coaches were always warning me. But the coaches, they can't follow you home. They can't be out with you every night when you're on the streets. They can only tell you after practice what you should do to stay out of trouble. When you go somewhere, you forget about all that. I didn't have all that in mind when I did the stuff I did.

I guess I was just an average kid getting into trouble. Parents tell you to do one thing, and you say, "OK, mom, I'm not going to do that." Then when she turns her back, you do it. I can't say that I totally respect my parents because if I did, I wouldn't have done all the stuff that I did. Maybe I do respect them, but when it came to getting into trouble, I would forget what they told me. I would just do what I wanted to. I wouldn't think about who it would affect, besides me. Now I think about who it would affect: my parents, my family, me, as well as other people.

When I started high school, I was pretty clean-cut. I was all excited about school. My freshman year, I had a little bit of fun. But that year I started shooting dice, hanging around with the wrong crowd. My sophomore year, I cleaned up my act a little bit because I realized what I was doing. Playing football cleaned me up somewhat. Then I started getting into trouble again. My first offense was serious; it was retaliation. I was young. I was with that wrong crowd again. I did what I had to do. And when I did that, it came down on me. I got locked up for attempted murder.

I was just walking down the mall, trying to meet girls. A guy bumped into me, and I asked him what was his problem. He got all mad and I guess he got all of his friends. I went to go home on the trolley and got jumped. I found out who he was, and one night he and his friends had a party, and we went over there and started fighting. People were getting hit over the head with mirrors and stuff, and some kid ended up getting in a coma. He came out of it and was all right, but me and about three of my friends got accused. Another friend, he had a real good lawyer, so he only got house arrest. But if you didn't have a good lawyer, you got sent to some kind of placement. They dropped the charges down to something like assault with a deadly weapon and four counts of assault. I got sent to a placement in San Jose for that. I did five months there. I got out. Then I got locked up again. I was in and out with, like, violation of probation and stuff like that. Now I'm here.

You can take out a lot of aggression in football. For me, it's good because all the time you would spend in the cottage, giving you time to do something wrong, you're out practicing on the field instead. You can still get in trouble on the football field, but this makes you want to do more with yourself. I would like to maybe get a scholarship. That's my goal. I lost my defensive position so I'm struggling right now. I guess I wasn't in shape when I got here, so I had my position taken away from me. I guess that's going to make me work harder to get it back. I'm going to be here next year. Hopefully I can start on the football team then, too.

I really don't know yet what I want to do. I like sports, but I know that I've got to get an education. In a way, I want to play sports, but I want to get an education first. Sometimes I can get lazy. I need somebody to stay on me all the time. When I get out, I know that I'm not going to have someone to stay on me like that. It's going to be hard. I know that this is my last placement before I get in the adult system.

I have a son. He's two months old. I haven't seen him since I got here. I have pictures and stuff, and I call home every week. His name is Junior. Amenweah Yuoh, Jr. Me and his mom, we have a good relationship, but it didn't work out. But we both know that we have a job to do. You don't have to like each other to take care of a child. I get along with her in a friendship kind of way.

My name is African. It's from Ghana. That's what my mom says. I guess my real dad is African. But I don't even know what he looks like. I don't know where he is. My boy is the main reason why I'm trying hard here. I don't want somebody else bringing him up. Somebody else brought me up. I'm not blaming my dad. But I don't want to do the same thing.

WHO'S GOT THE BALL?

"I don't think a single Boys Ranch player even laid a hand on him, folks!"

The announcer at the Bradshaw Mountain High School football stadium was gleefully throwing a little salt into the Spartans' open wound. It was late in the third quarter, and a Bear running back had dashed the length of the field with a kickoff. The announcer was right. The player had streaked down the turf untouched. Even though the extra point was wide right, the Ranch was now down 20–6, and maybe out.

It looked bleak for the Spartans. You could almost hear the hissing sound as air escaped from their balloon. The players sensed that they were watching their season end. Several had thrown down their helmets in frustration. Others were cursing, although they were wise enough to make sure that no staff were within earshot. It was freezing here in Prescott Valley, and the Ranch players were cold and discouraged. The Spartans seemed to just want the game to be over.

What a strange week it had been. It was as if the team had been on an emotional teeter-totter for days now. Up and down, up and down. It had started right after the Show Low game. The Ranch's first-round play-off opponent would be Bradshaw Mountain. The Spartans would have to travel to their field because the Bears had been the No. 2 seed in 3A West Region. The higher seed got the advantage of hosting in the first round. The Ranch coaches were certain that they had drawn the shortest straw of all the East Region teams in opening-round games. It was considered gospel at the Ranch that the East was the best 3A conference in the state. All season the coaches had talked about how, if they got to the play-offs, they wouldn't meet a team that was better than any they had played in the regular season. Bradshaw Mountain, however, was the exception. *The Arizona Republic* had even picked Bradshaw Mountain as its preseason No. 1 team. The Bears had finished the regular season 7–2 and been ranked No. 5 in the state Associated Press poll. One of their losses had been against a 4A school. The Bears had won six in a row. They had outscored conference opponents, 319–34. But what really had Gray on edge was that the Bears had one of the best quarterbacks in the state, and the Ranch had a defensive secondary that was consistently shredded by even marginally talented QBs.

The previous year, the Spartans had visited Bradshaw Mountain and gotten pounded, 46–19. It could have been worse. The coach was a class act and called off the dogs in the second half. The quarterback, who was the coach's son, had absolutely destroyed the Spartans. Standing on the sideline, Milbrandt had caught himself marveling at the perfect passes the kid threw, even though he was carving up his own team. "You hated to see him drop back because you knew that even if everybody was covered, he was going to run, and he could just kill you that way, too," Milbrandt added. By now the boy had thrown a state-record seventy-four touchdown passes and for nearly 5,500 yards in his four-year career. He also starred on defense, which was why Gray figured that he probably would end up being a Division I college player as a defensive back rather than a quarterback.

The Ranch looked to be in for a heck of a challenge. But when Moore went to a neutral site somewhere between Phoenix and Prescott Valley to exchange game films with the Bradshaw Mountain coach, he sensed that something was wrong. Gently trying to probe for information, Moore asked the coach how his son was doing, because earlier in the year the boy had suffered a minor leg injury. At the mention of his son, the coach began to tear up and explained that he wouldn't be playing Friday night. He had been hurt in the final regular-season game. At first, Moore figured that the coach was just trying to pass along some disinformation. But the more he thought about it, he became convinced that the man wouldn't make up something like that about his son. Sure enough, the news hit the *Prescott Courier* a couple of days later. The quarterback had suffered a broken arm in the fourth quarter of the last game. He was out for the play-offs, and his backup, a fourteen-year-old freshman, would start in his place.

The Spartans had caught a colossal break, so to speak. But Moore said it didn't matter one way or the other; the opponent wasn't what concerned him. The Spartans' real foe, he explained, was themselves. "We can go as far as we want to as long as we don't kill ourselves and get to fighting among ourselves," he said. As the week went on, those words would take on very real meaning. The Spartans had little time to reflect on how the quarterback's injury would affect Friday night's game. The Spartans were having their own problems. Bradshaw Mountain had lost one of its best players, but the Ranch had also lost one of theirs.

Sparkman had quit the team.

There was nothing understated about Juan. When he was having a bad day, everybody knew it. The Wednesday practice was a prime example. It started off harmlessly enough. The team had been working on reverse plays in which the wide receiver gets the handoff. It was the kind of gadget play that might have taken advantage of Sparkman's quickness. But Sparkman somehow kept ending up in the wrong position. When Gray corrected him, Juan started arguing. He threw his helmet down. He was told to pick it up. But Sparkman decided to pout and stomp off, refusing to respond to the coaches' questions and orders.

"Are you with us or not?" Gray asked. Juan said he wasn't. "So we decided to call it a season because we were heading for a confrontation," Gray said.

After practice, both Ta'ase and Gray talked to Sparkman again, but he continued to say that he was quitting. The mood was glum back in the coaches' office. Nobody wanted to lose Sparkman now. It was too close to the end of the season. He had made it this far, and it was important that he finish what he had started. The coaches weren't even that upset about losing Sparkman as a player. He was already having a disappointing season. When Gray took the job, everybody had told him that Sparkman would be one of the kids who would carry his team in the fall. Just wait until you see this kid Juan. He runs like the wind. He's got that football mentality. "Juan," Gray said, "was supposed to walk on water. But he's getting to the point where he's just figuring out that he's not what people were saying about him. I think that's why he's having a tough time right now." He had some moments. But, others like Elliott, McKissic, and Armstrong had become not only the stars, but the team leaders. As the year went on and Sparkman struggled, he became more and more frustrated. It must have been difficult to see the team finally coming together, knowing that he contributed only a minor part to its success. This was supposed to be his year, his team.

The worst moment came after the Show Low game, which Sparkman couldn't play because he was serving his one-game suspension for being ejected against Winslow. Elliott had taken over Sparkman's strong safety position in the defensive secondary and impressed the coaches. They planned to start Elliott there again in the Bradshaw Mountain game. They tried to explain to Sparkman that not only would this be better for the team, but it would free him up for more plays on offense. That was why they were working on the trick-play reverses in practice. None of that got through to Sparkman, however. His anger over losing his position just added to his general unhappiness about the whole season. He had made up his mind. He was done.

The coaches were almost as upset as Sparkman was. Every single one of them liked him. He might have been hard to handle sometimes, but there was something about Juan that made him worth the seemingly endless hassles. Maybe it was his infectious smile. Or perhaps it was the gut feeling people had that somewhere deep inside, there was a kid with a good heart. They could live without Sparkman the football player. But they didn't want to lose Sparkman the boy. They knew that this was the worst thing Sparkman could do to himself. And tragically, for Sparkman, this was a familiar pattern.

Milbrandt pointed to a bulletin board next to his office desk. There was a group picture from some sporting event years ago. In front was a younger, smiling Sparkman. He was maybe twelve years old. It was a reminder of just how long Juan had been here. In a very real sense, he was the son of every staff member at the Ranch. "This definitely isn't good for Juan," Milbrandt said. "But I truly feel that it's out of anxiety. Juan is so good at sabotaging what's good for him."

Milbrandt recalled a time when Sparkman lived at Robson House and even attended Mountain View High, a public school in nearby Mesa. Mountain View was one of the state's 5A football powers, and Sparkman had played on the school's junior varsity team. But then he got in trouble there. Sparkman's version of the events was that he and another Robson House resident "borrowed" a friend's truck. Sparkman said the other boy had permission to drive the truck sometimes.

Only on this occasion, the boy took the truck out of the school parking lot without asking. The truck's owner thought it had been stolen and called the police. The result was that Sparkman was pulled from the school and returned to the Ranch's main campus.

"Some of the decisions these kids make, you just wonder what they're thinking," Milbrandt said. "We give kids second and third chances. We give them an out so they can save face. There has to be more to this, because everything could have been settled with a simple 'Yes, sir.' But Juan kept running his mouth and arguing. There's got to be something going on with Juan right now."

Gray didn't know what was going on inside Sparkman's head. All Gray knew was that he felt lousy. In forty-eight hours, his team would be walking on the field in the state play-offs. This was what made all the long hours of watching film, designing game plans, and working on the practice field worthwhile. A season was like going off to war for a football coach. He said goodbye to his loved ones and told them he would be back, God willing, when it was over. That sort of commitment came with the territory. A coach put the extra time into the job because he always knows that the other coach is busy watching game film, looking for a weak spot in his team's armor. Gray's own son was a senior football player at another Mesa high school. Gray hadn't been able to watch him play all season because he was busy coaching his surrogate sons — the Spartans.

Gray had a nagging feeling that somehow he had failed one of those sons. He didn't sleep well that night, and it wasn't from the normal nervousness that comes when a pivotal game looms on the horizon. And when he finally did doze off in the wee hours, his last thoughts were not about Bradshaw Mountain, but about Juan Sparkman.

———

Thursday was a new day. As quickly as the dark clouds had blown in, they blew out. The first thing that morning, Sparkman showed up at the coaches' office. He had something to say to Gray: He was sorry.

After apologizing to Gray, Sparkman later addressed the whole team. He said he had let his emotions get out of control. He had said and done things in the heat of the moment that he now regretted. He just wanted to be part of the team, and he hoped everyone would welcome him back. They did, of course. The coaches were ecstatic. Gray said he was glad that Sparkman had decided to come back. But his ear-to-ear grin gave away that "glad" probably wasn't anywhere near a strong enough word to describe his feelings.

"Welcoming him back was probably the most therapeutic thing done for Juan since he's been here," Shofner added.

Now they could worry about plain ol' football again.

———

On the way to Prescott Valley, Spartan Pride passed several places that reflected Arizona's rugged history: Deadman's Wash, Horse Thief Basin, Bloody Basin. But it was unclear whether any of the boys paid much attention to those road signs. Arizona was home for none. They were just passing through. Their routine was the same on all of the long road trips: Get on the bus. Hold your bladder for a few hours. Get off the bus. Find a bathroom. Play the game. Get back on the bus and go to sleep on the journey back to the Ranch. They rarely complained about the trips. It was just part of life at the Ranch. It didn't really matter whether they liked it. They just did it.

"They're still a mystery to me," Gray said before the game. "I think they're a mystery to themselves, too. They don't even know where they are. They just get on the bus and wait until it stops. They have no idea where we are except that it's cold, so we must be in the mountains somewhere. These kids from Compton and San Diego, they don't know Bradshaw Mountain from Magic Mountain."

Bradshaw Mountain, as they would soon find out, wasn't nearly as much fun.

In the locker room before the game, the coaches talked among themselves about how they couldn't believe that they were here. A year earlier, they had been at Bradshaw Mountain with a team that was lucky to lose by only 27 points. Now they were back with a team that was in a position to win and advance into the state quarterfinals. Who could have imagined it? But while the coaching staff was downright giddy, the players didn't share their enthusiasm. As they got dressed, it was eerily quiet. They were walking around as if they were in a collective trance. Some had a look of terror. All year they had been talking about making it to the play-offs, and now that they were finally here it appeared that the fear of the unknown was getting to them.

As the Ranch players prepared to take the field, they heard the Bradshaw Mountain team yelling and chanting in their locker room.

"You guys who were here last year, this butt-whipping is owed," Allen growled to the players. "This is payback. Let them whoop and holler. We'll do our talking with our pads. Let's make 'em scream like stuck pigs." The words had seemingly little effect on the Spartans. They were still nervous and jittery. That was also how they would play.

It was a bad first half. On its first possession, the Ranch drove down to the Bradshaw Mountain 15-yard line with a McKissic-to-Harris bomb that went 53 yards, covering most of the distance. But there the drive stalled, and the Spartans gave up the ball on downs. Then Bradshaw Mountain promptly marched the ball back the other way on an eleven-play drive that used up most of the first quarter. The Bears' freshman quarterback sneaked in from the 1-yard line to cap the drive. The extra point made it 7–0. Bradshaw Mountain wouldn't score the rest of the half, but then neither would the Ranch.

The Bear defense was everywhere. Each time Peters, Elliott, Cabell, or McKissic carried the ball, there was a small army of black jerseys waiting for them. The Ranch's ground game had ground to a halt. The Spartans were listless, uninspired. There was no noise coming from the sideline, either. The lone bright spot was that the Ranch found itself down by only seven points when the horn sounded. It was, by far, the worst half that the Ranch had played all season. At halftime, Gray told the players that he was out of motivational speeches. They could yell at one another, but that wasn't going to do any good. They now had one half left. It was up to them to decide if it would be their last half of the season. Do you want to keep winning? Are you happy just getting to the play-offs? His goal was to be state champs. What was their goal?

Ta'ase and Allen, though, had no problems raising their voices to decibel levels normally associated with jet planes taking off.

"Hey, this isn't the right time to be pulling an attitude and start feeling sorry for your freaking selves!" Ta'ase shouted. "That's bullcrap! That's not gonna work. No way. You gotta be hungry, dammit. Find that hunger!"

"We've got these people thinking that they're going to win this game because we played like shit," Allen rumbled. "Now we have to take it away from them."

Back out on the field, nothing changed. The Ranch still couldn't move the ball. Then, with 3:11 left in the third quarter, the Bears capped a ten-play drive with another 1-yard plunge to make it 14–0 with the extra point. The big play of the drive was a flea-flicker, the sort of thing that would catch an inexperienced team like the Ranch by surprise. Faced with fourth-and-6 at the Ranch 23, Bradshaw Mountain lined up to run a play. But then the quarterback walked over toward a receiver and pretended to be shouting out instructions to him. While the Spartans were watching this, the Bears center snapped the ball to the lone running back, who then raced 9 yards for the first down.

At least that touchdown seemed to awaken the Spartans from their slumber. After the ensuing kickoff, McKissic completed a 36-yard pass to Sparkman, who had leaped over a defender to grab the ball out of his hands. On the next play, Cabell went off tackle to the right side and scampered 21 yards into the end zone. Andrade's extra point was wide left, but the score was now 14–6. There was still 2:40 left in the third quarter, so there was plenty of time for a rally.

Then came the kickoff return. A Bradshaw Mountain player took the kick at the 9 raced up the middle through a hole big enough to drive a truck through. The kick failed, but the score was 20–6. The home team's sideline was in pandemonium. The Spartans' sideline was silent. Even the coaches seemed momentarily stunned. Had this happened earlier in the year, the game would have been over. The Ranch would have folded like a tortilla. As it was, the Spartans looked as if they were ready to have the epitaph written on their football tombstone.

There was still a faint pulse, however. The Ranch returned the next kickoff at its own 42. Elliott then ran for 9 yards. Then he ran for 21 more. Cabell picked up 4 more tough yards. Those runs served to set up the play of the game, something the Spartans had been practicing all week. Gray decided to gamble. He owed the Bradshaw Mountain coach a trick play. So when the ball was hiked, McKissic swept left like he was going to run another option play. The entire Bear defense followed him. It appeared that they had him hemmed in behind the line of scrimmage near their sideline. There was only one problem: McKissic didn't have the ball.

Brian Coleman, the guard, had it. And he was rambling 24 yards, unnoticed, in the other direction and into the end zone.

Instead of snapping the ball to McKissic, Cody Jeffries had taken it out of the quarterback's hands and put it on the ground. There he shielded it with his, uh, ample rear end. When all the defenders reacted to McKissic's running to his left, Coleman picked up the ball and headed right. It was the old hidden-ball trick. It was also known as the Fumblerooskie. When it worked, the coach was a genius on the scale of a football Einstein. When it failed, especially in a situation like this, the coach often had to consider looking for a new place of employment. This time it was sheer perfection, and it got the Ranch back into the game in a hurry. When Elliott lowered his head and bulldozed into the end zone on the two-point conversion, the score suddenly was 20–14 with seconds still remaining in the third quarter. It was a ballgame again. The pendulum had begun to swing to the Ranch's side.

On the third play of the Bears' next possession, there was a mix-up on the handoff between the Bradshaw Mountain quarterback and a running back, and the ball dropped to the turf. It was recovered there by Yuoh. Four plays later, Cabell had scored on a 7-yard touchdown run. With 9:34 remaining, Andrade's extra point sailed straight through the uprights. The Ranch held a 21–20 lead.

From there, it was up to the Ranch defense. Bradshaw Mountain would have the ball three more times in the closing minutes. The Bears had possession for virtually the entire fourth quarter. But that didn't mean that they were moving it anywhere. The Ranch defense started putting on a heavy rush against the freshman quarterback, either sacking him or forcing him to hurry his passes. On each possession, the Bears offense sputtered. When the quarterback's final fourth-down pass fell harmlessly incomplete with four seconds left, it was party time for the Ranch.

"Now that's what I call a comeback!" Elliott shouted as he danced off the field.

If the Show Low game had been like dodging a bullet, then the Ranch had just eluded a cannon ball. It wasn't only that the Spartans had won. It was how they had done it. Most of their young lives, these kids had always taken the easy way out. When things got tough, they quit. To keep battling in the face of adversity, trusting that good things are bound to happen to you eventually, was a foreign idea. Yet they hadn't given up. They hadn't stopped trying. That third-quarter kick-off had scared the hell out of Gray. He saw all the Bradshaw Mountain players exchanging high fives. In twenty-five years of coaching, Gray said he had seen a lot of teams that just would have rolled over after that play and called it a season. These kids were different. They had something. Gray didn't know exactly what to call it. A team either has it or it doesn't. Then he found the phrase he was searching for: comeback spirit.

"Everybody in this place thought we were done," Gray said afterward. "They thought they had us. Everybody thought we were going to lay down. But these kids never gave up."

Gray took off his glasses and rubbed the sweat off his forehead with a sleeve.

"It's a hell of a ride with these kids," he said. "It's nonstop. Up-down. In-out. I've never seen anything like it."

That wild ride was just getting started.

My name is Stanley Moultry. I'm from Chicago. I'm seventeen. I've been here going on three months.

I'm from the West Side of Chicago. It's bad there. There, it ain't nothing but gangs and drugs and a lot of killing. I grew up with my father by the projects. My momma lived in a nice neighborhood. But my father lived near Cabrini-Green. My auntie lived in there, and I stayed there when I was small. That's the worst project in Chicago. I lived near there for like two or three years. Then we started moving around in the West Side. It wasn't as bad as Cabrini-Green, but I always used to go back there because my auntie was there, and she always wanted me to stay with her.

When I go back, I'm going to live with my mom. I ain't got my father. He died around May of this year. He had cancer. But my mom, she's going to help me find a place for me, my baby, and my baby's mom. I've got a baby coming. My girl, she's about six months along. I'm still with her. That's why it's hard to be here. I can't keep in touch with her the way I'd like to. I can't be on the phone with her anytime I want. Here, you gotta request to talk to her. I've only been able to talk with her once. But I write her, and she writes me back.

I ended up in the system because I was in a couple of racial fights. The school I was going to had a group called White Power, and they didn't like black people. Every time they'd see a black person walking by himself, they'd try to jump him. So I went to the office and told the principal, and I guess he thought I was telling a story because he wouldn't do nothing. So I took the law into my own hands. I found one of them and it was just one-on-one. I asked him, "What's up? Your boys ain't around, so we can do this now." Then me and one of my friends jumped in and we beat him up. At first, the probation officer said I could stay at home, but then my mom told the P.O. that I was having trouble around the house, too. Where I was living, a whole bunch of gangs wanted to kill me. They kept calling the house and threatening me. They told my mom that when they catch me, they was going to kill me wherever I was at. So my mom told my P.O. about that, and she got in touch with this program.

Why did they want to kill me? Because I was hanging around with the wrong people. They were getting into it with other people, and I was with them. In Chicago, the West Side gets into it with South Side or the North Side. If you go on their side and cause trouble, they come looking for you. They're going to get you even if you had nothing to do with your boys jumping their boys. It's payback.

I was in the gangs, but I wasn't out there gang banging the way other *people gang-bang. I was in a gang called Black Stone. It's like the Bloods, but they're older. I never got caught selling drugs or nothing. Well, I got caught selling drugs once, but they let me off because it was my first case. I was stupid. My friend was going to court and he had drugs on him, and I was stupid enough to carry them around. I know that the police in Chicago don't like me. I got pulled over on the street. They checked me and found the drugs on me. I wasn't thinking at the time.*

Usually I was hanging with my woman and stuff. But when I'd hang with my friends, they'd want to go start trouble. I'd be, "Let's go then." Sometimes I wouldn't do nothing, and sometimes I would. And when I'd think about it later, I'd say to myself: "You shouldn't have done that because you know it's going to come back to haunt you." But it would be too late. When I'd go to school, I'd get into a lot of fights. Guys would try to catch me alone or with my friends. They'd try to shoot you or stab you. Whatever they could do.

I started staying with my girlfriend. I was living with her family for a while, and seeing my momma on and off. You gotta walk and watch your back all the time. In Chicago, they won't do anything to you in the daytime. Well, maybe some of them will get you in the daytime. Those kind have been in trouble so many times that the law don't scare them. When you're walking at night, that's when they'll usually get you. They'll come up from behind and that's it. One of my friends saw these people in the daytime, and they didn't do nothing to him. But then they saw him at nighttime and they beat him and his girlfriend up. At nighttime, I would hang with my girlfriend. I wouldn't go outside with her because I didn't want nothing to happen to her because I knew that too many people wanted me.

I knew all the guys who were after me. They were going to the same school I was going to. But you can't do nothing but look at them. We got security guards in there, so they can't do nothing, although sometimes they'd push you. Or they'd wait until there wasn't a security guard around. I tried to watch my back, but I thought they were going to get me. My mom wanted to call the police, and I'd say no because the more I'd tell, the more it would come back to me. If I tell on them and they get arrested, they're going to come to my house next time. That's how it is. So I didn't tell.

Sometimes I wish I was back home, like when staff is getting on your back. You might know that it's good for you, but you'll still be thinking, "I want to go home." They're giving me discipline. They're giving me what my momma or my father should have been giving me when I was grow-

ing up. I used to get yelled at, but I would just walk away. Here, you can't walk away from it. You have to respond. I ain't never disrespected my mom or my dad. But I just did some bad things, and that's why I'm here.

I didn't know what I was getting into here. I asked them if it was a physical-restraint thing, and they told me in the interview that it wasn't. But now I know it is. I've seen a lot of people get physically restrained. I haven't been restrained yet, but I was close to getting it. I thought it was going to be a regular school. I didn't know that it was going to be all boys. I'm not used to doing all that PTing stuff. You gotta lock it in, look straight ahead, and you gotta walk a certain way. Back in Chicago, you didn't have to do any of that. You only did what you wanted to do. But it's good here. It just shows you that you can do better than the wrong stuff that you were doing back home.

You can walk around here without watching your back. Staff watches you 24-7. You know, twenty-four hours, seven days a week. You don't have to worry about nobody messing with you because everyone is worried about staff. You can't do nothing but get along with people here. Everyone is friends. We're all ABR here. I haven't heard no gang stuff yet.

I can avoid the people looking for me when I get back. My mom said nobody has been calling, except my woman. Besides, I got a year and half left here. With a baby coming, I gotta do what I gotta do in the program and not go back to my old ways. I need to start over and be a new man.

All I can do is try to change. And I'm trying.

UNEXPECTED HEROES

Cody Jeffries was the quintessential gentle giant. Although he was only fifteen, Jeffries stood 5 feet 10 and weighed 250 pounds. He had, well, a big derriere. In fact, after the trick play against Bradshaw Mountain, Gray went out of his way to give credit to Cody's butt for its role in hiding the ball before Coleman picked it up and ran. There was a roundness and softness to Jeffries that was reminiscent of a huge teddy bear. He was quick to smile. He sang in the Ranch's choir. Unassuming and quiet, he was the sort of boy who wouldn't speak until spoken to because he was inherently shy.

The only time Jeffries got on the wrong side of the coaches was for eating too many peanut-butter-and-jelly sandwiches. The coaches thought Jeffries, just a sophomore, had the potential to play college football, but they were worried that he might get too heavy. Controlling his weight was a constant struggle. Each time a coach chastised him for filling his plate too high at the pantry, Jeffries would shrug his shoulders good-naturedly and break out in a devilish grin. Jeffries was simply a nice kid. If anything, he seemed too nice to play football. To excel at the game, a player needs to have a nasty streak, especially if he's an offensive lineman who is expected to keep hurtling his body at somebody else on every play along the line of scrimmage. But there didn't seem to be a mean bone in Jeffries' wide body. But Jeffries, who had been at the Ranch for almost two and a half years, would point out that he hadn't always been so amicable.

"When I first got here, I had a temper," he explained. "I used to go off every day. I was always getting into fights and into trouble. I would start fighting with staff. I got restrained. I would AWOL all the time."

He had acted that way out of self-pity, he added. Jeffries was a Native

American from the Mohave tribe. He had grown up on a reservation in the small city of Parker, which is along the Arizona-California border on the Colorado River. It was a nice place to grow up, Jeffries said. There were a lot of open expanses. It was not, Jeffries explained, what most white people think of as the stereotypical reservation. It wasn't like other more destitute reservations that even he had heard about in his young life. People there were proud of their community. There were youth gangs in Parker, but they weren't into making serious trouble. So unlike the cities where most of the kids at the Ranch had been raised, kids didn't have to worry about being shot as they walked down a road in Parker. If more people came to his reservation, Jeffries added, society would have a different view of Native American life.

In many ways, Jeffries described a rather idyllic childhood — until, that is, he started talking about his family. Jeffries had two brothers and two sisters who were all younger than he was. He also had an aunt and an uncle who looked after him for a time. That was the extent of his family. He had never known his father. His mother had virtually abandoned Jeffries when he was about five. Since then, he had been a ward of the tribal court. He had been in and out of one foster home and group home after another. He had never been in any environment that could remotely be classified as normal.

"The last contact I had with my mother was about three or four years ago," he said. "She went to one of those homeless shelters. She was out in California somewhere. They asked her if she wanted to go back home, and they'd help her find a house, but she didn't."

Jeffries talked about his mom in the same monotone he might use to discuss the plays the team had worked on in practice that day or what he had for lunch. His voice was totally lacking in emotion. He explained that he had just learned to control his anger. He had steeled himself to the reality of his life. There was nothing he could do about it, Jeffries said, so he was moving on. "It doesn't really hurt to talk about it anymore," he added. But there was a time when it did. With that pain welling deep inside, he would take his frustrations out on others. Jeffries had always been a big boy; he had learned to use his size as a destructive force. He would become violent in school with little provocation. He fought with classmates. He would kick desks if he was mad at the teacher. He would run away from his foster parents.

Eventually, Jeffries was shipped from Parker to a foster home in Phoenix. After he walked away one day, he was sent to a group home.

There was another placement after that. Along the way he hung out with a gang for a short time, but eventually he decided that he liked thinking for himself. That, however, didn't mean he was avoiding trouble. "All those places I was in didn't want to deal with me," he said. "They kept expelling me. I was hoping they would throw me out of here, too, when I first got here."

Like most boys, Jeffries found the Ranch to be different from what he had expected. He thought it would be a working ranch with horses, cattle, and so on. He was disappointed to learn that there was a school here. He knew there were gang bangers from California at the Ranch, so he figured there would be fights all the time. "Then you see how people come together here," he said. "Everybody knows that this is probably their last chance to make something of themselves. And they basically don't let you fail."

Accepting that idea was a gradual process for Jeffries. He thought it took about eighteen months until he completely stopped bucking the Ranch's system. There wasn't a certain day when he looked at somebody and said, "*OK, you want to help me? Now I want to be helped.*" But he did stop fighting with the staff. He stopped trying to run. Slowly, he went from tolerating the Ranch to actually liking the place. He had two more years of high school, and he wanted to complete it at the Ranch. Jeffries had found an environment in which he could succeed. He was worried about what would happen to him in a public school. Jeffries was afraid he might begin the self-destructive cycle again. He was content to stay right where he was, thank you. He fit in here.

People, Jeffries said, constantly told him that they couldn't believe he hadn't always been a calm, quiet kid. They knew there had to be a reason he was at the Ranch, but the stories he told about himself were just so out of character for a young man who now looked incapable of stepping on an ant. Jeffries likened the process of change to playing football. The game takes patience, he explained. You can't learn it all at once. It takes a long time. But if you keep working at it, and dealing with the adversity, eventually you can become pretty good if you try. He had decided that he could be a good person, too, if only he tried.

A tribal scholarship would be waiting for Jeffries after he graduated from the Ranch. But he didn't want it. He wanted to earn his own way to college with a football scholarship. Like any normal fifteen-year-old who sees the future as full of wonderful possibilities, Jeffries had big plans for his life. He wanted to play pro football. If that didn't work out, he wanted to be a brain surgeon. More realistically, Jeffries knew one thing that he really wanted to do with his life. He understood that he had missed out on things growing up without parents. He was going to try and make up for that by being a good father to his own family someday.

"My aunt and uncle are proud of me," he said one day. Then he paused. "I think my parents would be proud of me, too," Jeffries added.

————

As Spartan Pride pulled into the Glendale Community College parking lot, it slowly passed the Monument Valley Mustangs team bus which had made the long journey down from the Navajo Indian Reservation. Jeffries watched the Mustang players and cheerleaders walking toward the stadium. With a grin on his face, Jeffries turned to Milbrandt and joked: "Navajos are nothing. We'll beat them and take their women next."

Finally, the Ranch had had a short road trip. Spartan Pride had to fight only the Friday afternoon rush-hour to get to the west side of Phoenix, where the Ranch's state quarterfinal game was being played at Glendale. Monument Valley was the team with the travel disadvantage. The Mustangs had to make a six-and-a-half-hour drive. "It's just good that we don't have to go up there," Gray said. "I just found Kayenta on the map for the first time."

Kayenta is on the Navajo reservation near the Four Corners region where the borders of Arizona, Utah, New Mexico, and Colorado all meet. More noteworthy, Kayenta is on the edge of the famed Monument Valley. The region is filled with the awe-inspiring red-sandstone buttes, mesas, arches, and monoliths. Because of its rugged natural beauty, Monument Valley is a favorite of Hollywood directors. The picturesque site had been a backdrop for movies since the old-time westerns, including John Wayne's *Stagecoach,* as well as such recent films as *Thelma and Louise* and *Waiting to Exhale.*

Despite the long road trip, several hundred spectators from Monument Valley had made the trip to see their team play. The fans, like the team itself, were almost all Native Americans. They knew their team was on the brink of doing something no reservation team had ever done in Arizona history: advance to the state semifinals in football.

Basketball was the sport of choice on Arizona reservations. During the Ranch's first football season, the Spartans had played four games against teams from various reservations around the state and had won all of them. Each time the Ranch had taken a solid lead, and the coaching staff had the sense that the other teams just gave up. Then, that winter, the Ranch would play eight basketball games against reservation teams and lost all eight. For whatever reason, Gray noted, basketball appealed to Native American kids more than football.

"Traditionally, the Indian reservation teams haven't been football powerhouses," Gray added. "That's not derogatory. It's just a fact. You can look it up." He was right. A Native American team had never won a state play-off game until the year before, when a reservation school from the town of Ganado in northeastern Arizona had won a 3A first-round game. It had been a landmark moment for Native American football.

Monument Valley was building on that success. The Mustangs, dressed in silver pants and helmets and red jerseys, were big and fast. They operated the rushing-oriented wishbone offense with precision. Their entire backfield could fly. It was no fluke that they had reached the state quarterfinals. They were 9–1 and had won the 3A North title. They had established their credentials late in the year when they played St. Johns, another one of the small towns in the White Mountains, in the last game of the regular season. For years the St. Johns Redskins had been beating up on the state's 2A competition. They had won three consecutive state titles before being moved up to 3A this season. St. Johns had carried a forty-four-game unbeaten streak — one of the nation's longest — into that game. Monument Valley ended that run with a victory. For an encore, the Mustangs recorded a convincing win in the first round of the playoffs.

So Gray knew the Spartans would not win this game easily. It didn't help that he was having trouble convincing the players that winning was important. Ever since the play-offs had started, the coaches had been on edge. All of them were former players themselves. They knew what being in the state quarterfinals meant. For a player, it was a once-in-a-lifetime opportunity. It didn't come around too often for a coach, either. If the Ranch had been a public high school, the locker room would be buzzing with excitement. The days counting down to Friday night would be like the final days before Christmas.

Gray couldn't understand why his players didn't seem excited. Football had become just another part of their daily routine. They slept in the same beds. They went to the same classes. They went on the same work crews. They went to the same meetings. They sat in the same places at the pantry. Their lights always went out at the same time. They were up at the same time each morning. Football practice was just another place they were supposed to be at a certain time. It was a strange existence, Gray thought. He wondered if the Ranch's extreme structure had sapped the joy out of the game for them.

The Spartans were doing everything that was asked of them in practice. Gray just wished they would savor the moment. In a week, or two, or three, the season would be over. Most high school football players would give anything to be in their position. It would be close to the culmination of a dream. But kids at the Ranch were different. Here they were, three victories away from a state title, and they barely seemed to care.

Gray marveled at how far the players had come just in terms of dealing with coaching. In the beginning, everything had been a confrontation. Now they were accepting what was told to them, maybe because they had figured out that the coaches knew what they were doing. Gray figured that this change, small as it might be, could only help them later in life. After all, one day they were going to have to take orders from their bosses. The fact that the team was having some success also had to improve the boys' self-esteem. Instead of getting kicked in the ass, they were receiving pats on the back. What kid wouldn't like that? At the moment, though, Gray wasn't interested in treatment. Coaches were supposed to win games, and he was desperately searching for something to motivate his team.

"I don't think they understand what winning the state championship would mean," he said earlier in the week. "They just do what they're told. They win, so they stay and keep practicing. They have no idea what they're doing. They act just like they did a month ago. They're on the field because they're supposed to be. Here I am going crazy, but they're not. There's no rah-rah. It's just not in them."

The boys' attitude worried Gray to no end. He wanted to see that same Spartan team that had played against Winslow. For some reason, Winslow had gotten under their skins. It was hate at first sight. Some button had been pushed, and it showed in the final result. The Spartans had hurt Winslow physically. They had wanted the win that night. The Spartans he now saw were indifferent.

After Thursday's practice, Gray had a heart-to-heart chat with the team. Take a moment and look at yourselves, Gray said. Think about the situation you're in. You're one of eight teams left playing. You're going to be playing in a nice stadium. There will be a big crowd there. This is something you have accomplished. We've got a good team. We've been able to overcome bad things. This is something nobody can ever take away from you. This memory will be with you the rest of your lives. This will be a big night for me, too. I've been coaching for twenty-five years now, and this is the closest I've come to a state championship. It means a lot to me because this group of young men is special. We're not a dumb football team. We run a multiple offense with multiple formations. We run a check system on defense. We are one of the best football teams in Arizona. We're not the same team that lost those early games. We're just learning how to play. But you must have that desire inside you, too.

Later, Gray would say that he could have sworn he was talking to a brick wall.

Shofner had been at the Ranch longer than most staff. He had been in the business of treating troubled kids for years. He couldn't figure out what was going on, either. Deep down, he was just an old jock who had played small-college football. Adrenaline was coursing through his body. Meanwhile, he was watching kids around him stifling yawns. "Sometimes I think we brainwash them to the point where they lose some of their fire," Shofner said. "They never fight in practice. Never. We've got this reputation for having the meanest, gang-banging SOBs, and they're not like that on the field. But they should be excited about this because the day they lose, the next day a lot of them will be heading back down to Oracle. And that won't exactly be a highlight in their lives."

As it turned out, there was a noticeable change in the boys' demeanors as the 5 o'clock kickoff approached on Friday. It was hardly the change that Gray had hoped for. While the coaches were fidgety in the locker room, the players were walking around with a blatant devil-may-care attitude. They were talking loud and joking with one another. It was the complete opposite of the way they had acted before the Bradshaw Mountain game. One boy had even forgotten his cleats back at the Ranch. When Pat Castillo, the team's assistant trainer, couldn't find an extra pair, he asked the player if he was in the Civics program.

"Yes, sir," the boy responded.

"Then you better get your combat boots on, son," Castillo said.

The other kids found this incredibly funny and turned up the volume on their chatter even higher. It wasn't until Moore went over and told everyone to shut the hell up that silence descended on the locker room. Were they overconfident? Did they just not give a damn? Were they tired of football and eager for the season to be over? Gray didn't know. If he hadn't yet figured out what made them tick, he probably never would. Maybe the boys would wake up after they had been knocked back on their butts a few times.

It didn't take long for that to happen.

In the first series of the game, McKissic hobbled off the field with a sprained ankle. As the trainers and a local doctor, who had volunteered his services to the team, examined the ankle, McKissic sat perched on a folding table. In obvious pain, McKissic's head was buried in his hands. When he occasionally looked up to see what was happening on the field, the agony was etched on his face. The reaction among the players was like that of troops who have just watched their commanding officer fall in battle. They kept glancing back over their shoulders to see what was happening to their quarterback.

Suddenly, there wasn't anything to laugh about.

As the trainers wrapped McKissic's left ankle with tape, Todd Harris jogged out on the field. One of the Spartans' best athletes, he had played wide receiver all season. Although he was the backup quarterback, Harris had taken just one snap in the first ten games. McKissic had played so well all year that they hadn't needed to use Harris. Yet, Kush, who had been coaching the quarterbacks early in the year, loved the way Harris threw the ball. Although McKissic clearly was the more polished of the two, Kush had always thought that Harris had the potential to be a great high school quarterback. Only sixteen, Harris would get his chance after McKissic graduated.

The only knock against Harris was his inexperience. No one had any idea how he would react in this high-stress situation. The hopes of the entire Ranch had been thrust upon his slender shoulders. Regardless of the fact that Harris was already the father of a little girl, had been a Crip for years, and was at the Ranch for having committed such crimes as strong-arm robbery and grand theft auto, at this moment, as he stood in the huddle, he looked like a scared teenager.

His bad case of nerves showed quickly. In his first series, Harris fumbled a snap from center, and Monument Valley recovered. On the

Spartans' third possession, McKissic limped back out on the field. He had convinced the medical staff and coaches that he could give it one more try. But almost immediately, he swept right on an option play and was tackled hard out of bounds on the track that surrounded the football field. When McKissic finally got to his feet, he could barely walk. He looked like an old man trying to hobble across the field back to the Spartan sideline. He would be a spectator for the rest of the game, his contribution limited to shouting encouragement while leaning on crutches.

The Ranch's chances now rested in the hands of Harris.

Fortunately, they began to look like able hands. Harris had settled down. The Spartans had a golden scoring opportunity late in the second quarter. In Mustang territory, Harris found a wide-open Miller, who was playing tight end, in the middle of the field with no one around him. It would have been a sure touchdown . . . if only Miller had held on to the ball. On the next play, with just seconds left in the half, Harris sent a tight spiral to Sparkman in the corner of the end zone. It slipped through Juan's hands.

As the teams jogged off the field at halftime, they were deadlocked in a scoreless tie. It had been a sloppy first half. The schools had made six turnovers between them. The ball had been on the ground much of the first two quarters. But there was a reason for that, too. There was some ferocious hitting going on. The Monument Valley defense attacked like a pack of hungry wolves. As soon as Elliott, Cabell, or Peters shook off one defender, there were three more waiting for them. The Mustangs were stacking eight or nine men on the line of scrimmage, daring the Spartans' untested backup quarterback to throw the ball. So far, that strategy had paid off.

Meanwhile, the Ranch defense was doling out punishment of its own. The Spartans had broken the Monument Valley wishbone. They were forcing the Mustangs to throw the ball, and each time the Monument Valley quarterback faded back to pass, he saw the imposing sight of Armstrong, Yuoh, Reggie Miles, and Marcus Thompson barreling down on him. The Spartans had hit him so hard several times that he was slow to get back up on his feet.

After the Spartans made the long walk back to the locker room, Moore couldn't wait to get into the face of his running backs' faces. The venom he spewed could be heard in every corner of the room, echoing off the metal lockers and through the shower stalls. "Y'all were laughing before the game," Moore scolded. "But that shit isn't funny now, is it? You were laughing, thinking this would be a piece of cake. But now you know better. That Indian team is physical. They're big. They've hit you. So now what are you gonna do about it?"

Instantaneously, that became the theme. Each position coach began yelling at his players: *What are you gonna do about it? You want the season to end tonight? Do you want it to end this way?* By the time Gray addressed the team for a last-minute pep talk, they didn't need to be screamed at anymore. It was time for soothing words of encouragement. Let go of the first half, he told them. Everybody has dropped the football at some point in his life. The important thing is to catch the next pass. Harris is good enough to get the job done, but we've got to help him. Somebody, he concluded, is going to have to step up and make a big play for us.

It almost was Sparkman. Early in the third quarter, Reggie Miles recovered yet another Monument Valley fumble at the Mustang 26. The Ranch got a first down and eventually faced a third-and-6 situation at the Mustang 11. Harris lofted a high pass to the back of the end zone. Sparkman leaped over a defender and pulled down the touchdown pass. At least that was the way it looked until a yellow flag fluttered to the turf. The play was waved off by officials. Sparkman had been penalized for offensive pass interference, and that put the ball all the way back on the 27-yard line, with the Spartans now facing fourth down. It appeared that the Ranch had blown yet another scoring opportunity.

Gray's message at halftime had been that somebody was going to have to come through for them. Charles Williams was then given his chance to be that somebody. Williams tended to be a loner. He seemed to get along with everyone, but more often than not, he could be seen out and about the Ranch by himself. Unfailingly polite, he had large eyes that seemed to take in everything around him. During games, those eyes were often trained on the coaches. Williams hadn't received much playing time during the season. He would patiently wait on the sidelines, never complaining but always close enough so that the coaches knew he was there, watching.

Deep down, Williams believed he was a great football player. He was one of the few kids who had played the game at a public school before coming to the Ranch. He was perhaps the fastest boy on the team. He should have been the Spartans' big-play receiving threat, except for one problem: Williams was tentative on the field. He had a condition that some coaches refer to as "alligator arms"; he wouldn't extend his arms while trying to make a catch, thus exposing his body to harm. While he often talked about how well he had played at his previous school, he seemed to lack self-confidence on the Spartan practice field. That fit a pattern. Williams, after all, had been the boy who was so terrified of attending the Civics program that he had faked his way into a wheelchair.

Williams had yet to catch a single pass all year. But with Harris now playing quarterback for the injured McKissic, the Ranch needed another wide receiver. Gray called Williams's number. It was a simple crossing route. Williams ran a couple of steps straight toward the end zone, then made a sharp cut toward the middle of the field and turned his body. Harris fired the ball to him in midstride. Williams caught it and didn't stop sprinting until he was brought down at the Monument Valley 5. First down, Spartans. A face-mask penalty on the Mustangs tacked two more yards on the play, advancing the ball to 3-yard line. Meanwhile, Williams jogged back to the huddle with a confident gait that suggested he had been doing this all season.

A quarterback sneak by Harris pushed the ball to the one-yard line. Then the Monument Valley defense stiffened. On second-and-goal, Elliott was stopped for no gain up the middle. On third-and-goal, Peters was stopped for no yardage in the same place. It was like one of those Saturday-morning cartoons in which Wile E. Coyote runs smack dab into a canyon wall while chasing the Roadrunner. The Spartans had gotten nowhere.

So now it was fourth-and-goal from the 1-yard line. It was decision time for Gray. He elected not to try a field goal and gave it one more shot into the heart of the Monument Valley defense. This time, Elliott went off-tackle to the right side, found a little crack, and burrowed his way into the end zone. The scoreless deadlock had been broken. Andrade's extra point try was blocked, but at least the Ranch now held a 6–0 lead. A gale-force sigh of relief blew through the Spartans' sidelines. Finally, the Ranch had drawn blood. As the third quarter wound down, the comedy of errors continued. There was another Mustang fumble. Then an interception thrown by Harris. Then yet another fumble by Monument Valley, this one recovered near midfield.

That last turnover set the stage for further heroics by Williams. On the first play of the fourth quarter, he ran a streak pattern down the sideline. In other words, he ran as fast as he could as Harris tried to get him the ball. He did. Harris launched a cannon throw that Williams, who had outrun his defender, sprinted underneath. Williams caught the ball as softly and as carefully as if he were catching a falling baby. The play went for a 45-yard touchdown. The two-point conversion attempt failed, but the Ranch led 12–0.

Over on the Spartans' bench, teammates were hoisting Williams up into the air. Bob Thomas, who as usual was prowling the sideline, could barely contain himself as he joined the impromptu celebration. "That's so good for his development," he said. "Charles was so scared when this season started. Look at him now."

Williams had done his part. It was now up to the defense to hold on to the lead. Just like the previous week against Bradshaw Mountain, the unit was on the field for most of the fourth quarter. The clock was again the Spartans' friend. Although the Mustangs managed to move the ball, their run-oriented offense was eating up valuable time. One Mustang drive ran out of gas at the Ranch 28 when Monument Valley's quarterback threw a bad pass on the fourth down that was forced by the heavy rush of Yuoh. Later, as the fourth quarter slowly ticked away, Monument Valley began throwing on every down. The Mustangs managed to put together a sixteen-play drive that reached the Spartans' 13. But it was there that Armstrong and his teammates really began introducing themselves to the Mustang quarterback on an up-close-and-personal basis. First it was Armstrong sacking the quarterback. Then it was Armstrong and Reggie Miles forcing a poor throw. Finally, it was Armstrong and Yuoh, who hurried a fourth-down pass that fell incomplete.

Yet it still wasn't over. An Elliott fumble gave the Mustangs the ball back with two minutes left. Two plays put the football on the Ranch 3 with 1:21 left. A twelve-point lead seemed insurmountable, but stranger things had happened in high school football. The fact that the Ranch was even here on this night was proof of that. In the huddle, the Ranch defenders weren't worried about losing the game. Rather, they wanted to preserve the shutout. On the next play, Armstrong helped make sure that they wouldn't as he bolted up through the middle and sacked the quarterback for a 3-yard loss before he even had a chance to turn and plant his feet. Two plays later, on fourth down, Sparkman ran down a running back from behind at the 7 to seal the

12–0 outcome.

The Ranch had done it again. It was as if the Spartans had received the official blessing of the football gods. Somehow, they had managed to find a way to win without their starting quarterback. They were making a most improbable play-off run. After the two teams lined up to shake hands, the lights from TV cameras shined on Gray at mid-field. Reporters with blow-dried hair were looking for an explanation of how a team from a reform school in just its second year of playing football could already be in the state semifinals.

"Never in my wildest dreams did I imagine that after twenty-five years in coaching I would finally get to the Final Four with a team from the Arizona Boys Ranch," Gray admitted. "It's amazing, and I don't even know how we're doing it. I've learned just to sit back and watch. It's easier to take that way."

Meanwhile, newspaper reporters sought out Harris and Armstrong. They had been the obvious stars. Harris had played brilliantly. One writer who covered high school sports noted that if there were a better prep defensive lineman in the state this year than Armstrong, he hadn't seen him yet. Armstrong simply had decided that the Spartans weren't going to lose. The Spartans were just as tired as the Monument Valley players were late in the game, Armstrong said. But the difference, he added, was that you could see in their eyes that they were whipped. "They could have beaten us there in the fourth quarter, but we wouldn't let them," Armstrong told reporters.

It was a chaotic scene. The two teams playing in the second game of the doubleheader were preparing to take the field for their warm-ups. The Spartans lined up by twos and slowly made their way through the crowd of people. It was then that Allen started talking. He was addressing his comments to the Spartans, but his booming voice was loud enough that the players from the other teams could hear him. "Now comes the fear," he growled. "People have seen us now. They've seen us come back and beat the hell out of people. They know who you are now."

Almost forgotten in the postgame revelry was Williams. But Gray didn't forget him. Outside the locker room, Gray leaned against a wall while he waited for the players to shower and get dressed. The look on his face suggested that he was afraid he would awaken from this remarkably sweet dream. He kept coming back to one word over and over again: unbelievable.

"We continue to find some way to come out on top," Gray said.

"Tonight Charles Williams comes from nowhere. Where's he been all season? But tonight he was there for us. He's come a long way. He was petrified all year. He's not really one of the guys around here. But we said throw it to Charles and see what happens. It was great to see him come through. He's got those big ol' eyes, and he's always looking at you, waiting for his chance. Well, tonight he made the most of it. This is something he can really use."

A few minutes later, Williams emerged from the locker room and headed toward the bus. Gray walked over and put both hands on his shoulders. He had made two great plays and pulled the team's chestnuts out of the fire, Gray told him. He had saved the Ranch tonight. "Yes sir," Williams immediately said. At the Ranch, it's a mandatory, knee-jerk response to answer an adult that way. After a while, it's like breathing. Kids don't even think about it. But while Williams said nothing else, his handsome face gave him away. He was beaming as he turned toward the bus.

The Spartans didn't stick around for the second game between Snowflake and Safford, the 3A South champion. Instead, the team would be headed directly to a Mexican restaurant for a postgame meal. There were just too many things that could happen if they hung around, Gray explained, most of them bad. These were sixteen- and seventeen-year-old kids who hadn't seen any girls for who knew how long, he added. The Ranch team bus was heading out of the parking lot even before the opening kickoff of the second game. The Spartans missed seeing Safford methodically take apart Snowflake, 32–12.

My name is Luis Collazo. I'm eighteen years old. I got here on October 6, 1994. I've been on the main Ranch for about seven months. Before that, I was down in Civics. I'm gonna be going home in December. I'm from San Diego.

This is good for me. I'm getting a plan together to go to college. I'm going to live with my sister. I don't want to live where I was, with all the gangs in my neighborhood. I don't want to be in the same area. I'm going to go to community college in Chula Vista.

I used to live in southeast San Diego. There's gangs and everything there. I would just hang out with my friends in the neighborhood and gang-bang and stuff. My gang was Shelltown. Some of the older people in my neighborhood controlled the drugs and whatever. That's how all the fighting would start. And we don't get along with all the other neighborhoods, like the next street over. That's the way it's been for a long time.

Being in a gang, to me, was fun. I liked doing what I did. Being here does change the way you think. I can see that being here has saved me from being arrested for something else. We were getting out of hand. I got caught for something else that wasn't that bad compared to some stuff. It was assault with a deadly weapon. What was I doing when the cops caught me? What do you think? Running. It was just something that happened with somebody we didn't get along with from another gang.

I was at another program before this one, then I got out and got arrested again for a probation violation, and that's why I ended up back here.

That stuff is all I ever did. We'd just like to drink. Or we'd go out looking for fun and things got out of hand or we'd see somebody that we didn't like. We did what we had to do. I kind of enjoyed it. Around here, they make us out as some kind of terrorists or something. But I look at it as people just doing something that they enjoyed. If they didn't like it, they wouldn't be doing it.

My brother used to be hanging around with gang members, and he's quieted down. He's got a wife. I'd like to do that. A lot of my friends already have three strikes. They're only eighteen or nineteen. They're doing life. These are kids that I used to hang out with. I talked to my P.O. yesterday, and he told me that they might be able to get me off gang suppression back home. That's a unit that monitors the gangs in the neighborhood. They go to your house and start messing with you too much. You can't wear any gang clothes. You can't have certain pictures or drawings. They try to be all friendly and get to know you and everything that goes on in the neighborhood, and then they try to get you. You give them too much information, and it catches up to you. My P.O.'s going to go to the judge and try to get me off that.

I think about what it's like back there. I talk to staff, and they suggested to stay out here. But I don't want to do that. All my family is back there, and I've been gone a long time. I've got my parents, three brothers. One's locked up. I've got two sisters, including one who's going to USD [University of San Diego]. She's gonna be a lawyer or something. She's helping me with college.

What I've learned here is to respect people for what they are. It shouldn't matter what color clothes they're wearing or whatever. I remember when I first got in juvenile hall, and I saw my mom crying and everything. I know how me and my brothers would get her so upset. I know that if I get locked up again, I'll probably never see her again. My parents tried everything with me, but nothing worked. They tried to keep me away from that stuff. But I was stubborn. I've already been gone about three years in places like CYA and here. At least I like it here better than at Civics. You're like a robot there. Here, you can be more normal. It's more realistic.

I guess what's different now is that I get along with people that I never got along with before. I've left all that stuff behind me. I've dropped it. I know that there's still people out there who want to get me. That's why it's going to be hard going home. They know me from those days when I was just hanging out with my friends. But I need to avoid them because I know that I can make it out there.

I was supposed to be going home in August, but I wasn't ready. I didn't have a plan or nothing. I was just going to go back to where I used to live. They gave me until December to think about it. I didn't want to go back there without a plan, because it would have been just the same thing. Now I can get my head straight.

I guess I think all that gang stuff is just stupid. I think about all the things that happen in the neighborhood and how we don't get along with other neighborhoods and I think it's stupid. I think about all the people I used to be with who are locked up now. When I went home on a visit, I saw some people I used to hang with and they wanted to know where I had been. They said, "Let's go out." I just said, "No, I'm beyond that. I'm just here to see my family." I've basically changed.

I'm kind of scared to go home. I don't know what college is like. I've never even been to a normal high school. I'm sure it's structured. If I go there and mess up on my grades, then that will be it for me.

I've got a plan. But plans can always fail, right?

HALLELUJAH, HALLELUJAH, HALLELUJAH!

In most places around the country, a long summer is something to be savored. Not in Arizona. The natives can't wait for the arrival of winter. It brings the mild temperatures that make everyone in the Snow Belt jealous. But some years winter takes its sweet time in arriving. This was one of those years. It was the third week of November and the afternoon temperature was still topping out at 86 degrees. The only people sweating more than the players and coaches during Monday's practice were the trainers, who had been filling and refilling the water caddies and then straining to pull them around the field.

After practice, Gray sat his players down for one of his coach-to-team chats. They had already gone over the film of Friday night's game at lunch. It hadn't been a pretty sight. The Ranch hadn't played particularly well against Monument Valley. Gray told the players that it said something to win when they were not having their best night. But do that again this Friday, he added, and they were going to be embarrassed.

"Where is Safford?" Gray asked after the players had a minute to catch their breath following the practice-ending wind sprints.

Guesses came fast and furious.

"North."

"West."

"South."

"Close," Gray said. "It's east of here. Here's something else you probably don't know. Of all the high schools in Arizona, Safford has the third-winningest team in state history. I can't ever remember a Safford team that wasn't in the state play-offs. They turn out a lot of good college football players, too. So they've got a good program."

The kids who had played the previous season could testify to that. This was to be another one of those rematch games that the Ranch had been playing all year. The season before, Safford had spanked the Spartans, 33–0. Evidently, the Safford coach valued the concept of sportsmanship because the Ranch staff said the final score could easily have been worse, like 100 to nothing. Mercifully, they had gone easy on the Spartans. This year the Bulldogs were even better. They had won the 3A South title and now were 10–1.

Gray gave the players something to chew on before they went to dinner. He decided to play an old coach's trick and tell them a fish story. He said that he had heard through the grapevine that the Safford coach and the Blue Ridge coach were already planning to exchange game film after Friday night's games because "everybody" knew they were the two schools that would meet in the state finals. That was how little everyone thought of the Spartans as a team, Gray added. But if that got their blood boiling, the players didn't show it as they headed off to the locker room. There was none of the "Well, we're going to show them" talk. Maybe it was just impossible to con kids who had spent their entire lives trying to con the system. Nonetheless, Gray hoped the tale would achieve the desired effect.

"It was just a white lie," Gray said. "I need an ornery bunch of kids." Then Gray thought for a moment. "Heck, I could tell them that Safford is the main headquarters for the Ku Klux Klan," he said. "And I might have if I thought it would help us win."

One thing that would surely improve the Ranch's chances of winning was a healthy McKissic. Although he still had a noticeable limp, he had completed the practice and it looked as if he would be ready to play by Friday.

———

It is, Thomas said, almost like the Super Bowl around here. The football team had unified the entire Ranch. At least that was the growing feeling among the staff and kids who weren't on the football team. The players, however, continued to be less than enthusiastic. Thomas claimed he knew why they were expressing so little excitement about being in the state semifinals.

"I don't mean this in a funny way at all, but running from cops and ducking bullets is probably the only thing they've done to get that adrenaline rush," Thomas said. "Football is a brand-new experience. We ex-jocks sit around and can't figure them out. But they don't experience pressure. They've seen things on the street corner that most people have never seen. They've seen friends get shot. Add to it that we teach so much self-control here. When they score, they just flip the ball to the referee. But sometimes you need to let loose. You need that in sports. Sometimes our control works against us."

As was his habit, Thomas had stopped by to catch the last portion of a midweek practice. He also wanted to grab some tape of Safford to see what the Ranch would be up against on Friday. When it was noted that this was something that Jerry Jones might do, Thomas just chuckled. It was a chance for him to laugh after what had been a rough couple of days.

"You know," he said, "there's two ways to get out of Boys Ranch. You can either claim to be beat on, or you can try to commit suicide." A boy who had played on the JV football team had just attempted the second option a few days earlier by slashing his wrist with a razor. Luckily, he had been taken to a hospital in time to save his life. Now he was back home in Indiana to be reevaluated by juvenile authorities there. A psychiatric institution complete with a medicine cabinet full of psychotropic drugs would probably be in his immediate future, Thomas said. "It's a tragedy," he said. "But he got a call from his mother and that set him off. This program will help him. He needs to be here." Chances are, Thomas added, we'll never see that boy again.

There was something else, too; something far less important than a boy's nearly taking his own life. Nevertheless, it bothered him. He reached into his pocket and pulled out a copy of a fax. It had been sent to Thomas by a friend. It was a letter to the editor that had appeared in a small newspaper in the White Mountains that served the Show Low area. The headline read: "Wrong Values Rewarded."

To the editor:

A typical team versus an atypical team. The typical Arizona high school football team (in this case, Show Low High School) arrived for the game on a typical yellow school bus with a typical Taco Bell pregame meal lying leaden in the pits of their stomachs. They meandered onto the playing field dressed in typical jeans, T-shirts and tennis shoes wondering how many fans or family would make the 200-mile trip to watch this crucial game. These are the typical rural American boys. Sons of ranchers, clerks, real estate agents, insurance agents, teachers, etc., who, along with worrying about jobs, grades and family, also try to play football at a level acceptable to themselves, coaches and family.

The atypical team (Arizona Boys Ranch) arrives on a new $200,000 bus emblazoned with "Spartans" on the sides, a carefully planned, catered meal already coursing through their systems. They are marched onto the field in formation, wearing matching game-day shirts, slacks and brand-name shoes. They also wonder if family members will show up for this homecoming game. These are tough boys, convicted of crimes including rape, aggravated assault, robbery and the rest of the criminal spectrum, who are provided the best equipment, training and coaching that money can buy.

As the Show Low fans arrive, they trickle into the stadium in family units and one larger as the band takes its place. They too are nursing Taco Bell or McDonald's drinks and food as they settle into their seats.

The Boys Ranch student body arrives from the three different campuses: one in Queen Creek, one in Oracle, and one in Payson, riding in at least 29 new Ford vans. They, along with their guards, form up and, accompanied by a corps of drummers, march into the stadium making a lap around the track. There, they are treated to a catered meal of barbecued meat, potatoes, rolls, drinks, salad and even a cake for dessert. Family is invited to join in (the public also, for $3 a head) and a festive mood fills the stands.

Onto the field charge the teams, Show Low proudly wearing new uniforms, but underneath the pads, T-shirts and shoes that don't match, but some have seen more than this season, being hand-me-downs from older brothers or cousins who have played the game in the family tradition. ABR has all new, matching equipment, right down to their shoelaces.

The Show Low coaching staff, typical of most rural Arizona high schools, consists of a physical education teacher, a special education teacher and three volunteers from the community. These men have provided a game plan to be used against the Spartans and their staff, comprised of an Arizona Hall of Fame collegiate and former NFL coach, three ex-NFL players and 10 other assistants..

Team money could and did buy a win. As the jubilant Boys Ranch boys lined up to be marched back to their "home," I couldn't help but feel this is sick and wrong. Was justice served on this evening?

A team of good, young men with positive societal values, supported by local taxpaying citizens, has just been taught a lesson in justice by a team of youths who have scorned society, flaunted their disdain for law and order, and have been sentenced as incorrigible and menaces to that society. The same society that gives them anything and everything they need, at taxpayer expense, to make their experience at this "prison" a rewarding experience.

As the lights are turned off and darkness takes over the field, I think that it is right that justice is blind, for the game played on this night was a travesty before her. The darkness existed long before the lights went out.

It was signed by a man from Show Low.

Thomas didn't know where to start with his rebuttal. How about that the football program was not funded with a dime of taxpayer money? Or that the Ranch wasn't a prison? Or that these boys never had the rock-solid family support that kids in Show Low enjoyed? Or maybe that they were supposed to feed kids only gruel? Or . . . the bus. It was the line about the "new $200,000" bus that really frosted his cake. The letter writer was referring to trusty ol' Spartan Pride, the bus with the radiator that constantly overheated on the way up mountains, often leaving the Ranch players and coaches stranded on the roadside until the engine cooled sufficiently, the bus that didn't have a working gas gauge. "But because it looks good with a nice paint job, people think that we're filthy rich," he added. Thomas knew he had to consider the source. It was only one letter to the editor. It was just one person's opinion. Most any letter gets printed, because no newspaper wants to be perceived as suppressing free speech, something every editor holds near and dear to his or her heart.

But Thomas wondered how many other people out there agreed with this letter writer's line of thinking. There had been other minor accusations throughout the course of the season that had annoyed him as well. The JV team had a fourteen-year-old boy who stood about six feet four. Every week opponents commented that the boy had to be at least eighteen. One time a woman from an opposing school asked Gray if it was true that the Spartans were using nineteen- and twenty-year-old kids on the team. Thomas had also heard that other schools suspected the Ranch was recruiting throughout the juvenile court system. In fact, Thomas did hope the day would come when judges steered promising athletes toward the Ranch instead of to Glen Mills, but not because it would help the Spartans, but because the Ranch was proving athletics could be used to help change kids with even the worst behavioral problems. "What makes us different from the other facilities like this is that we hardly ever turn anybody down," Thomas explained. "We take kids that Glen Mills won't, and we can help them." Some people just want to throw these boys on society's trash heap and leave them there, Thomas added. Maybe that's the only solution that would make them happy.

Later, over at the pantry, what quickly had been dubbed "the Letter" was the hot topic of conversation among the coaches. Like Thomas, they suspected that this lone writer was expressing the sentiments of others. It was frustrating. Here these kids were trying to do things the right way and enjoy an opportunity every other boy in America got, and still they were being slammed for who they were. Ta'ase may have been the most upset of all. He was a Mormon, and Show Low had a substantial Mormon population. He noted that the first thing you saw when you drive into town was a towering Mormon church. His religion taught him not to pass judgment on others, he said, yet that was exactly what those people were doing. Some people wouldn't even give the Ranch a chance to prove itself or give these boys a chance to show how they've changed.

Perkins added: "If we were 0–9, nobody would be saying anything. It's only a problem because we're beating people."

That, of course, went to the heart of the matter. The Spartans weren't supposed to win. They were expected to be little more than a tackling dummy, a gimme victory for other schools in the 3A East Region. So there had to be a reason they were winning, people thought. They must have some unfair advantage over the clean-cut kids in the public schools: money, coaching, equipment, something. And while they were at it, shouldn't those juvenile delinquents be doing something more productive like breaking rocks instead of learning the nuances of the power sweep?

"If they could beat these kids and keep their self-esteem down, then everybody would be happy," Gray said. "But now that we're beating them and ruining their self-esteem, it's a problem."

Gray had known the football program would be criticized. It was only a matter of time. He was different from much of the Ranch staff in that he had spent all of his teaching career in public schools. He knew how they worked. He understood the bureaucracy involved and how some parents would react when their boys did poorly on the playing fields. All that had surprised him was that opponents were closing ranks against the Ranch so soon. But then even he hadn't expected the Spartans to be this good this fast.

"These little rumblings are just the beginning," Gray said as he pushed his meal tray away from him. "The morality side is starting to line up, and we're going to have to answer questions. We're going to hear about whether or not it's right for kids who have had behavior problems to take away opportunities from the 'good' kids of the state. We're hearing questions like, 'Why should my kid be playing against those convicts?' We're going to have parents who don't want their kids to play against them. They're going to say: 'These kids have made mistakes, so why are we rewarding them?'

"Unfortunately, I believe it's human nature to want to keep these kids down," he continued. "Why should these kids who have robbed, raped, done drive-by shootings be rewarded? It really comes down to a debate about crime and punishment. It will be interesting to see if we become an outlaw team that's a bastard stepchild that bounces around from league to league because nobody wants to be associated with us. We're going to face the heat because there's almost nobody else in the country that's doing this. In my mind, what it comes down to is this: Do you want these kids to move next door to you after they get out and be the same people they were when they went in, or do you want them changed? These people who want to keep punishing them seem to think that coming to the Ranch and playing football is some big privilege. Well, it's not."

Lono Hill had been quietly taking in the coaches' discussion from the other end of the dinner table. As he got up with his meal tray, he offered a simple suggestion: "Hey, if they want to beat us, tell them to work harder."

———

The rest of the week fit a familiar pattern. The players went through the motions at practice, acting sullen and lifeless. The coaches fretted that some kids had already called it a season in their heads. Elliott was walking off the practice field one day when he was asked how he was feeling. "You know how it is," he responded. "Just another day at the Ranch."

But Friday, November 17, wasn't just another day. It was the day of the state semifinals. The two 3A games would be played at Mesa Community College, a nice junior-college facility just a short bus hop from the Ranch. The early game would match unbeaten and No. 1–ranked Blue Ridge against Globe. The Ranch would face Safford in the nightcap.

Because the junior college was so close and there were sure to be distractions when the team got to the stadium, Gray decided to arrange the schedule so the Spartans arrived when the first game was ending. That way, they could walk right onto the field for their warm-ups. That meant he would have his pregame talk with the team back in their own locker room, before the players got on the bus. He wanted them to be thinking about what he had to say on the trip to Mesa. Gray wanted them to ponder the concept of fear.

He wasn't talking about what you feel when somebody is breaking into your house, Gray explained to the players. He was talking about a feeling you get in your gut. Some people have a fear of losing, a fear of failure. That's when you don't have self-confidence. That's when you doubt yourself. There's also fear of rejection. You want to satisfy people: friends, family, people you know in your cottages. You don't want to let people down.

All those feelings are normal, Gray continued. But there should be no fear in this room. It took courage to come out for this football team.

"Most of you had never played before," Gray said. "But we're here tonight because you brought us this far. That's why when we get on that bus, expect to win. It all comes back to self-esteem. A lot of those who have had only negative reinforcement in their lives lack self-confidence. But you have to believe in yourself. What you've done is special. I've never had a team improve like this. I believe in destiny. Before I came here, my life was a little down. I had been coaching at a high school where they got rid of me. Last year I was at Mesa Community College, and I was down on the list of assistants, just helping out with the defensive line. I believe I'm here for a reason. So what if nobody else expected us to be here in the state semifinals? Everybody thought they were going to beat the Boys Ranch's butt. That's why we were put in the 3A East. Now that we've established ourselves as winners, we've got every crybaby wondering what advantages we have. Well, all we do is work harder than everyone else. So losing is a foreign thought. We expect to win tonight."

Gray said all this in a calm tone of voice. Yet, for the first time in weeks, each player hung on his every word. Every eye followed him as he walked around the confined space of the locker room. He had struck upon a subject that each boy could grab hold of. Maybe fear, not lack of interest, had been the problem all along. For most of their young lives, these boys had been told that they were worthless. Then suddenly they were pretty good at something. Maybe they were having a hard time dealing with that success. Or maybe they were worried about having that success taken away. What would happen if and when they finally lost? Would everyone look down on them again? It was a frightening prospect. Perhaps their aura of cool indifference — like the pose a young hood might strike as he was being taken into a police station in handcuffs — was their way of masking the jumbled emotions they felt inside.

When Gray was finished, there was absolute silence in the room. The only sound was the breathing of some fifty boys and coaches. Gray broke the quiet with the announcement of one last order of business: his choice for captains. He picked four, including Sparkman and Armstrong. Gray had his reasons. "I picked Tamar Armstrong because he's had some tough times," Gray explained. "But he represents what we're all attempting to do here: improve ourselves. And Juan has been here a long time, longer than anyone else. He represents what the Boys Ranch is all about: trying."

The Spartans arrived at MCC just as the first game was concluding. Wearing their home white jerseys, they went through their usual pregame routine of stretching and drills. There would be a formal ceremony before kickoff in which players from the Ranch and Safford squads would line up at midfield and be introduced individually. But just before taking the field, the team gathered around Elliott under some trees just beyond the north end zone.

"We've come this far, let's not let it get away," he said. "Let's go out there, win tonight, win the state championship next week, and then go home and get on with our lives."

It went bad for the Ranch almost from the start. Cabell fumbled on the Spartans' first possession. Safford then turned the ball over on downs. But on their second possession, the Bulldogs ran the ball down the Ranch's throat. Safford methodically marched over the Ranch defense on a drive that had all the thrills of a chess match. On eleven consecutive plays, the Bulldogs rushed the football. Safford must have seen something on film because they kept running off-tackle to the left side, which was straight at Marcus Thompson, who was the Ranch's smallest defensive lineman. When a Bulldog running back darted into the end zone from 14 yards out and the extra point was kicked, Safford held a 7–0 lead late in the first quarter. After the Ranch couldn't move the ball on three plays and had to punt, Safford went right back to work. This time it was an eight-play drive, seven of them running plays to the same soft spot. And the same running back pushed his way into the end zone from three yards out. The extra point was blocked, but with 9:37 remaining in the half, the Ranch was already down 13–0.

Finally, the Spartans' offense came to life. After the Ranch returned the kickoff to its own 35-yard line, McKissic, who was showing no signs of his ankle injury from the week before, completed a 19-yard pass to Sparkman. Then Peters took a handoff up the middle and broke it for 23 yards. McKissic found Charles Williams open for a pass that would gain 19 more, putting the ball on the Safford 4. All that precision would go for naught, however. In a sign of things to come, Safford demonstrated wickedly vicious defense near the goal line. Blue-and-white-clad players swarmed, eager to put a helmet on the ball-carrier. Peters struggled to gain one yard up the middle. McKissic forced his way for two more on a quarterback keeper. But disaster struck when Cabell took a pitch to the right side on third down. A Safford defender was there right after the ball arrived in his hands, and Cabell was tackled for a 7-yard loss back at the 8. On fourth-and-goal, McKissic barely got off a poor pass under a heavy rush that Elliott dropped. The drive had amounted to nothing.

The Spartan defense yielded one first down before forcing the Bulldogs to punt. But the Safford punter uncorked a 65-yard booming spiral that put the Ranch all the way back on its own 25 with 3:04 left in the half. Nothing was going the Ranch's way on this night. Yet twenty-one seconds later, the Ranch was on the scoreboard. That's how long it took McKissic to find Williams with a 75-yard scoring pass. The Ranch coaches had found a big-play weapon in Williams, and they were determined to keep using him. Williams simply beat his defender on a deep pattern, caught the pass from McKissic, then raced into the end zone. Andrade's extra point made it 13–7. Williams had done it again. So instead of heading into halftime on the verge of being routed, the Ranch was down by just six points.

In their typical fashion, the Spartans would have to avoid further disaster in the final moments of the half. Cabell had muffed a Bulldog punt, and Safford recovered the ball at the Ranch 11 with 1:38 left. But, the Ranch defense had managed to push Safford back out of field-goal range just before half.

As the Spartans headed back to their retreat under the trees beyond the end zone, they weren't happy campers. Safford was a good team, maybe even better than they were. But so far, the Ranch was beating itself. The Spartans had already fumbled the ball away twice and had 40 yards in penalties. Once again, Elliott took the leadership role among the players as the coaches met several yards away to discuss adjustments and changes in strategy. "We're going to win this game," Elliott said. "It's not negotiable. The first half is over. This half is ours."

When Gray emerged from the coaches' huddle, he was livid over how the Spartans had gone into a panic and given up two early touch-downs. And there had been bickering again in the defensive huddle. It appeared that they never were going to solve that problem. Fingers had been pointed. To play off an old line, the Spartans had seen the enemy, and it was themselves. Gray moved to apply a tourniquet to make sure there was no further bleeding from self-inflicted wounds.

"We haven't learned a damn lesson all year," Gray thundered. "Not one. We can't win if we turn on ourselves. We're in this together. If you get frustrated, you can't take it out on each other. Bad things are going to happen. If you want a cakewalk, then you better play against a lot less team than Safford. There's a reason why they're 10–1. If we don't start working together, we don't have a chance. But if we work togeth-er, there's no question in my mind that we can beat them. Now I'm looking at your faces and I'm trying to figure out if you guys really know where you're at. You're one half of a football game away from making it into the Arizona state championship. We're down 13–7. The last time I looked, that was six points. Is that something we can measure up to?"

"Yes, sir!" came the automatic response.

"Then let's go do it," Gray answered.

As the Spartans jogged back to their sideline, it was almost 9:30 P.M. The temperature had plunged, and spectators in the stands were huddling to keep warm. A light fog had begun to roll in. As the brightness of the lights was softened by the mist, the stadium took on an almost surreal quality. Colors were dulled. Combined with an eerie feeling in the air, the scene was reminiscent of an Alfred Hitchcock film.

On the sideline, Allen went up to one player after another, slapping their helmets or lightly punching the tops of their shoulder pads. Over and over, he repeated the same message. "This is your destiny," he kept saying. "It's right here within your reach. You control it. Make it happen."

It had been a weird football game so far, and it was only about to get more bizarre. Eight minutes into the third quarter, Safford struck again. The Ranch had been moving the ball down the field, but a McKissic pass sailed through the hands of Harris and right into the arms of a Safford defender. A Ranch personal foul was tacked onto the play, and the Bulldogs took over at the Spartan 25. Four plays later, that same Safford running back notched his third touchdown of the game, this one a 15-yard run. Now it was 19–7. Yet it was the two-point conversion try that symbolized the kind of evening it had been for the Ranch. Safford reached into its bag of tricks. The quarterback pitched the ball to a running back, who then took a few steps to the right before pulling up. It was a halfback pass. The Ranch had it trapped perfectly as several players converged instantly on the boy with the ball. But somehow the running back eluded three Spartans long enough to throw up a prayer across the field. Not only did the Safford quarterback catch the ball in another crowd of Spartans, but he then scooted his way through the mob and into the end zone. The Safford sideline erupted. Ranch players kicked at the turf in frustration. It was now 21–7.

The situation quickly got even worse. On the Ranch's next possession, McKissic was sacked and fumbled. Safford recovered the ball at the Ranch 33-yard line with 1:47 left in the third quarter. The Ranch was digging itself into a deep hole, maybe even a Grand Canyon–size crater. But on Safford's second play, there was a bad handoff exchange. The ball ended up on the ground, then Walik Smith landed on top of it. From there, the Ranch embarked on its longest drive of the night. Elliott ran for 12 yards. Williams caught a 9-yard pass. A couple of penalties pushed the Ranch backward, but McKissic found Lono Hill wide open in the middle of the Safford secondary and he rambled 24 yards. Corey Luster spelled Elliott and ran for 8 more. Then McKissic took over. He ran left on an option play, faked a pitch, and turned upfield when he saw a crack in the defense. McKissic gained 23 yards on the play before he was tackled at the Safford 2. Two plays later, Jovan Davis scored from 1 yard out. Andrade's extra point made it 21–14 with 8:19 left in the game. It wasn't over yet.

Three plays later, Safford fumbled again. This time Yuoh recovered the loose ball at the Bulldog 49 with 7:11 remaining. Lady Luck, that fickle mistress, had abandoned the Safford sideline and sashayed over to the Ranch's side of the field. The Ranch quickly moved the football to the Safford 22 with two first downs. But then the Spartan offense became bogged down. There was a holding penalty. A McKissic pass was almost intercepted. Two short-yardage running plays left the Ranch facing a fourth-down-and-9 situation with 3:27 left. McKissic faded back to pass and tried to throw across the field, but the weak throw was deflected at the line of scrimmage by a Safford defensive lineman and the football fell harmlessly to the earth. The Bulldog defensive players danced their way off the field. Victory was within their grasp.

It looked grim for the Spartans. There was 3:24 remaining in the game, and the Ranch had just one time-out left. Safford had the ball at its own 21-yard line. A couple of first downs by the Bulldogs would probably be enough to run out the clock, and the Spartans' season would be over. The fans on the Ranch side of the field, who had been raucous all evening, were quiet. The fog that hung over the field was a fitting accompaniment for their depressed mood. It had been a heck of a ride, but now their team's season looked to be ending.

Safford ran two safe, conservative running plays up the middle that together gained 6 yards. The Bulldogs now faced third-and-4 with 2:23 left. Gray called his last timeout. He slowly made the short walk out on the field, as if he were trying to delay the inevitable as long as possible. When he reached his defense, the unit huddled around him. He told his players that the next play would probably go outside, something that had worked well for Safford most of the night. It also was something that might eat up some clock, too. So Gray called a cornerback blitz. It was a risky play. When the ball was snapped, the cornerbacks would leave their receivers and rush directly toward the backfield. If a cornerback was in the right place at the right time, he might make a big play and force the Bulldogs to punt the ball away. But if Safford surprised them and decided to pass, their receivers would be wide open. Or if it were a running play and the back got past a Ranch cornerback outside, he probably wouldn't stop running until he reached the end zone because there wouldn't be any defenders downfield close enough to stop him.

Just as Gray was walking off the field, he turned and offered one last instruction to his cornerbacks. The running back would be carrying the ball in his outside arm to protect it. Remember to try and strip it from him. Don't just tackle him. Go for the ball. Make something happen.

When the Safford quarterback did take the snap from the center, he wheeled to his right and handed off the ball to the running back who had scored all three Bulldog touchdowns. He went wide, just as Gray had guessed. Ed Williams, the Ranch's left-side cornerback, did just as he was told and blitzed. There was confusion for a moment about what happened next. The play had headed toward the Safford sideline, so it was difficult to see from the Spartans' side of the field as players began to collide into one another with a savage fury. But then suddenly, magically, inexplicably, Cabell had the ball and was running in the other direction before he was pulled down at the Safford 19. Williams had done exactly as he was told. He had gone for the ball when he hit the running back. The impact of the collision had dislodged the ball from the Safford player's arms and Cabell plucked it out of the air on the fly. Call it luck, good fortune, or maybe even a miracle of biblical proportions, but the Ranch still had a chance.

The Spartans made the most of the unexpected opportunity. McKissic scrambled for 7 yards. Davis ran for 3 more. Then Elliott, his legs pumping like pistons, muscled his way into the end zone from 9 yards out with just thirty-four seconds left. The score was 21–20. Now it was the Safford fans who were stunned into silence as the Ranch fans erupted with shouts of glee.

The question was what to do now. Kick the extra point and take the game into overtime, or say what the hell and try to win the game now when things were going the Ranch's way? After some quick discussions with his coaches, Gray elected to go for the two-point conversion.

He'd win the game or lose it right here. But as the Ranch players ran up to the line of scrimmage, a yellow flag was tossed into the night sky. The Spartans had taken too much time. A 5-yard delay-of-game penalty was assessed. That changed the situation. Gray wasn't left with much choice. He sent Andrade onto the field. No kick was ever a sure thing with him. Andrade did his best, but you just never knew where the ball was heading when instep met leather. This one would be even harder. With the penalty, this extra point was basically a 25-yard field goal attempt.

The Ranch sideline held its collective breath as Andrade's leg swung like a pendulum toward the ball. His kick went up and sailed straight through the uprights, dead-solid perfect. It was as if he had been doing this for years, not four months. That tied the score at 21. After a squib kickoff, Safford fell on the ball for one play.

It was on to overtime.

Anyone who has ever watched a Sunday-afternoon football game probably could recite the NFL's sudden-death overtime rules from memory. If a game is tied after regulation, there is a coin flip to determine which team gets to receive the kickoff. The first team to score wins. Well, the rules are different in high school football. The Ranch and Safford would be settling matters with something called an Arizona Play-off. None of the Spartans had ever heard of such a thing, of course, so the coaches had to bring the team together on the sideline to explain the system. One team would get the ball at the 10-yard line. It would have four plays to score. The team could score a touchdown or try to kick a field goal. Then the other team would receive four plays to do the same. Whichever team scored the most points would win. If it was still tied after each one had its chance, the process would be repeated. Spartan players began to nod as the rules of this new game began to sink in.

Now, in this format, it is a big advantage to have the ball last. That way, a team knows exactly what it has to do to win. Gray realized this. If the Ranch won the coin flip, which it did, he wanted Safford to have the ball first. But Armstrong, who was serving as the lead captain, indicated that the Ranch would take the ball first, which is what the Ranch always did when it won a pregame coin flip. Gray had neglected to tell Armstrong about the change in strategy. So the Ranch would begin the overtime on offense at the 10. Elliott went up the middle for 1 yard on the first play. Then Cabell went off tackle for 5 more. Elliott again went into the heart of the Safford defense for an additional 2 yards. There was just nowhere to run inside. It was fourth-and-goal from the 2. Kick the field goal or go for it? Gray had shown himself to be a gambling man by nature all season. That wouldn't change now. Besides, he didn't think three points would be enough to win. On fourth down, McKissic was hit behind the line of scrimmage and fumbled before he could pitch the ball to Elliott. The Safford defense had held.

On the sideline, AIA officials who were there as observers couldn't believe that Gray had elected not to go for the field goal. "And that's it for the Ranch," one said quietly. "He must not understand the rules because he just lost his team the game. It's a shame." Thomas and several other Ranch administrators who had been stalking the sideline had come to the same conclusion. Only they weren't as circumspect in showing their emotions. They were visibly distraught. *Why not kick the damned field goal? What the hell is he thinking? That way, you at least make them have to score a touchdown to beat us!* They had a point. Now all Safford had to do was kick a short field goal and the Ranch's season would be history.

The Bulldogs didn't even have to risk a play. They could just kick the ball right away. But there was indecision on the Safford sideline. First the Bulldogs called one time-out, then a second. Finally, they decided to run a couple of plays and see what happened. On first down, a pass fell incomplete after a heavy Ranch rush forced the Safford quarterback to hurry his throw. On second down, Safford's star running back was bottled up for a 1-yard gain. Now, the Safford coaching staff figured they should stop fooling around, send the field-goal team on the field, and finish this thing.

The snap was good. The hold was good. The kick was up. Everybody in the stadium contorted their bodies to the right as they followed the trajectory of the kick toward the uprights. All eyes descended on the two officials stationed under each post. They glanced at each other ever so briefly and then began to wave their arms furiously. The kick was wide right by inches, they ruled. It was still a tie game. The stadium was in an uproar. The Safford fans couldn't believe the kick had been missed. The Ranch fans couldn't believe it, either. But that didn't stop them from celebrating. Even the AIA officials looked at one another as if to say, "What the hell is going on here?"

Because the game remained deadlocked, the teams would do the Arizona Play-off all over again. The Ranch got the ball back at the 10.

This time Elliott went off tackle for 7 yards on first down. But then as Cabell was dropped for no gain, this drive began to take on the appearance of déjà vu. The Ranch had seen this before. Peters lowered his head, went up the middle, and was stopped within inches of the goal line. The Safford defense simply would not yield the end zone to the Spartans. It was fourth down again. Gray decided to go for it again. Later, he would explain that there comes a point where a coach has to let his players know that he believes in them. This time, his faith was rewarded. Peters, the powerful little fullback, pushed his way into the promised land. For the first time all night, the Ranch held the lead. When Andrade's extra point split the uprights, making the score 28–21, a flag was thrown. A Safford player had run into Andrade after the kick. So because of the personal foul penalty, now the Bulldogs would be getting the ball on the 25-yard line instead of the 10 to begin their last chance.

The Ranch was on the verge of an upset. Back on the sideline, the players from the offensive unit were already congratulating one another. That proved, however, to be premature. On their first play, the Bulldogs sent all their receivers and running backs deep. Somehow a receiver had broken free in the end zone and a pass was heading in his direction. The Ranch's Judas Ervin got there just a split second before the ball arrived on the scene to get a hand in the receiver's face and force him to drop the ball. Gray was left screaming on the sideline: "How'd that guy get open? Who didn't have his man?" Gray didn't get an answer, and on second down, Safford did the same thing. A desperation pass was tossed into the end zone. This time Cabell was there. He got a hand on the ball, and tipped it away . . . and into the waiting hands of a Safford receiver.

Touchdown, Bulldogs. The Ranch's lead had been shaved to 28–27.

Once again, there had been an incredible reversal of fortunes. But neither side had time to celebrate or curse its fate. Safford had to decide whether to kick the extra point to tie the game again or go for the victory with the two-point conversion. It wasn't an easy call. The Bulldogs' kicker had just missed that short field goal and had had an extra point blocked earlier. Even worse, the Safford quarterback had been hurt on the touchdown play when he was buried by the Spartan defensive line after just getting away the pass.

A strange quiet fell over the field as Safford lined up to kick the extra point. On the Ranch sideline, some kids held hands, while some said prayers. Others couldn't stand to watch and turned their heads away. McKissic was down on his hands and knees. It was, he would say afterward, as if time stood still.

Finally, just before the snap, Safford shifted out of the kicking alignment. A running back, who had been squatting down on one knee as the holder, stood up and took the hike from a shotgun formation. Safford was going for two. The game would come down to this play. Bulldog receivers and backs flooded into the end zone, with Spartan defenders in hot pursuit. Everyone may have been running a precise pattern, but it looked like sheer confusion. The Safford running back with the ball dropped back a couple of steps and drifted to the right as he surveyed the field, urgently looking for an open teammate before his offensive line collapsed under the weight of the Ranch's relentless pass rush.

Then the running back found somebody.

In the back of the end zone, a tight end had broken free of the coverage. The running back saw him and lofted a pass in his direction. Spartan defenders instantly saw the hole in their defense and tried to break to the ball. But they wouldn't get there in time. The Safford tight end reached high into the air, stretched his body vertically, pulled the football out of the sky, and came down.

He caught the ball. His feet also landed out of bounds — barely.

Two officials, who were right on top of the play, were waving their hands frantically across their chests. The catch was no good. Video replays would indicate that they made the correct call. But the tape would also show something else: exhausted Safford players slumping to the ground. Their bitter defeat had proved correct the axiom that football is a game of inches. At the same moment, Ranch players could be seen rushing onto their field, throwing their helmets high into the late-evening sky, as they jumped up and down in a spontaneous outburst of pure joy.

Over three hours after the game had begun, the final score was the Ranch 28, Safford 27.

The Spartans were going to the state championship game.

The party was interrupted momentarily when the Safford players, in classy fashion, came over and shook hands with the Spartans and wished them luck in the title contest. Then it was back to the revelry. The players picked up Gray in the end zone. He kept shouting: "Not now! Next week!" But they wouldn't listen and refused to return him to the ground. Mike Smith lifted Andrade up. It was his kicks that had helped make the difference. Players kept hugging one another and mugging for the TV cameras and newspaper photographers. Eventually, Gray got his feet planted on the ground again and the players took a knee in the end zone. First Mike Miller wanted to say something. Miller had been one of the boys who had gotten frustrated in the first half and had begun to run his mouth. He apologized for doubting the squad and said it meant more than anything to him to be playing with these teammates and coaches. Then it was Gray's turn.

"You guys are something else when it comes to testing the limits and waiting until the last minute to get the job done," he said. "But if anybody can overcome that much adversity and still come out ahead, it's you guys. There were so many times that we could have said that we were out, that we were done, that we're not going to win this. But you didn't quit. Don't forget that. And I don't know who's watching out for us, but I'm going to keep following him."

Father Mitchell had an idea about whom the team was following. His white hair ruffled, he entered the circle of players and raised his thin voice to make a request. Before they did another thing, he said, he wanted them to do something for him: shout "Hallelujah" three times.

"Hallelujah, hallelujah, hallelujah!" responded the players.

Slowly, the natural high began to wear off. The players knew that it was time to get serious again when they were told to line up for the walk back to the bus. As they left the field, Gray spied the Blue Ridge coach and went over to shake his hand. The two men congratulated each other and quickly began negotiations for the exchange of game film. The top-ranked Yellowjackets had improved their record to 12–0 by crushing Globe in the other semifinal, 60–8.

It was enough to bring a coach back down to reality.

My name is Andre Hughes. I'm eighteen years old. I'm from San Francisco. I've been here about seventeen months.

When I first got here, it was hard. This can be a real frustrating place. They expect a lot out of you. There's a lot of work crews. You march everywhere. This wasn't the kind of place that I expected it to be. But I ended up here because I was doing all the wrong things: robbing people, selling drugs. This is my fourth placement. I was at two other ranch places, and I was at a group home. This is the best place because staff really takes more time to get to know you. They don't just give you food and a place to sleep. They really want to help you. Staff members will go out of their way to make sure you're doing OK and to talk to you. They want to get involved with you.

When I first got here, I was in Civics. Then I came up to main campus to play football. I was at the main Ranch for ten months. Then I got in trouble and had to go back down to Oracle. There was some adversity. I had gotten comfortable in the system here, but that shook me up. That's when I really started giving this place a chance. It's been about six months now that I've been doing the right thing. Now I've got my plan. I don't want to go back home. I want to stay here and maybe go to Mesa Community College.

I don't want to go back to San Francisco because of, you know, trouble. I don't have problems with people looking to kill me or nothing. But it won't be good for me to go back. There's just not much back there for me, like a job. The temptations would still be there. I'd probably be tempted to go back to my old ways. I don't even want to deal with those temptations.

I grew up in the projects, but they weren't the real bad ones. There were some bad people there, but there were more good people living there than bad. The trouble started when I was about eleven years old. That's when my mom started using drugs. It changed our whole family. Up to then, I'd had a good childhood. I was going to a Catholic school. It was pretty normal. But then that all changed. I started going out and selling drugs to support my little brother and sister because my mom wasn't doing it. From there, I started getting high all the time, and drunk, and robbing from people and getting in trouble. My dad wasn't around because he was in prison. See, I thought I was being a man doing this stuff. But I wasn't. I was robbing stores. I was robbing people. I was carjacking. Sometimes it was for the money. Sometimes it was just for the feeling of power that I held over people, scaring them.

I would go into a program and learn about doing the right thing in life, and then I would go back to my same ol' ways on the street. I knew that there was another way, doing right and being positive, but nobody else was doing that. None of my friends were doing it.

My dad's in a federal prison out in Phoenix. He's got a few more months there; then he has to go back to San Quentin for eighteen more months. It will have been fifteen years for him in January, so he hasn't been around since I was little. My grandmother tried her best to take care of us, but she couldn't. So I had to step in. I would get groceries and clothes for my brother and sister. I would get them toys. I tried my best to put food in the refrigerator because my mom, the drugs were controlling her mind. So I did try to do some good.

I don't talk to my mom much because I don't like to talk to her when she's using drugs. It upsets me. Something else that upsets me is that I've got a son out there and I haven't talked to him in a long time. That hurts me. He's in San Francisco with his mom. She and I, we don't get along too well. She's a pretty good person. But it's just that she's not the kind of person I can spend the rest of my life with. Lately, I haven't talked to her much. My son's name is Angelo. He's three years old. I miss him.

What do I think of football? It's a fun game, but it can be kind of stressful because we're here. C'mon now, we're not a normal high school. At a normal school you don't wake up at 6 o'clock in the morning, clean up the barracks, go to inspection, then march to breakfast all before school. Then you go to class, then it's three hours of football practice. Then we have work crew after that. I'm not complaining, but it can be hard. You want to win, but you're not into it as much as you should be, either. You're not here to play football. You're here to deal with your issues.

I couldn't have imagined being the person I am today. I've learned how to work. They told me I was a hard worker on the work crews in Civics. I worked in Rave Reviews; that's the discount store that the Ranch runs. The Ranch even got me a job at Arby's.

I wouldn't have been talking about myself like this even ten months ago. I would have answered questions and stuff, but it wouldn't have come from the heart. When you first get here, you put a wall up around yourself. You don't want to let anyone inside. You don't want to hear it when staff tells you that you're going to change here. The first thing you say is, "I'm not changing." But then when you're here awhile and do some positive things, you realize that you can do some good things and you don't have to spend your life in jail being miserable. The Ranch makes you see

that if you have opportunities, you can take advantage of them. I'm start-
ing to see the light. And the clearer that light gets, you realize how impor-
tant it is to do the right thing.

If you think about it, the Ranch is a little community unto itself. Some
people haven't changed here and won't change. But I ignore those people
when they talk to me and try to start something. I do get mad, don't get
me wrong. I'm not a perfect angel. I have gotten in fights. But that was a
long time ago. I've learned to love myself more than to get in that kind of
trouble.

Tim Elliott and I went to MCC [Mesa Community College] today. It
was a nice trip. We got to visit with staff, some coaches, some guidance
counselors. We even took placement tests. I think that's where I want to go
to college. They seemed to like us. But it's hard coming from the Boys
Ranch. Tim and I were out looking for apartments near school and they
asked us where we were from and we said Boys Ranch. You could just see
it in their eyes that they didn't want us there. They didn't say anything, but
you knew. Suddenly they started saying we had to have stuff that they
knew we couldn't possibly have, like proof of employment for six months.
They kept putting up these obstacles. It's all because of what they've heard
about Boys Ranch.

People need to know what the Ranch is really like, what we're really
doing here. If they don't, then it's hard for people like us just getting out
and trying to make it in the world the right way.

THE END OF THE BEGINNING

It was Thanksgiving week, and a parade of visitors had been making their way to the Ranch's practice field. A Phoenix TV crew appeared one day to do a profile on the Spartans. It was rare for a 3A program to get that kind of media coverage. Usually the small schools were dwarfed by the attention paid to the 4A and 5A programs. But the Ranch's story was beginning to turn some heads. The unique nature of the program made it good human-interest material. For a change, the Ranch was making headlines for reasons that didn't include accusations of abuse.

The usual suspects were rounded up and herded toward the TV cameras — Elliott, Armstrong and McKissic. Elliott, strangely enough, didn't like all the attention. Like a hermit crab, he preferred the safety of his shell. He was wary in interviews and would carefully analyze every question before offering a safe response. Most of all, he just wanted reporters to bother someone else. "How come everybody wants to talk to the same people?" Elliott groused. "We got other guys on the team who can play. It's not just me."

There was one guest, however, that week that Elliott was eager to meet: the head football coach at MCC [Mesa Community College]. He had come out to talk with the players who would be graduating from high school in December and May. As the team had progressed in the play-offs, Gray had begun fielding more and more inquiries from colleges. Miller was only fifteen, for instance, and would be just a sophomore at a normal high school. Yet he was already getting questionnaires from Division I schools. One day, Miller had come to Gray's office and explained that he wanted to play college football. All right, Gray said, then this is what you need to do. And for the next ten minutes, Gray had explained Proposition 48, the academic standards that all incoming freshmen must meet to play at an NCAA Division I university. He talked about core classes and minimum grade-point averages and the SAT entrance exam. When Gray finally came up for air, a bewildered Miller explained in a shy voice that he just wanted to know if Gray thought he might be good enough to play someday. Gray put his hand on Miller's shoulder and said, yes, he believed that he would be good enough. But talent wouldn't matter, he added, if he didn't give his academics attention, too.

Gray had called the MCC coach, a man whom he had worked for the previous year, and told him that he might want to take a look at some of the Ranch kids because his competitors at other Arizona junior colleges were already sniffing around. "I'm not telling you where to go to school," Gray told the players before introducing the coach after an early-week practice, "but junior college is a great door to walk through and a great place to start." Elliott, for one, was determined to charge through that door.

Finally, a familiar face appeared at practice one afternoon: Kush. Since the first Blue Ridge game, Kush hadn't had much to do with the team. He had attended most of the games, but he always sat in the stands with fans. He stayed away from the sideline and the coaches. While his health wasn't great, Kush maintained that he wasn't a sick man, either. He had simply learned that there were limits to what his body could handle. Coaching football exceeded those boundaries, he explained. Besides, Kush had come to the conclusion that he didn't have the right personality to coach high school kids. It takes patience, something he admitted having precious little of when he stepped on the field.

"Did I expect they'd be here?" Kush asked rhetorically. "Hell, no. Going into the 3A East, with the caliber of competition they were going to have, I'm shocked they even made the play-offs. But I've been pleasantly shocked."

Some people look at football and see a game. Not Kush. He saw life. To Kush, the earth was flat — the exact dimensions of a football field, complete with sideline makers, end zones, and goal posts. He sincerely believed that football had saved his life and made him who he was. He believed football could provide kids at the Ranch with that same chance, as well as something else: redemption. "The key is that they acquire confidence here and then transfer it to other parts of their lives," Kush said. "If nothing else, they have learned not to quit. But you can also learn skills on the football field that will help you in life, stuff like perseverance, determination, playing with pain, working with others, learning what it takes to succeed. Football is reality. There's no bullshit to it."

Kush hadn't been the only doubter, of course. None of the coaches ever expected to get to the state finals. A few months earlier, their goals had been modest: be competitive, don't get embarrassed. Now they were on the threshold of completing the most remarkable of seasons. They were 9–3. Their team hadn't lost since late September. This bunch of inexperienced misfits was one step away from winning a state championship. No wonder the coaches joked among themselves about how they could probably sell the movie rights to their story to Disney. But then Gray would add that Disney wouldn't be interested because the tale would be considered too unbelievable. Just about the only coach who wasn't giddy about the prospect of playing in the state title game was Moore. Yet he also epitomized perfectly how the play-off run had caught all of them by surprise. He had missed the better part of the previous two weeks after undergoing ankle surgery to repair an old football injury. Moore had scheduled the operation months in advance. Understandably, he hadn't thought he would be coaching football in late November. Now he was hobbling around the field on medication to take the edge off his pain.

The players were more stunned than anybody by their accomplishments. A few, like Letua, thought they should never have lost those games early in the season. But they were the exceptions. The majority would just shake their heads when asked if they had ever thought that first day in August, when they were sweating through three-a-day workouts in triple-digit heat, that come late November they would be knocking on the door of a state title. Most of the players would have been happy with a winning record. What they had done was almost beyond their comprehension. They still may have lacked the passion of a normal high school squad, but what they had accomplished over the last three months finally was beginning to hit them. "It's been kind of shocking, but we worked for it, too," McKissic said. "I didn't think we'd have the opportunity to be here. But as the year progressed, we kept getting better and better. I knew in the very first game we might be better than we thought. I just didn't know that we would be this much better."

If an award was given to the nicest kid on the football team, it probably would have gone to either Cody Jeffries or Lono Hill. Like Jeffries, Hill always seemed to be smiling, although like everyone else here, he had a history. He ended up in the juvenile court system in San Diego after he got drunk one night with some of his fellow gang homeboys and started beating a kid he didn't know. Hill didn't remember much about what happened, but witnesses had IDed him in the assault. Hill couldn't explain why he had done it or why he had joined a gang in the first place. He only knew that while he had been violent and angry then, he was different now.

"I figured we'd just win a couple of games and get killed in the rest," Hill said. "I'm glad I stuck it out. I wanted to quit back in the three-a-days. I've been thinking that football has shown me that I can make it. I can do things. I'm thinking about enrolling in junior college. I never thought that I could hack that. But if I can do football, then maybe I can do that, too. I'm starting to really believe in myself, that I can do something with my life, something more than just sit on a street corner. I never felt like that before."

He added that someday he was going to tell his kids about playing in the state championship football game. He was worried that they might not believe their old man, so he was hoping for a little proof. Thomas had spoken to the team before the play-offs and promised the players that if they did win the state title, he would make sure they got championship rings.

"I want a ring," Hill said, that omnipresent grin crossing his face.

———————

Gray had a newfound appreciation for the Bible story of David and Goliath, and right now he was holding the slingshot and looking for a smooth stone. The hulking giant standing across the valley was Blue Ridge. What word could he find to describe the Yellowjackets? Great? Unreal? Awesome? They all applied. Before their first game back in September, Gray had looked at film of Blue Ridge and decided that the 1995 Yellowjackets were not the same team that had won the state title in '94. Gray still agreed with that assessment. Only now he had decided that the Yellowjackets were even better.

For a team from such a small, remote school, the Yellowjackets had a remarkable core of good athletes. On top of that, they were well coached. They made opponents pay for their miscues, while they simply didn't make very many mistakes. There was a good reason for that. Kids on the team had been playing football together since the seventh grade. Before each season, the team would spend a week in southern California. They would practice hard twice a day and then spend the rest of their time on the beach. In the spring, they spent another week at something called Mountain Camp, where, in the words of Blue Ridge coach Paul Moro, "We try to kill them." They would do backpacking, play games of paint-ball war, anything that worked them to exhaustion. Each year, Moro said, he would end up with eighteen to twenty-three players on his team, which was a low turnout for a 3A school.

"It's too hard," Moro said. "A lot of schools want everybody to play football. Well, a lot of people want to be in the Army, too. But only a few want to be in the Rangers. We're the Rangers. We're an elite football team. We're not a normal football team." The numbers backed up Moro's boasting. Blue Ridge's winning streak had reached twenty-five consecutive games. But even more impressive was how the Yellowjackets had won. They had not even been challenged all year. Blue Ridge had outscored opponents 528–48 on the season. When you played the Yellowjackets, you knew what you were in for. They would beat you, and they would beat you bad. "They will get up on you and not let up," Gray said. "They will pound you when you're down. When you play them, they'll keep you down, and that's fine. I've got no problem with that. It's my job to prevent them from scoring seventy on us."

Gray had tried to play it straight against the Yellowjackets in the third week of the season. He had attempted to run the ball right at them with their array of running backs. The result was that the Spartans got whacked, 31–0. This time Gray planned to pull out every gadget in the playbook: reverses, options, halfback passes. Gray needed some big plays. They've had it too easy all year, Gray believed. We need to rattle their cage. Maybe it would shake their confidence if they were suddenly down by a couple of touchdowns. "We're riding the long-shot horse here," he said. "We need to trick them. Our offense is going to be the Fumblerooskie. We're going to razzle. We're going to dazzle. Then we have to hope our defense plays the game of its life."

Anyway, that was the plan.

The telegram was taped to the window in the coaches' office. It was addressed from Blue Ridge. "We're going to win by forty. Don't even bother showing up." Gray didn't know who had sent it, but he suspected somebody from the Ranch's staff in the Ranger Corps, which was a ninety-day shock program for juvenile offenders based near Payson, had written it to fire up the players. But if the Spartans were upset about the telegram, they kept it to themselves. Most didn't even look at it as they passed by the office before and after practice. Perhaps they just saw through the cheap motivational ploy.

But Gray got their attention after Tuesday's practice. He had already announced that everyone was going to play in Friday night's game. Everyone had helped the team get this far, so every player was going to be able to say that he had been on the field in a state championship game. Gray said he owed it to all the players for taking him this far. Then he noted that the team was looking like state champs, too. Everyone else can doubt you, he said, but we're going to set them straight and let them know who plays for the Ranch. With that, Gray pulled out a No. 76 jersey with the name of reserve lineman Bouakhao Dovangchompa on the back.

"We've had everybody's name put on the back of their jersey," Gray said. "They're not going to need a program to know who you guys are Friday night."

———

The sun was going down as practice came to an end on Wednesday, the day before Thanksgiving. It was one of those glorious Arizona sunsets when every color in the spectrum reaches out across the sky. Next to the practice field, a work crew had just marched in with rakes and shovels on the shoulders of some boys and others marched in a row as they pushed a formation of wheelbarrows. They had come from the direction of the new football field. The stadium was beautiful. The stands and lights were up. A turf of emerald green had been planted. The track surface was even Spartan green. A soccer field nearby with lights had also been completed. All that remained was for the gymnasium to be built, and ground was scheduled to be broken on that in the spring. When finished, the sports facility would have cost about $1.5 million to build. Thomas was always quick to point out that the complex was being constructed with donations, so taxpayers didn't have to reach for their wallets. The Ranch no longer would have to play its basketball games over at the Williams Air Force Base gym or host "home" football contests at area schools. In fact, the Ranch could have played the Show Low game on this field, but Thomas had wanted to wait. He preferred to hold off until next fall before formally dedicating the Frank Kush Athletic Complex.

The two staff members watching over the work crew instructed the boys to line up next to the field and then relax at parade rest. All the boys in the crew wore yellow shirts, indicating that they had violated some portion of the Ranch's code. One of the boys was Jerrold Smith, who liked to call himself "The Hitman." He had played on the JV all season. When the squad's season ended, Smith had gotten restless and gone AWOL. Now he was back and clothed in yellow.

Smith served as a reminder of football's place at the Ranch. It wasn't why boys were here. It was important, but only as a tool and only for a short time. All that would last would be the memories and perhaps some lessons gleaned from the game. One way or another, the season would be over for everyone late Friday night when the state title game concluded over at MCC. Then football would be in everyone's rearview mirror. The boys, though, would still be at the Ranch. Many would still be struggling. All would be trying to find their way. For every other high school football team in America, the end of the season meant the end of the hard work, the conditioning, the pain. Not at the Ranch. As one member of the Civics staff, who was up from Oracle to watch over the kids from his program, said: "Monday will be a wake-up call when we get the football players back. We'll be PT'ing 'em. We'll take care of those prima donna football attitudes."

Shofner was standing within earshot. "And there's a lot of distance between the P and the T," he added.

Meanwhile, the yellow shirts had been marched away to the pantry for dinner. Jerrold Smith never looked back. Everyone at the Ranch knew that a resident never turned his head when he was marching, especially if he was wearing yellow.

———

As the final minutes ticked away before the game, the Ranch locker room was silent except for the sounds of cleats scraping on the floor, the flushing of toilets, and the hushed sound of whispering. Then

Gray called the players over and delivered his last pregame talk of the season.

He spoke in an even, measured voice. There was no fire and brimstone. There was no attempt to fire up the troops before they rushed onto the field. He barely even talked about football.

Before we go out there, Gray began, I want you to take a minute and think of what this season has been about. Think back to when we were practicing three times a day, when we were working in the 115-degree heat. When practice started, you didn't even know how to line up in formations correctly. The center could barely snap the ball to the quarterback without fumbling it. None of you grew up next door to each other. You all come from different parts of the country, different backgrounds, different problems, different lives. Yet you joined together to become good enough as a team to play in the state championship game.

Football may end tonight, Gray continued, but what you've learned from football and what the Boys Ranch is all about is just beginning for you. You've learned about the positive people that you can be. Most of your lives, people thought that you couldn't do anything, you wouldn't amount to anything, you were bums, you would probably be criminals your whole life. But you *are* somebody. Everybody in this room should feel important. Before the season, you were told that this football team wouldn't win. Look where you are now. That's why I say that this is just the beginning for each and every one of you. You're just understanding what you're capable of doing. When you leave the Ranch and you have people tell you that you can't do this and you can't do that, just remember back to this season. The idea is exactly the same. You can't let adversity stop you. You haven't let adversity stop you on the football field. There's no reason to let it stop you in the world. I'm here to tell you that you're pretty damn remarkable young men.

Then Gray paused to look around the locker room.

This football team has been about one thing, he continued. We coaches have known it all along. It's been about making you realize that you can achieve anything you want in life if you just open your minds to the possibilities. That's what we're going to do tonight. We're going to open our minds up and win the state championship. But no matter what happens, they can't take away our pride, they can't take away our self-respect, they can't take away who we are. A lot of you guys are leaving the Ranch in December, and I firmly believe that the success you've had on the football field is going to help you when you're ready to go out there because now you know that you are somebody.

———

If this indeed had been a Hollywood movie, there would have been a fairy-tale finish to the season. The Ranch would have taken the field and dethroned the defending champ. The last scene might have featured McKissic throwing a game-winning touchdown pass, or maybe Armstrong forcing a fumble to save the game, or perhaps even Elliott sprinting into the end zone. Gray would have been carried off the field as inspirational music played in the background as the credits began to roll.

But this was reality.

When the game was over, there were no tears and no real anger. There were a few small displays of frustration. Some helmets slammed to the turf. There were a few harsh words involving maternal themes. But mostly the Spartans handled their defeat with grace. When they were told to line up to shake the hands of the two-time state champions, the Blue Ridge Yellowjackets, they did so quickly. Sparkman was among those leading the way. At the postgame trophy ceremony, the Spartans all offered polite applause as the Yellowjackets held up the spoils of their victory — the title trophy.

Perhaps it would have hit the players harder had the game been closer, if this had been a narrow loss that had gone down to the final minutes. But it wasn't. Blue Ridge, just like in its first game against the Spartans, dominated from start to finish. Or maybe it was, as Mike Smith would say afterward, that these kids had dealt with real hard knocks before coming to the Ranch. This would hardly register on their personal Richter scales of emotional earthquakes.

The 41–13 final score accurately reflected the contest. Gray would say later that he knew about halfway through the first quarter, when his offense could do absolutely nothing on the Spartans' first two possessions, that it would be a long night. The Ranch had broken out the trick plays, and Blue Ridge had methodically broken each one. The lone bright spot had been Elliott. The score was already 21–0 when, on the last play of the first half, he took a kickoff on the left side of the field, ran right, picked up a wall of blockers, and didn't stop sprinting until he reached the end zone 80 yards later. It had briefly given the Ranch some hope.

But the second half was more of the same. This time the Ranch had no miracle comeback. The Blue Ridge defense left McKissic running for his life. As Gray made good on his promise to let everyone play, the Yellowjackets' offense took advantage of the Ranch's inexperienced reserves by turning the game into a rout. The final nail in the Spartans' coffin was a Blue Ridge touchdown run with just nine seconds left in the game. Gray had not expected any mercy, and none had been given.

That meant, however, that there would be one final kickoff. And on the last play of the season, Elliott set a state title game record by returning yet another kick for a touchdown, this one for 76 yards.

Back in the locker room, Elliott addressed his teammates. He had not let go of the runners-up trophy since it landed in his hands. He wore a Spartans cap on his head and a broad grin on his face. He felt good about the season, and he wanted to make sure that the rest of the Spartans did as well. "We were No. 32 before the season, and we finished No. 2," he told them, holding the trophy up high. "There ain't no reason to be hanging our heads. We don't need no ring. So let's keep our chins high."

As the players went about getting showered and dressed, the atmosphere in the locker room gradually became looser. The noise level rose. The players started joking with each other. It was apparent that in some ways the weight of the world had been lifted from their shoulders. More than a few boys simply were happy that the season was finally over. Armstrong was among those who had talked to the coaches earlier in the week about the tremendous pressure he was feeling. Everyone at the Ranch had been counting on them, and it had been difficult to deal with that. At this moment, though, Armstrong was flashing the biggest smile of the season. "I can look in the mirror at myself," he said. "Hard work got us this far. Hard work got me this far."

Not far away, teammates were giving Elliott a hard time, telling him that he better have enjoyed those two touchdowns because they were his last ones. In junior college, they needled, he was going to be converted to a safety, where he wouldn't get the chance to run with the ball. "Just watch me when I intercept the ball," Elliott countered.

Even the normally stoic McKissic was visibly happy. "I'm not going to be upset about this," he said. "No, sir."

Those who took the loss the hardest, though, were the coaches. They knew how close the Spartans had come and the opportunity that had been lost. This might have been the only time in the coaches' careers that they would get this far in the play-offs. But Gray refused to show his disappointment. He didn't want the players to feel they had let anybody down. He went through the locker room, shaking hands, slapping backs, hugging players. "I'm going to feel good about this season, and I'm going to feel good about these kids," he said quietly.

The defeat was slowly forgotten. These were just normal teenagers, enjoying each other's company. Some were already talking about the upcoming basketball and wrestling seasons. Their conversations had turned to the pizza parlor where the team was being taken for a postgame meal. A few even joked that back home they weren't going to believe that they had played in the Arizona state championship football game.

This would be one of the last times this group would be together. Maybe only a dozen would be back next season. The Ranch would have to start from scratch again next year. There would be another meeting where Gray would ask how many kids had played organized football and only a handful would raise their hands. The same trials and tribulations would start again with a new batch of troubled boys.

Most of the kids in this room would be long gone by then. They were heading back to the Outs, where the real game would begin. Only then would they find out if football had been more than a mere game that had kept them busy for four months or if they had really learned something. The true final score for this team — the only one that really mattered — wouldn't be known for years.

As they boarded the bus, the lights on the football field flickered out.

EPILOGUE

Eight days after the state championship game, the Frank Kush Roast and Celebrity Golf Classic was held. It was in part to honor Kush, who would be heading to New York City the next week for a formal dinner honoring his induction into the College Football Hall of Fame. It was also used as a vehicle to raise money for the new athletic complex. Thomas never missed a trick when it came to fund-raising. The roast gave friends and former players a chance to take their best shots at Kush. John Jefferson, who went on from Arizona State to a long NFL career as a wide receiver, noted that Kush had left his mark on all his former players. "We probably all have the medical bills to prove it, too," Jefferson added. "Before I got here, other players told me that Kush liked to reach out to his players. Well, little did I know that meant reaching for my face mask and pulling it off my helmet."

John Mistler, another ASU wide receiver who would later play for the New York Giants, remembered one day when he dropped a pass in practice and then, to his horror, saw Kush stop the workout, point at him, and start screaming to an assistant. "Who recruited that jackass?"

"You did, Coach," answered the assistant.

"Well, then I'm a bigger jackass," Kush countered, stalking away.

Charity roasts are supposed to give everyone a chance to poke good-natured fun at the guest of honor. In this case, the people who had come from around the country to skewer Kush seemed to be pulling their verbal punches. Maybe it was out of respect — or maybe it was out of fear that Kush might have them running laps around the resort later that night. As former ASU and Dallas Cowboy quarterback Danny White said, "The thing you have to understand about Frank is that it's not easy to act like a complete and total jerk when, deep down, you're not a complete and total jerk."

Joe Garagiola, who served as master of ceremonies, could only shake his head as the roast became more of a testimonial dinner. "Frank," he said, "you'll be lucky if you get out of here tonight without being canonized."

In all, more than $250,000 was raised that weekend for the Kush complex.

———

In mid-December, the team banquet was held. Because Gray didn't believe in individual awards, no trophies were given out for most valuable player and such. Everyone, Gray explained, had been valuable. Five players had made the 3A East first-team all-conference squad, however. Letua and Armstrong were named on defense, and McKissic, Elliott, and Marcus Thompson, a starting guard, were first-teamers on offense. The honor roll didn't end there. Elliott, Yuoh, and Andrade, the kicker who couldn't kick at the beginning of the season, were named to the 3A all-state team. Then there was one more honor for Armstrong. His hard work had definitely paid off. He had been named first-team all-Arizona, which consisted of the best players in the state regardless of school size.

This had been a dream season for the coach, too. Gray had begun the year with some doubts about whether or not he could coach high school football anymore. In many ways, the Ranch had been his last chance as well. In a newspaper story written about him after he was named the state's 3A Coach of the Year, Gray said he hadn't witnessed any miracles that season. But he had seen a group of kids from tragic backgrounds hold their heads high, and seeing the pride they took in playing football had meant a lot to him.

At the banquet, each player's name was called as he walked up and received a varsity letter. Gray had a brief story to tell about each one. He saved the best for Walik Smith. Gray said that during the season, his wife would shake him in the middle of the night. When he woke up, Gray would ask, what's wrong? Well, she'd say, "You were shouting out, 'Walik, Walik! You're lined up wrong!'" Everyone laughed, including Walik.

One other memento of the season wouldn't arrive for another few weeks. After the state championship game, when the team went out to eat, Thomas had stood up and told the players how proud he was of them. What the heck, Thomas had added, I'm gonna get you guys rings anyway. State runners-up rings would be arriving sometime after the first of the year.

"I hope you don't misunderstand this gathering here," Gray told the team. "It's not just because we won a lot of football games. It's because you're winners in the truest sense of the word, and it has nothing to do with victories."

————

The hearing chamber at the House of Representatives at the Arizona state capitol was packed. It was standing room only, so an adjoining room had to be opened up as well. It was December 20, and state lawmakers had scheduled a public hearing to air concerns about the actions taken by the Department of Economic Security against the Ranch. State representative Robert Burns had called a hearing of his legislative committee after the McDonald report was brought to his attention. "I have read at least 90 percent of the report, and the findings, in my opinion, point to unacceptable behavior," Burns said. "I believe they point to flaws in our regulatory system."

Citing the pending civil suit filed by the Ranch, DES officials said that they could not answer questions at this time. But Eric Bost, the agency's assistant director, did read a prepared statement. He noted that it was the state's duty to investigate allegations of abuse at facilities that it licensed. He said that of the fifty-nine investigations of alleged abuse at the Boys Ranch, thirty-seven had been found not to be substantiated. But, he added, "The department continues to have concerns about Arizona Boys Ranch compliance with licensing standards and compliance with state reporting statutes. Currently, there are twelve allegations of abuse at Arizona Boys Ranch that are under investigation. . . . The department agrees that many of the residents of Arizona Boys Ranch are serious juvenile offenders and that Arizona Boys Ranch meets a significant need. However, some methods used in dealing with serious juvenile offenders may conflict with licensing standards for child welfare agencies in Arizona."

Then, for the better part of three and a half hours, Ranch supporters pummeled the Child Protective Services branch of the DES, accusing it of bias and incompetence and of blatantly trying to close down the facility. Two probation officers from California spoke, saying they had no concerns about the Ranch but questioned some of the methods of state case workers who interviewed them about cases of alleged abuse involving boys they had placed there. Both said they wondered if the state workers really understood the kind of kids they were dealing with and repeatedly warned that they should view any allegations these boys made with a high degree of skepticism.

A probation officer from Alameda County said that one of the residents who had AWOLed and accused the Ranch of abuse was now in a California prison. "An investigator at the prison asked him about his experience at ABR," she said. "He said, 'Yes, I was abused there. They made me exercise.' That was what he thought abuse was. But he also conceded that maybe if he had stayed at the Ranch, he wouldn't be where he is today."

A current resident of the Civics program spoke. If there was abuse at the Ranch, he asked, why did he return voluntarily nine months after Alameda County was forced to pull its kids, including him?

McDonald, the attorney who had investigated the program, presented the Ranch's case. He made an analogy between the Ranch's philosophy and the approach taken with Helen Keller. McDonald reminded everyone that nobody, including her parents, could reach or control the blind, deaf, and mute girl. But remember, he said, how her teacher — the miracle worker — finally broke though to Keller with a regimen that combined both discipline and love. "It's important to know that when Helen Keller spoke her first word, she didn't run to her parents, she ran to the miracle worker," McDonald said. "This program is about pay me now or pay me later. It's about how it's a lot better to grab a kid by the seat of the pants and make him run now than it is having that same kid at the end of a police officer's six-shooter years from now."

The most poignant moment occurred when a mother spoke. With a quivering voice and fighting back tears, she talked about how she had lost her son somewhere along the way. She considered it her fault because she had been a drug addict while he was growing up. She had gotten herself clean and sober, but by then her son was running with a gang and she couldn't reach him. She said she knew it was only a matter of time before he would be shot by a rival gang member or by a cop. I knew there was a good boy in there somewhere, but I just couldn't find him, she said. But the Ranch did find him. He hadn't liked it at first, but slowly he had changed. The Ranch was tough, but it was fair, she said. He had graduated from the program and was now in his third semester of college. I can never repay the Ranch for what it did for me or my son, she said.

At the end of the hearing, two other men who ran group homes for juveniles in Arizona said that they had not experienced any problems with any overzealous state workers and that maybe the legislators were getting a slanted view of CPS because only one facility in the state — the Ranch — seemed to have trouble with the agency. But another state representative named Stan Barnes had a sharp retort to that just before the hearing ended.

"The reason why Boys Ranch is getting all this attention is because they are daring to fight city hall like no one else has fought city hall before," he said. "They have stuck their necks out. Places like Boys Ranch serve a real need, and we need to protect the reputations of the people servicing that need. You know, a few centuries ago, it was witches. A few decades ago it was communists. Now it's abusers. They might not stone people like they used to, but the damage is still done."

The next day, the members of the Arizona Boys Ranch December class of 1995 received their high school diplomas. Dressed in Spartan green caps and gowns, seventeen graduates, including twelve who had played on the football team, made up the class. Among them were Elliott, Cabell, Breer, Hughes, Peters, and Armstrong. Fittingly, Armstrong was the first one to march into the chapel. He couldn't contain the wide smile on his face. A few minutes later, he would experience a preacher's dream. He would address a full chapel.

The most heartfelt moment of his speech came when he read a quote about the tension between love and rage. Using Frankenstein as an example, Tamar noted that human beings tend to indulge their rage, when their desire for love remains unsatisfied. The words meant something to Armstrong because when he had arrived at the Ranch, he resisted at first because of the rage that had been welling up inside of him for years. He had learned to overcome it. With the help of the Ranch's staff and teachers, he had reached this moment. You made us understand and change, he said. And for that, speaking for my graduating class, we say thank you. Later, after pictures had been taken of the new graduates throwing their caps in the air, Armstrong shook hands with Gray. "I have come a long way in a short time," Tamar told him.

As important as commencement is at any high school, the ceremony that took place the next morning, on December 22, was the one that the residents of the Ranch wait for with real anticipation: program graduation. This one is for all the boys who have successfully completed their programs at the Ranch. Most of the staff were present. Only Allen, the intense coach who said he found Ranch graduations far too sad to attend, was noticeably absent. The chapel had such an overflowing crowd, including the residents of the main campus, that many in attendance were forced to sit in a back room and watch the ceremony on TV monitors. There were thirty-five graduates, including all the boys who had received their high school diplomas the previous afternoon. It was a tradition that each one stand and say a few parting words. Most thanked the Ranch staff or a particular adult with whom they had been especially close.

When it was Elliott's turn, he addressed his remarks to his mother, who had made the trip from California. "I'd like to thank my mom, who stuck by me in the good times and in the bad, especially when I was nuts," he said. "I wouldn't be standing here today without you." Then his gaze left his mother and turned to the rest of the crowd. "And to my friends, take care of business," he said. "If you want to do good here, you've got to give some, and you've got to take some."

Thomas had the last word. He couldn't make any promises about what was going to happen to these boys, he said. Seven out of ten were going to make it. The others would fail, he added bluntly. Those were the cold, hard statistics. "There are parents out there today who are scared to death, and you'd be fools not to be terrified," he said. "You're wondering, 'Is my son going to act out there the way he did at Boys Ranch or is he going to go back to the gang life?' We don't know the answer to that. But we do know that each and every one of these young people can be successful because they've proven it here. Every one of these young men wants to do well, and they will if they choose to do so. But the real work begins now, and they know that."

When graduation was over, the boys began to scatter to the wind. Plane tickets were handed out. Goodbyes were said.

Among those left behind was McKissic. He wasn't scheduled to leave the Ranch until August. If Thomas had his way, McKissic would be spending another full year here. According to a normal high school calendar, McKissic was only midway through his junior year, and Thomas wanted him to graduate with his proper class. That, of course, would mean than McKissic would be around to play football again next season. But McKissic was ahead academically. He also was adamant about leaving as soon as he could. Apparently he had discovered that he didn't meet the Air Force Academy's high standards because now his goal was to attend Eastern Arizona. "He's too young to be going out there," Thomas said. "He needs to graduate when he's supposed to, when he's eighteen. But he's been here awhile, and like all good kids, it's nice to leave here." Thomas would become even more concerned when, a few months later, McKissic got the hard news that his mother had passed away in California. But even through that tragedy, Shaune remained insistent that he wanted to go as soon as possible.

Others were going now. Walik Smith was heading back to San Diego, where he planned to attend junior college. "In a weird kind of way, I guess I'm sad," he said. "These people here really helped me."

Hughes would be attending MCC. Peters had a job lined up locally and would be moving into an apartment with his mother. Cabell would be leaving for Eastern Arizona the first week in January. He intended to play football there. Cabell had not gotten a football scholarship, but he had received enough financial aid to attend the school. "I'm excited and nervous," Cabell said. "I don't know what to feel. It's all mixed up right now. But I sure am glad to be graduating." Breer was going back to Oceanside, where he would be starting a job at a golf club factory making $8 an hour. One of the conditions of his employment was that he take a weekly P-test. "That's a urinalysis test," he explained. There was one other thing he wanted to do soon: get that "FTP" tattoo removed from his upper arm. "It never really suited me," he said.

The Outs awaited all of them. The two who really couldn't wait for what was beyond the Ranch's property were Armstrong and Elliott. Both had full football scholarships waiting for them at Arizona Western, a junior college in Yuma, three hours to the west along the California border. Gray liked the idea that the boys were going to Western because players there lived in dorms and there were probably fewer temptations in that small desert city than in the metropolitan Phoenix area. Gray had taken them, along with Sparkman and Charles Williams, to meet with the head coach at Western the previous week. Armstrong and Elliott were immediately offered full rides. If Sparkman and Williams graduated in May, as planned, they might get scholarships, too. The four had taken placement exams while visiting the school. Gray had been surprised by the results. Sparkman, by far, had graded out the highest during the testing. "He's got all that fire and spirit," Gray said. "He's the one kid that even Civics couldn't bust. Yet he's also the one who has the most upstairs that could take him the farthest."

The trip to Western was not without some conflict, though. While the football coach really wanted the Ranch kids, school officials had some concerns, not about accepting them as students but about allowing them to live in the dorms. They wanted to know exactly what Armstrong and Elliott had done in their past to warrant a stay at the Ranch. Gray, citing privacy laws, respectfully declined to tell them. Maybe it would be different if you asked every dorm resident detailed questions about his previous criminal record, Gray said. You can't single out these kids for that kind of interrogation. In the end, the school relented, and in just three weeks, Elliott and Armstrong would begin their first semester of college.

"I pray that they don't have a hard time, but I think they will," Gray said. "These kids are the first ones to make the transition. They'll be gone from the Ranch, away from people they know, away from this routine of having someone watch you all the time. Being thrown out into the world from here is like being thrown into a swimming pool. You're going to have to swim. We just tossed Tim and Tamar into the water."

Gray added that the magnitude of the impending changes in their lives hadn't hit the boys until it was time to pile into the van for the long trip back to the Ranch from Yuma. After they got on the highway, Gray said he realized that it was really quiet in the back, and he stole a glance in the mirror.

"All four of their heads were on each other's shoulders," Gray said. "They were all huddled together."

It reminded Gray of a litter of puppies snuggling up to one another so they could feel safe.